# The Origins of the Cold War

# PROBLEMS IN
# AMERICAN CIVILIZATION

*Under the editorial direction of*

the late **Edwin C. Rozwenc**

Amherst College

# The Origins of the Cold War

**Second Edition**

*Edited and with an introduction by*

## Thomas G. Paterson
University of Connecticut

**D. C. HEATH AND COMPANY**
Lexington, Massachusetts   Toronto

For my son, Thomas Graham Paterson, Jr.

# PREFACE

Since the publication of the first edition in 1970, scholars have been prodigious in their research and writing on the origins of the Cold War. Happily, too, the generous reception by teachers and students of the first effort has encouraged this revised anthology. About half of the selections in this volume are new; they were chosen for their command of respect, thoroughness of information, lucid writing style, and spirited interpretation. Also I have added maps, cartoons from several countries, and illustrations. The chronological chart has been revised and expanded. Both the chronology and maps have been designed to include all important dates and names mentioned in the text. I have rewritten the Introduction and all the headnotes, and I have enlarged and updated the bibliography. The wide range of viewpoints and issues and the large number of selections will permit flexible use of this book. Care has been taken to avoid setting up contrived or false debates. I am grateful for the kind cooperation of the authors and publishers of the works included herein and for the suggestions and assistance of J. Garry Clifford, Holly V. Izard, Edwin Rozwenc, and Theodore A. Wilson.

Thomas G. Paterson
University of Connecticut

# CONTENTS

# I THE PARTICIPANTS DEBATE THE ORIGINS

# II THE TROUBLESOME ISSUES: SECURITY AND ECONOMIC RECOVERY

viii                                                      *Contents*

# III THE ROOT CAUSES: THE SCHOLARS DEBATE

# ILLUSTRATIONS

# INTRODUCTION

With the defeat of Germany and Japan in 1945, the Big Three alliance of Great Britain, Russia, and the United States crumbled with alarming speed and impact. The diplomatic impasse and anxiety that followed soon were labeled the Cold War, a phrase made popular by Walter Lippmann in 1947 with the publication of a book by that name. To those Americans who nurtured hopes of peaceful postwar international affairs, the collapse of the wartime coalition and the rise of Soviet-American tension were shocking and largely unexpected. For others, however, the antagonism was disturbing but anticipated, and for some people, perhaps desired. The history of twentieth-century Russian-American relations was not comforting to anyone, because before 1945 they often were characterized by aloofness, suspicion, ideological hostility, economic friction, jilted hopes, and even armed conflict. The quest for national security and economic development (and reconstruction) on the part of both nations were common themes in that history and in the postwar period as well.

The successful Bolshevik Revolution of 1917 precipitated Russia's decision to withdraw its weary people from World War I. To France, Britain, and the United States, the decision to end the war on the eastern front appeared catastrophic. Some observers believed in fact that the Bolsheviks were German agents. American and European leaders considered the Marxist ideology an anathema and regarded the Bolshevik seizure of foreign properties in Russia as intolerable. They feared the triumph of the revolution, its possible spread, and its conspicuous challenge to the capitalist world order. To keep Russia in the war and to weaken the Bolsheviks, the United States contributed about five thousand soldiers in 1918–19 to an

Allied intervention in Northern Russia. Another ten thousand Americans invaded Siberia and were not withdrawn until 1920. President Woodrow Wilson also funnelled economic assistance and weapons to anti-Bolshevik forces. Soviet leaders would not easily forget that at a time of national peril the United States intervened in their civil war and thereby prolonged it. American participation in an economic blockade of Russia before 1920 also put trade on a troubled footing from the beginning. Russia too was excluded from the peace conference at Versailles. At home in America a destructive Red Scare brought anticommunism to a feverish level. Thus, deep scars were imprinted on Soviet-American relations right at the start.

Although Great Britain opened diplomatic relations with Russia in 1924, American recognition was not extended until 1933. Yet recognition did not smooth diplomatic ripples, for American leaders soon complained that Russia was fomenting international revolution through the Comintern. Nor did Americans appreciate Soviet criticisms of capitalism when capitalism was on its knees in the Great Depression. Through the 1930s the two nations failed to reach agreement on the issue of Russian debts ($636 million) owed to American nationals, corporations, and the United States government. Soviet leaders refused to compensate American companies for confiscated properties after the revolution. Nor did Soviet-American trade improve markedly as some had anticipated. The ghastly purges orchestrated by Joseph Stalin disgusted Americans. The diplomacy leading to World War II further embittered relations. Not invited to the Munich Conference of 1938, Russia felt isolated and vulnerable and rejected the appeasement agreement. The Nazi-Soviet pact of the following year, in which two dictators carved up helpless Poland, and Russia's seizure of Finnish territory in the winter war of 1940–41, confirmed American beliefs that Adolf Hitler and Joseph Stalin were two of a kind—brutal and aggressive.

After 1941, Communist Russia and capitalist America formed an alliance of convenience for national survival. But the anti-German coalition constantly was torn by strife. The United States and Britain failed to fulfill their 1942 promise to Russia of a second front to relieve the Russians from carrying the burden of the fighting. That front finally came at Normandy in June 1944. The Russians were grateful but their frightful wartime loss of several million lives (some estimates run as high as 20 million) made them think the worst about the delay: that many people in the West were realizing their publicly stated hope that Germany and Russia would annihilate one another while the West happily watched. Squabbles over Lend-Lease shipments, the surrender of Italy, and Soviet liberation and occupation of Eastern European countries also divided the Allies.

The Big Three wartime conferences at Moscow (1943), Teheran (1943), Bretton Woods (1944), Dumbarton Oaks (1944), Yalta (1945), and Potsdam (1945), although bringing agreement on the need for a second front, a World Bank and International Monetary Fund, a United Nations organization, the temporary division and long-term punishment of Germany, and Russian entry into the war against Japan, left many divisive questions unanswered in the imprecise language of the agreements. The postwar administration of Germany and Japan, German boundaries, reparations, governments and elections in Eastern Europe (especially Poland), trade and monetary policy, and the management of the United Nations awaited more precise formulation. In short, a long history of troubled relations lay behind the breakup of the World War II alliance.

Despite that bleak history, there were enough examples of Soviet-American accommodation to suggest to many Americans that the wartime coalition might be perpetuated and that intense postwar conflict was not inevitable. There were bound to be differences, but not necessarily the extremes of heated rhetoric and bombastic propaganda, military alliances, arms races, nuclear threats, direct confrontations, interventions in the Third World, neglect of domestic programs, overreaction to critics and suppression of civil liberties, and above all else, the abandonment of diplomacy. Shared concerns about national security and economic development at times had brought together the two ideologically-opposed nations and, conceivably, it could happen again, argued some Americans.

After the removal of American troops from Russia in 1920, a period of courtship had ensued. The United States encouraged Japan to withdraw its forces from Siberia and to return Northern Sakhalin to Russia. Ideology was shunted aside as trade between the state-controlled economy of Soviet Russia and American businessmen increased. Leading American corporations placed representatives on the American-Russian Chamber of Commerce and Moscow established a trading corporation (AMTORG) in New York to purchase American products. To the surprise of many, Henry

Ford signed a Soviet contract in 1929 for the construction of an auto-
mobile plant in Russia. In the early 1930s, after Soviet-American
trade had declined sharply, some leaders thought that Russia might
help the United States out of the depression by buying American
goods. Furthermore, at that time America and Russia saw each other
as possible bulwarks against an expansionist Japan. So in 1933,
after a hiatus of sixteen years, official diplomatic relations between
Washington and Moscow were opened. In 1937 a Russian-American
trade agreement gave further evidence of some cooperation.

Following Germany's attack upon Russia in 1941, the United
States extended valuable Lend-Lease aid (totalling over $10 billion
for the war period). Realizing the importance of this aid to their
survival, the Russians were appreciative and hoped that economic
assistance could continue after the war to help repair the massive
damage. Although the wartime alliance was often rancorous, ideology was played down as Marxist and capitalists merged their common security interests vis-à-vis Germany. There was also general
understanding among Allied leaders Winston Churchill, Joseph
Stalin, and Franklin Roosevelt that after the war each major country
would, in a reflection of power realities, watch over a sphere of influence. Russia sought to eliminate one irritant by disbanding the
Communist International in 1943, and on the whole, temporarily at
least, Americans moderated their anti-Communist sentiments during
the war.

As Russia and the United States jockeyed for secure international
positions in 1945, troublesome issues broke out in alarming fre-
quency. The dropping of the atomic bomb in August introduced a
new, frightening weapon which intruded into diplomacy. The issue
of international control versus American monopoly was corrosive.
The prospects of postwar aid to Russia dwindled as the United
States attempted to apply economic pressure for diplomatic concessions and rejected a Soviet request for a large loan. Trade de-
clined as each power sought to use its economic resources for
political advantage. The erstwhile Allies clashed in the World Bank,
International Monetary Fund, and United Nations, where American
voting power became dominant and the Soviets resorted to the veto.
In Eastern Europe, the Soviet Union pressured governments and
eventually engulfed Poland, Hungary, Rumania, Bulgaria, and
Czechoslovakia. In early 1946, in a classic case of great power com-

petition, the United States and Russia vied for control of the government and oil of Iran and thus generated an international crisis. The
division of Germany became permanent as the occupying powers
squabbled over reparations and began to create separate economic
and political institutions in their zones.

The Truman Doctrine of 1947 brought American intervention in a
Greek civil war, military assistance to Turkey, and a simple doctrine
called containment. Europe continued to suffer from the devastation
of the war, and when the United States responded with the Marshall
Plan, the question of Soviet participation in a European recovery
program became paramount. Ultimately Communist countries, under
pressure from Moscow, could not accept the American terms and
boycotted it. In 1948–49, the Communist coup in Czechoslovakia,
the Berlin blockade and airlift, and the creation of the North Atlantic
Treaty Organization further solidified antagonistic spheres and
divided Europe. Crises in Asia, especially in China and Vietnam,
spawned American fears that Russia was masterminding a plot of
global conquest. How in such a short time had the Allies become
such bitter rivals?

The leading participants in these events disagreed vigorously
about the origins of the postwar dissension. Harry S. Truman, Winston Churchill, and Clark Clifford, for example, strongly blamed an
aggressive and obstinate Soviet Union for the coming of the Cold
War. Joseph Stalin, on the other hand, decried the rise of an expansive and uncompromising Anglo-American bloc which refused to
recognize legitimate Soviet security fears. Internal critics like Henry
Wallace and Walter Lippmann pointed to the responsibilities of both
powers in neglecting opportunities for peaceful solution.

Historians have in essence followed the outline of the debate as
delineated by the participants. There are two major schools of
thought on the origins of the Cold War, although it must be emphasized that neither school is monolithic. The members of the traditional, conventional, orthodox, or liberal school hold that the United
States was largely blameless and helpless, that responsibility for
conflict lay in Moscow, that Russia, not America, harbored expansionist goals, and that there were no workable policy alternatives for
the United States in the face of Soviet intransigence. The Cold War
was inevitable and the containment of Soviet communism was a
necessity, both morally and pragmatically. Although they accept in

varying degrees and argue in differing levels of sophistication some of these contentions, in their selections below and in other works, Adam B. Ulam, Walt W. Rostow, Klaus Epstein, Joseph M. Jones, Robert H. Ferrell, Arthur M. Schlesinger, Jr., and Melvin Croan are representatives of the traditionalist interpretation.

The other school of interpretation has been variously labelled revisionist, New Left, or radical. The first term is the broadest and clearly defines the thrust of the school—a revision of heretofore commonly held assumptions about the origins of the Cold War. The other terms carry political connotations and are applied usually to those members of the revisionist school who argue that the system of American capitalism produces an imperialism which is perpetrated by an elite decision-making group. As with the traditionalist school, revisionists do not agree among themselves and the labels are becoming less useful as the two schools utilize the newly opened historical documents and take the best from each other to develop a more thorough and more profound view of the origins of the Cold War. One exciting feature of the debate is that it is constantly moving beyond imprecise labels to new questions and new research.

Revisionists generally accept a number of propositions. Although they recognize hostile Soviet actions, they do dispute the contention that Russia alone was the cause of tension. These scholars find such an explanation too simple, one-sided, and negligent in explaining America's responsibility. They point to the overwhelming strength of an expansionist United States which used its power to shape an American-oriented postwar world at a time when much of the rest of the world was devastated and weak. They suggest, too, that Russia was uncertain in its policy in the crucial 1945–46 period. In those years the Cold War was not inevitable and Washington ignored or rejected alternative policies which might have produced some accord. Finally, they contend that the global containment doctrine was an overreaction to a minimal threat. The studies by Gar Alperovitz, Thomas G. Paterson, Barton J. Bernstein, Richard J. Barnet, Stephen Ambrose, Athan Theoharis, William A. Williams, and Gabriel and Joyce Kolko fall generally within the revisionist category. H. Stuart Hughes, Norman Graebner, Robert W. Tucker, and Gaddis Smith fall somewhere between the two schools.

A number of broad questions divided participants and will continue to divide scholars. What were the root causes of the Cold War? What were the comparative places in the conflict of ideology, a reading of the "lessons" of the past and actual historical experiences, economic expansion and competition, irrational fears, quality of leadership, personality, domestic politics, and traditional great power rivalry? What, if any, were the grand postwar strategies and governing principles of the major powers? Was the Cold War inevitable? Or were there viable alternatives? Would different tactical decisions have made a difference in avoiding or reducing tension? Which nations and leaders were responsible for the Cold War? Or was responsibility shared? What were the comparative strengths and weaknesses of Russia and America? Did either side actually threaten the other? If so, what was the threat? When did the Cold War start?

Questions about Soviet foreign policy will continue to be debated. What motivated the Soviet Union? Were internal imperatives or external pressures uppermost? How important was Communist ideology in the formulation of Soviet policy? What were Russia's primary postwar objectives? Were Stalin's perceived needs and personality crucial? What influence did the experiences of World War II have on Soviet leaders? Did Russia have a plan for the subjugation of neighbors or for the subversion of Western Europe? Was communism a monolith? Was Russia aggressive or isolationist? Did Russia have legitimate security fears?

Questions about American foreign policy also will continue to arouse controversy. What motivated the United States? What role did ideology and rhetoric play? What were the roots of American anticommunism? Was America counterrevolutionary? Did capitalism and class structure determine policy? What "tools" did the United States have with which to build its desired postwar world? Did Americans adhere to or practice universalism or a sphere-of-influence approach? What effect did World War II have on American thinking? Was the United States expansionist? Did the United States embrace multilateralism? What influence did public opinion have on policy making? Did Truman's diplomatic style and personality influence American behavior? Who made foreign policy? Were decisions made haphazardly or accidentally, or by deliberate, rational choice? Was there continuity or discontinuity between Roosevelt and Truman?

The three sections of readings which follow provide both historical data and interpretations of these questions. The first part develops the debate among contemporaries and introduces most of the Cold War issues. Part II chronologically and topically studies these issues to demonstrate the continuity of crisis and the common themes of national security and economic recovery. The last part includes selections which tackle the major interpretive question of the root causes of the Cold War.

Common abbreviations in Cold War history include Cominform (Communist Information Bureau), Comintern (Third Communist International), EAM (Greek National Liberation Front), ECA (Economic Cooperation Administration), ECE (Economic Commission for Europe), EDES (National Republican Greek League), ELAS (Greek National Army of Liberation), ERP (European Recovery Program), FDR (Franklin D. Roosevelt), GNP (Gross National Product), JCS (Joint Chiefs of Staff), NATO (North Atlantic Treaty Organization), NEP (New Economic Policy), NSC (National Security Council), OSS (Office of Strategic Services), SAC (Strategic Air Command), U.K. (United Kingdom), UNRRA (United Nations Relief and Rehabilitation Administration), USSR (Union of Soviet Socialist Republics), V-E (Victory Day in Europe), and V-J (Victory Day in Japan).

# Chronology

**1944**  *June:* Normandy invasion. *July:* Bretton Woods Conference. *August–October:* Dumbarton Oaks Conference. *October:* Churchill-Stalin sphere-of-influence agreement at Moscow. *November:* Franklin D. Roosevelt elected to fourth term with Harry S. Truman as Vice-President. *December:* Battle of the Bulge.

**1945**  *January:* USSR requested loan. *February 4–11:* Yalta Conference. *February:* Cease fire in Greek civil war. *April:* Jacques Duclos letter; Roosevelt's death; Truman-Molotov argument. *May:* German surrender; cessation of Lend-Lease to Russia; Harry Hopkins mission to Moscow. *June:* U.N. Charter signed at San Francisco. *July:* James F. Byrnes became Secretary of State; U.S. recognition of Communist government in Poland. *July 17–August 2:* Potsdam Conference. *August 6:* Atomic bomb on Hiroshima. *August 8:* USSR declaration of war against Japan. *August 9:* Atomic bomb on Nagasaki. *August 28:* USSR requested loan. *September 11–October 2:* London Foreign Ministers meeting. *October 27:* Truman's Navy Day speech. *November:* Communists defeated in Hungarian national elections. *December 16–26:* Moscow Foreign Ministers meeting.

**1946**  *January:* U.N. Atomic Energy Commission formed; Iran charged Russia with interference in its internal affairs; Russia charged Britain with interference in Greek affairs. *February:* Joseph Stalin election speech. *March:* U.S. found "lost" Russian loan request; Winston Churchill's Fulton speech. *April:* Soviet troops left Iran. *April–October:* Paris Peace Conference meetings. *May:* Greek civil war began again; Lucius Clay halted German reparations to USSR. *June:* Baruch Plan; Bikini atomic tests began. *August:* USSR sought base from Turkey; U.S. charged Poland with failure to create democracy. *September:* Henry Wallace speech and departure from Cabinet; Clark Clifford report on U.S.-USSR relations. *November:* Republicans captured Congressional elections; U.S.-China treaty. *November 4–December 12:* New York Foreign Ministers meeting. *December:* Anglo-American fusion of German zones.

**1947**  *January:* George C. Marshall became Secretary of State. *February:* British notes on Greece and Turkey. *March:* Communists began subversion of Hungarian government; Truman Doctrine. *March 10–April 24:* Moscow Foreign Ministers meeting. *May:* Aid to Greece-Turkey bill signed by Truman. *June:* Marshall Plan speech at Harvard. *July:* USSR rejected Marshall Plan at Paris; publication of George F. Kennan's "X" article on containment. *August:* Polish-Russian trade agreement. *October:* USSR created Cominform. *November 25–December:* London Foreign Ministers meeting. *December:* Brussels Conference on European defense; Interim Aid to Europe bill signed; Greek regime outlawed EAM and Communist Party.

**1948**  *February:* Brussels Treaty signed; coup in Czechoslovakia. *March:* Senate passed Marshall Plan; USSR walked out of Allied Control Council in Germany charging destruction by other three powers;

House passed Marshall Plan. *April:* Truman signed European Recovery Act of $5.3 billion; Committee of European Economic Cooperation formed. *June:* Currency reform announced in western zones of Germany; Berlin blockade by USSR; Yugoslavia expelled from Cominform. *November:* Truman elected President.

1949 *January:* Truman suggested idea of Point Four program; USSR set up Council of Economic Assistance (Comecon); Dean Acheson became Secretary of State. *April:* NATO organized. *May:* West German federal constitution approved; Berlin blockade lifted. *July:* Truman signed NATO Treaty. *August:* U.S. White Paper on China. *September:* Federal Republic of Germany established (West); USSR exploded atomic bomb. *October:* People's Republic of China proclaimed; Greek civil war ended. *December:* Chiang's government completed evacuation from mainland to Formosa.

1950 *January:* Truman authorized hydrogen bomb development. *January–August:* USSR boycotted U.N. Security Council. *February:* Joseph McCarthy opened anti-subversive attacks; USSR-China treaty of friendship and defense. *April:* NSC-68. *June:* Outbreak of Korean War.

# I The Participants Debate the Origins

*Harry S. Truman*

# AMERICAN POWER AND PRINCIPLES

*When Harry S. Truman became president after Franklin D. Roosevelt's death on April 12, 1945, Truman had had little experience with diplomacy. But he held basic assumptions about America's postwar international position and became more sure than most about the correct interpretation of the ambiguous wartime agreements (especially Yalta). After less than two weeks in office, Truman personally laced into Soviet Foreign Minister V. M. Molotov with charges of bad faith. The stunned diplomat complained that "I have never been talked to like that in my life." The president, famous as a partisan for the verbal brawl, retorted: "Carry out your agreements and you won't get talked to like that." He confided one week later: "I gave it to him [Molotov] straight 'one-two to the jaw.'" Roosevelt, with a diplomatic style far different from Truman's, certainly would have handled Molotov less abruptly, and the historian is tantalized by the question whether Roosevelt's departure marked a significant shift in American diplomacy. Then, too, many historians have pointed to the different diplomatic styles between Russians and Americans and have attributed part of the postwar tension to that difference.*

*In New York City, on October 27, 1945, Truman summarized American foreign policy before a record-breaking Navy Day crowd which had witnessed earlier an impressive review of American military power. His speech was both tough-minded and conciliatory, but disappointingly vague. Truman asserted that the United States held high principles and possessed enviable power, a combination which would permit no "compromise with evil." British Prime Minister Clement Attlee went so far as to remark that had an American president made such statements in 1914 and 1939, there would have been no world wars. American power and principles would be sorely tested in the near future, and the question for the student of the Cold War is how well both stood up.*

... The fleet, on V-J Day, consisted of twelve hundred warships, more than fifty thousand supporting and landing craft, and over forty thousand navy planes. By that day, ours was a seapower never before equalled in the history of the world. There were great carrier task forces capable of tracking down and sinking the enemy's fleets, beating down his airpower, and pouring destruction on his war-making industries. There were submarines which roamed the seas, invading the enemy's own ports, and destroying his shipping in all the

From *Public Papers of the Presidents of the United States: Harry S. Truman, 1945* (Washington, 1961), pp. 431–38.

oceans. There were amphibious forces capable of landing soldiers on beaches from Normandy to the Philippines. There were great battleships and cruisers which swept the enemy ships from the seas and bombarded his shore defense almost at will. . . .

Now we are in the process of demobilizing our naval force. We are laying up ships. We are breaking up aircraft squadrons. We are rolling up bases, and releasing officers and men. But when our demobilization is all finished as planned, the United States will still be the greatest naval power on earth.

In addition to that naval power, we shall still have one of the most powerful air forces in the world. And just the other day, so that on short notice we could mobilize a powerful and well-equipped land, sea, and air force, I asked the Congress to adopt universal training.

Why do we seek to preserve this powerful Naval and Air Force, and establish this strong Army reserve? Why do we need to do that?

We have assured the world time and again—and I repeat it now—that we do not seek for ourselves one inch of territory in any place in the world. Outside of the right to establish necessary bases for our own protection, we look for nothing which belongs to any other power.

We do need this kind of armed might, however, for four principal tasks:

First, our Army, Navy, and Air Force, in collaboration with our Allies, must enforce the terms of peace imposed upon our defeated enemies.

Second, we must fulfill the military obligations which we are undertaking as a member of the United Nations Organization—to support a lasting peace, by force if necessary.

Third, we must cooperate with other American nations to preserve the territorial integrity and the political independence of the nations of the Western Hemisphere.

Fourth, in this troubled and uncertain world, our military forces must be adequate to discharge the fundamental mission laid upon them by the Constitution of the United States—to "provide for the common defense" of the United States.

These four military tasks are directed not toward war—not toward conquest—but toward peace.

We seek to use our military strength solely to preserve the peace of the world. For we now know that this is the only sure way to make our own freedom secure.

That is the basis of the foreign policy of the people of the United States.

The foreign policy of the United States is based firmly on fundamental principles of righteousness and justice. In carrying out those principles we shall firmly adhere to what we believe to be right; and we shall not give our approval to any compromise with evil.

But we know that we cannot attain perfection in this world overnight. We shall not let our search for perfection obstruct our steady progress toward international cooperation. We must be prepared to fulfill our responsibilities as best we can, within the framework of our fundamental principles, even though we recognize that we have to operate in an imperfect world.

Let me restate the fundamentals of that foreign policy of the United States:

1. We seek no territorial expansion or selfish advantage. We have no plans for aggression against any other state, large or small. We have no objective which need clash with the peaceful aims of any other nation.

2. We believe in the eventual return of sovereign rights and self-government to all peoples who have been deprived of them by force.

3. We shall approve no territorial changes in any friendly part of the world unless they accord with the freely expressed wishes of the people concerned.

4. We believe that all peoples who are prepared for self-government should be permitted to choose their own form of government by their own freely expressed choice, without interference from any foreign source. That is true in Europe, in Asia, in Africa, as well as in the Western Hemisphere.

5. By the combined and cooperative action of our war allies, we shall help the defeated enemy states establish peaceful democratic governments of their own free choice. And we shall try to attain a world in which Nazism, Fascism, and military aggression cannot exist.

6. We shall refuse to recognize any government imposed upon any nation by the force of any foreign power. In some cases it may be impossible to prevent forceful imposition of such a

## The Participants

Winston Churchill, Harry S. Truman, Joseph Stalin. *(U.S. Army photograph)*

Clark Clifford and Harry S. Truman. *(Courtesy, Clark M. Clifford)*

Henry A. Wallace. *(Courtesy, University of Iowa Libraries, Iowa City)*

Walter Lippmann. *(Courtesy, the Yale University Library and* The Washington Post)

government. But the United States will not recognize any such government.

7. We believe that all nations should have the freedom of the seas and equal rights to the navigation of boundary rivers and waterways and of rivers and waterways which pass through more than one country.

8. We believe that all states which are accepted in the society of nations should have access on equal terms to the trade and the raw materials of the world.

9. We believe that the sovereign states of the Western Hemisphere, without interference from outside the Western Hemisphere, must work together as good neighbors in the solution of their common problems.

10. We believe that full economic collaboration between all nations, great and small, is essential to the improvement of living conditions all over the world, and to the establishment of freedom from fear and freedom from want.

11. We shall continue to strive to promote freedom of expression and freedom of religion throughout the peace-loving areas of the world.

12. We are convinced that the preservation of peace between nations requires a United Nations Organization composed of all the peace-loving nations of the world who are willing jointly to use force if necessary to insure peace.

Now, that is the foreign policy which guides the United States. That is the foreign policy with which it confidently faces the future.

It may not be put into effect tomorrow or the next day. But nonetheless, it is our policy; and we shall seek to achieve it. It may take a long time, but it is worth waiting for, and it is worth striving to attain.

The Ten Commandments themselves have not yet been universally achieved over these thousands of years. Yet we struggle constantly to achieve them, and in many ways we come closer to them each year. Though we may meet setbacks from time to time, we shall not relent in our efforts to bring the Golden Rule into the international affairs of the world.

We are now passing through a difficult phase of international relations. Unfortunately it has always been true after past wars, that the unity among allies, forged by their common peril, has tended to wear out as the danger passed.

The world cannot afford any letdown in the united determination of the Allies in this war to accomplish a lasting peace. The world cannot afford to let the cooperative spirit of the Allies in this war disintegrate. The world simply cannot allow this to happen. The people in the United States, in Russia, and Britain, in France and China, in collaboration with all the other peace-loving people, must take the course of current history into their own hands and mold it in a new direction—the direction of continued cooperation. It was a common danger which united us before victory. Let it be a common hope which continues to draw us together in the years to come.

The atomic bombs which fell on Hiroshima and Nagasaki must be made a signal, not for the old process of falling apart but for a new era—an era of ever-closer unity and ever-closer friendship among peaceful nations.

Building a peace requires as much moral stamina as waging a war. Perhaps it requires even more, because it is so laborious and painstaking and undramatic. It requires undying patience and continuous application. But it can give us, if we stay with it, the greatest reward that there is in the whole field of human effort.

Differences of the kind that exist today among nations that fought together so long and so valiantly for victory are not hopeless or irreconcilable. There are no conflicts of interest among the victorious powers so deeply rooted that they cannot be resolved. But their solution will require a combination of forbearance and firmness. It will require a steadfast adherence to the high principles which we have enunciated. It will also require a willingness to find a common ground as to the methods of applying those principles.

Our American policy is a policy of friendly partnership with all peaceful nations, and of full support for the United Nations Organization. It is a policy that has the strong backing of the American people. It is a policy around which we can rally without fear or misgiving.

The more widely and clearly that policy is understood abroad, the better and surer will be the peace. For our own part we must seek to understand the special problems of other nations. We must seek to understand their own legitimate urge toward security as they see it.

The immediate, the greatest threat to us is the threat of disillusionment, the danger of insidious skepticism—a loss of faith in the effectiveness of international cooperation. Such a loss of faith would be dangerous at any time. In an atomic age it would be nothing short of disastrous.

There has been talk about the atomic bomb scrapping all navies, armies, and air forces. For the present, I think that such talk is 100 percent wrong. Today, control of the seas rests in the fleets of the United States and her allies. There is no substitute for them. We have learned the bitter lesson that the weakness of this great Republic invites men of ill-will to shake the very foundations of civilization all over the world. And we had two concrete lessons in that.

What the distant future of the atomic research will bring to the fleet which we honor today, no one can foretell. But the fundamental mission of the Navy has not changed. Control of our sea approaches and of the skies above them is still the key to our freedom and to our ability to help enforce the peace of the world. No enemy will ever strike us directly except across the sea. We cannot reach out to help stop and defeat an aggressor without crossing the sea. Therefore, the navy, armed with whatever weapons science brings forth, is still dedicated to its historic task: control of the ocean approaches to our country and of the skies above them.

The atomic bomb does not alter the basic foreign policy of the United States. It makes the development and application of our policy more urgent than we could have dreamed six months ago. It means that we must be prepared to approach international problems with greater speed, with greater determination, with greater ingenuity, in order to meet a situation for which there is no precedent.

We must find the answer to the problems created by the release of atomic energy—we must find the answers to the many other problems of peace—in partnership with all the peoples of the United Nations. For their stake in world peace is as great as our own.

As I said in my message to the Congress, discussion of the atomic bomb with Great Britain and Canada and later with other nations cannot wait upon the formal organization of the United Nations. These discussions, looking toward a free exchange of fundamental scientific information, will be begun in the near future. But I emphasize again, as I have before, that these discussions will not be concerned with the processes of manufacturing the atomic bomb or any other instruments of war.

In our possession of this weapon, as in our possession of other new weapons, there is no threat to any nation. The world, which has seen the United States in two great recent wars, knows that full well. The possession in our hands of this new power of destruction we regard as a sacred trust. Because of our love of peace, the thoughtful people of the world know that that trust will not be violated, that it will be faithfully executed.

Indeed, the highest hope of the American people is that world cooperation for peace will soon reach such a state of perfection that atomic methods of destruction can be definitely and effectively outlawed forever.

We have sought, and we will continue to seek, the attainment of that objective. We shall pursue that course with all the wisdom, patience, and determination that the God of Peace can bestow upon a people who are trying to follow in His path.

*Winston S. Churchill*

# THE IRON CURTAIN DROPPED BY RUSSIA

*Winston S. Churchill was no longer British prime minister on March 5, 1946, when he startled many Americans with his frank but polite iron curtain speech in Fulton, Missouri. Although many Americans shared his conviction that the United States should retain its monopoly of the atomic bomb, as well as his apprehensions about Soviet behavior, they were critical of his appeal for a virtual Anglo-American alliance. They liked his candid anti-Soviet language, but some critics pointed out that in condemning Russia for its influence in Eastern Europe, Churchill ignored British predominance in Greece and the empire. Truman stated in a press conference three days later that he had no prior knowledge of the contents of the speech. Actually he had read it on the train to Missouri and commented then that it was "admirable" and "would make a stir." For some observers, Truman's presence on the platform signified American endorsement of Churchill's remarks. Indeed, the Fulton address can be considered a "trial balloon," for Churchill stated publicly what some American officials had been uttering privately. Exactly two months earlier, Truman had concluded that "I'm tired of babying the Soviets."*

From the *Congressional Record*, 79th Cong., 2nd sess., 1945–46, 92: A1145–47.

The United States stands at this time at the pinnacle of world power. It is a solemn moment for the American democracy. With primacy in power is also joined an awe-inspiring accountability to the future. As you look around you, you feel not only the sense of duty done but also feel anxiety lest you fall below the level of achievement. Opportunity is here now, clear and shining, for both our countries. To reject it or ignore it or fritter it away will bring upon us all the long reproaches of the after-time. It is necessary that constancy of mind, persistency of purpose, and the grand simplicity of decision shall guide and rule the conduct of the English-speaking peoples in peace as they did in war. We must and I believe we shall prove ourselves equal to this severe requirement. . . .

Before we cast away the solid assurances of national armaments for self-preservation, we must be certain that our temple is built, not upon shifting sands or quagmires, but upon the rock. Anyone with his eyes open can see that our path will be difficult and also long, but if we persevere together as we did in the two World Wars—though not, alas, in the interval between them—I cannot doubt that we shall achieve our common purpose in the end.

I have, however, a definite and practical proposal to make for action. Courts and magistrates cannot function without sheriffs and constables. The United Nations Organization must immediately begin to be equipped with an international armed force. In such a matter we can only go step by step; but we must begin now. I propose that each of the powers and states should be invited to dedicate a certain number of air squadrons to the service of the world organization. These squadrons would be trained and prepared in their own countries but would move around in rotation from one country to another. They would wear the uniform of their own countries with different badges. They would not be required to act against their own nation but in other respects they would be directed by the world organization. This might be started on a modest scale and a grow [*sic*] as confidence grew. I wished to see this done after the First World War and trust it may be done forthwith.

It would nevertheless be wrong and imprudent to entrust the secret knowledge or experience of the atomic bomb, which the United States, Great Britain, and Canada now share, to the world organization, while it is still in its infancy. It would be criminal madness to cast it adrift in this still agitated and un-united world. No one in any country has slept less well in their beds because this knowledge and the method and the raw materials to apply it are at present largely retained in American hands. I do not believe we should all have slept so soundly had the positions been reversed and some Communist or neo-Fascist state monopolized, for the time being, these dread agencies. The fear of them alone might easily have been used to enforce totalitarian systems upon the free democratic world, with consequences appalling to human imagination.

God has willed that this shall not be, and we have at least a breathing space before this peril has to be encountered, and even then, if no effort is spared, we should still possess so formidable a superiority as to impose effective deterrents upon its employment or threat of employment by others. Ultimately when the essential brother of man is truly embodied and expressed in a world organization, these powers may be confided to it. . . .

There is . . . an important question we must ask ourselves. Would a special relationship between the United States and the British Commonwealth be inconsistent with our overriding loyalties to the world organization? I reply that on the contrary, it is probably the only means by which that organization will achieve its full stature and strength. There are already the special United States relations with Canada and between the United States and the South American republics. We also have our twenty years' treaty of collaboration and mutual assistance with Soviet Russia. I agree with Mr. Bevin that it might well be a fifty-year treaty. We have an alliance with Portugal unbroken since 1384. None of these clash with the general interest of a world agreement. On the contrary they help it. "In my Father's house are many mansions." Special associations between members of the United Nations which have no aggressive point against any other country, which harbor no design incompatible with the charter of the United Nations, far from being harmful, are beneficial and, as I believe, indispensable. . . .

A shadow has fallen upon the scenes so lately lighted by the Allied victory. Nobody knows what Soviet Russia and its Communist international organization intends to do in the immediate future, or what are the limits, if any, to their expansive and proselytizing tendencies. I have a strong admiration and regard for the valiant Russian people and for my wartime comrade, Marshal Stalin. There is sympathy and good will in Britain—and I doubt not here also—toward the peoples of all the Russias and a resolve to persevere through many differences and rebuffs in establishing lasting friendships.

We understand the Russian need to be secure on her western frontiers from all renewal of German aggression. We welcome her to her rightful place among the leading nations of the world. Above all, we welcome constant, frequent, and growing contacts between the Russian people and our own people on both sides of the Atlantic. It is my duty, however, to place before you certain facts about the present position in Europe.

From Stettin in the Baltic to Trieste in the Adriatic, an iron curtain has descended across the continent. Behind that line lie all the capitals of the ancient states of Central and Eastern Europe. Warsaw, Berlin, Prague, Vienna, Budapest, Belgrade, Bucharest, and Sofia, all these famous cities and the populations around them lie in the Soviet sphere and all are subject, in one form or another, not only to Soviet influence but to a very high and increasing measure of control from Moscow. Athens alone, with its immortal glories, is free to decide its future at an election under British, American, and French observation.

The Russian-dominated Polish government has been encouraged to make enormous and wrongful inroads upon Germany, and mass expulsions of millions of Germans on a scale grievous and undreamed of are now taking place. The Communist parties, which were very small in all these eastern states of Europe, have been raised to preeminence and power far beyond their numbers and are seeking everywhere to obtain totalitarian control. Police governments are prevailing in nearly every case, and so far, except in Czechoslovakia, there is no true democracy.

Turkey and Persia are both profoundly alarmed and disturbed at the claims which are made upon them and at the pressure being exerted by the Moscow government. An attempt is being made by the Russians in Berlin to build up a quasi-Communist party in their zone of occupied Germany by showing special favors to groups of left-wing German leaders. At the end of the fighting last June, the American and British Armies withdrew westward, in accordance with an earlier agreement, to a depth at some points of 150 miles on a front of nearly 400 miles, to allow the Russians to occupy this vast expanse of territory which the Western democracies had conquered.

If now the Soviet government tries, by separate action, to build up a pro-Communist Germany in their areas, this will cause new serious difficulties in the British and American zones, and will give the defeated Germans the power of putting themselves up to auction between the Soviets and the Western democracies. Whatever conclusions may be drawn from these facts—and facts they are—this is certainly not the liberated Europe we fought to build up. Nor is it one which contains the essentials of permanent peace.

In front of the iron curtain which lies across Europe are other causes for anxiety. In Italy the Communist party is seriously hampered by having to support the Communist-trained Marshall Tito's claims to former Italian territory at the head of the Adriatic. Nevertheless, the future of Italy hangs in the balance. Again, one cannot imagine a regenerated Europe without a strong France....

However, in a great number of countries, far from the Russian frontiers and throughout the world, Communist fifth columns are established and work in complete unity and absolute obedience to the directions they receive from the Communist center. Except in the British Commonwealth, and in the United States, where communism is in its infancy, the Communist parties or fifth columns constitute a growing challenge and peril to Christian civilization. These are somber facts for anyone to have to recite on the morrow of a victory gained by so much splendid comradeship in arms and in the cause of freedom and democracy, and we should be most unwise not to face them squarely while time remains.

The outlook is also anxious in the Far East and especially in Manchuria. The agreement which was made at Yalta, to which I was a party, was extremely favorable to Soviet Russia, but it was made at a time when no one could say that the German war might not extend all through the summer and autumn of 1945 and when the Japanese war was expected to last for a further eighteen months from the end of the German war. In this country you are all so well informed about the Far East and such devoted friends of China that I do not need to expatiate on the situation there.

I have felt bound to portray the shadow which, alike in the West and in the East, falls upon the world. I was a minister at the time of the Versailles Treaty and a close friend of Mr. Lloyd George. I did not myself agree with many things that were done, but I have a very strong impression in my mind of that situation, and I find it painful to contrast it with that which prevails now. In those days there were high hopes and unbounded confidence that the wars were over, and that the League of Nations would become all-powerful. I do not see or feel the same confidence or even the same hopes in the haggard world at this time.

On the other hand, I repulse the idea that a new war is inevitable, still more that it is imminent. It is because I am so sure that our fortunes are in our own hands and that we hold the power to save the future, that I feel the duty to speak out now that I have an occasion to do so. I do not believe that Soviet Russia desires war. What they desire is the fruits of war and the indefinite expansion of their power and doctrines. But what we have to consider here today while time remains, is the permanent prevention of war and the establishment of conditions of freedom and democracy as rapidly as possible in all countries.

Our difficulties and dangers will not be removed by closing our eyes to them; they will not be removed by mere waiting to see what happens; nor will they be relieved by a policy of appeasement. What is needed is a settlement, and the longer this is delayed, the more difficult it will be and the greater our dangers will become. From what I have seen of our Russian friends and allies during the war, I am convinced that there is nothing they admire so much as strength, and there is nothing for which they have less respect than for military weakness. For that reason the old doctrine of a balance of power is unsound. We cannot afford, if we can help it, to work on narrow margins, offering temptations to a trial of strength. If the Western democracies stand together in strict adherence to the principles of the United Nations Charter, their influence for furthering these principles will be immense and no one is likely to molest them. If, however, they become divided or falter in their duty, and if these all-important years are allowed to slip away, then indeed catastrophe may overwhelm us all.

Last time I saw it all coming, and cried aloud to my own fellow countrymen and to the world, but no one paid any attention. Up till the year 1933 or even 1935, Germany might have been saved from the awful fate which has overtaken her and we might all have been spared the miseries Hitler let loose upon mankind.

There never was a war in all history easier to prevent by timely action than the one which has just desolated such great areas of the globe. It could have been prevented without the firing of a single shot, and Germany might be powerful, prosperous, and honored today, but no one would listen and one by one we were all sucked into the awful whirlpool.

We surely must not let that happen again. This can only be achieved by reaching now, in 1946, a good understanding on all points with Russia under the general authority of the United Nations and by the maintenance of that good understanding through many peaceful years, by the world instrument, supported by the whole strength of the English-speaking world and all its connections.

Let no man underrate the abiding power of the British Empire and Commonwealth. Because you see the 46 million in our island harassed about their food supply, of which they only grow one-half, even in wartime, or because we have difficulty in restarting our industries and export trade after six years of passionate war effort, do not suppose that we shall not come through these dark years of privations as we have come through the glorious years of agony, or that half a century from now, you will not see 70 or 80 millions of Britons spread about the world and united in defense of our traditions, our way of life, and of the world causes we and you espouse. If the population of the English-speaking commonwealth be added to that of the United States, with all that such cooperation implies in the air, on the sea, and in science and industry, there will be no quivering, precarious balance of power to offer its temptation to ambition or adventure. On the contrary there will be an overwhelming assurance of security. If we adhere faithfully to the charter of the United Nations and walk forward in sedate and sober strength, seeking no one's land or treasure, or seeking to lay no arbitrary control on the thoughts of men, if all British moral and material forces and convictions are joined with your own in fraternal association, the high roads of the future will be clear, not only for us but for all, not only for our time but for a century to come.

## Joseph Stalin
# THE HOSTILE ANGLO-AMERICAN ALLIANCE

*Shortly after Churchill's speech, the Russian newspaper* Pravda *interviewed an extremely agitated and hyperbolic Joseph Stalin, the tough, often callous ruler of Soviet Russia since the 1920s. George F. Kennan, chargé d'affaires in the American Embassy in Moscow, reported that the interview was the "most violent Soviet reaction I can recall to any foreign statement." About a month earlier, on February 9, Stalin had delivered an alarmist election speech asserting that the capitalist system bred wars and that the Russian people, to remain strong, would have to make sacrifices under a new Five Year Plan. Mindful of the horrible human and material costs of World War II and alert to the problems of security and economic reconstruction, Stalin was particularly sensitive about his nation's borders, and neighbor Poland suffered under Soviet occupation. Repeatedly Stalin pointed out that Germany had attacked Russia through the Polish corridor. "It is not only a question of honor for Russia, but one of life and death," he said earlier at the Yalta Conference. The United States and Britain, he angrily charged, were ganging up to deny Russia future security. Truman rejected an opportunity to discuss the troubling interview when he dismissed a press conference question: "I can't read Russian, and I don't know whether that is the right translation or not, so I have no comment to make."*

Q. How do you assess the last speech of Mr. Churchill which was made in the United States?

A. I assess it as a dangerous act calculated to sow the seed of discord among the Allied governments and hamper their cooperation.

Q. Can one consider that the speech of Mr. Churchill is damaging to the cause of peace and security?

A. Undoubtedly, yes. In substance, Mr. Churchill now stands in the position of a firebrand of war. And Mr. Churchill is not alone here. He has friends not only in England but also in the United States of America.

In this respect, one is reminded remarkably of Hitler and his friends. Hitler began to set war loose by announcing his racial theory, declaring that only people speaking the German language represent a fully valuable nation. Mr. Churchill begins to set war loose also by a racial theory, maintaining that only nations speaking the English language are fully valuable nations, called upon to decide the destinies of the entire world.

The German racial theory brought Hitler and his friends to the conclusion that the Germans, as the only fully valuable nation, must rule over the other nations. The English racial theory brings Mr. Churchill and his friends to the conclusion that nations speaking the English language, being the only fully valuable nations, should rule over the remaining nations of the world.

In substance, Mr. Churchill and his friends in England and the United States present nations not speaking the English language with something like an ultimatum: "Recognize our lordship voluntarily and then all will be well. In the contrary case, war is inevitable."

But the nations have shed their blood during five years of cruel war for the sake of liberty and the independence of their countries, and not for the sake of exchanging the lordship of Hitler for the lordship of Churchill.

It is, therefore, highly probable that the nations not speaking English and which, however, make up an enormous majority of the world's population, will not consent to go into a new slavery. The tragedy of Mr. Churchill lies in the fact that he, as a deep-rooted Tory, cannot understand this simple and obvious truth.

There is no doubt that the setup of Mr. Churchill is a setup for war, a call to war with the Soviet Union....

Q. How do you assess that part of Mr. Churchill's speech in which he attacks the democratic regime of the European countries which are our neighbors and in which he criticizes the good neighborly relations established between these countries and the Soviet Union?

A. This part of Mr. Churchill's speech is a mixture of the elements of the libel with the elements of rudeness and lack of tact. Mr. Churchill maintains that Warsaw, Berlin, Prague, Vienna, Budapest, Belgrade, Bucharest and Sofia, all these famous cities and the populations of those areas, are within the Soviet sphere and are all subjected to Soviet influence and to the increasing control of Moscow.

Mr. Churchill qualifies this as the "boundless expansionist tendencies of the Soviet Union." It requires no special effort to show that Mr. Churchill rudely and shamelessly libels not only Moscow but also the above-mentioned states neighborly to the USSR.

To begin with, it is quite absurd to speak of the exclusive control of the USSR in Vienna and Berlin, where there are Allied control councils with representatives of four states, where the USSR has only one-fourth of the voices.

It happens sometimes that some people are unable to refrain from libel, but still they should know a limit.

Secondly, one cannot forget the following fact: the Germans carried out an invasion of the USSR through Finland, Poland, Rumania, Bulgaria and Hungary. The Germans were able to carry out the invasion through these countries by reason of the fact that these countries had governments inimical to the Soviet Union.

As a result of the German invasion, the Soviet Union has irrevocably lost in battles with the Germans, and also during the German occupation and through the expulsion of Soviet citizens to German slave labor camps, about 7 million people. In other words, the Soviet Union has lost in men several times more than Britain and the United States together.

It may be that some quarters are trying to push into oblivion these sacrifices of the Soviet people which insured the liberation of Europe from the Hitlerite yoke.

But the Soviet Union cannot forget them. One can ask, therefore, what can be surprising in the fact that the Soviet Union, in a desire to ensure its security for the future, tries to achieve that these countries should have governments whose relations to the Soviet Union are loyal? How can one, without having lost one's reason, qualify these peaceful aspirations of the Soviet Union as "expansionist tendencies" of our government?

Mr. Churchill further maintains that the Polish government under Russian lordship has been spurred to an unjust and criminal spoliation against Germany. Here, every word is a rude and offensive libel. Contemporary democratic Poland is led by outstanding men. They have shown in deeds that they know how to defend the interests and worth of their homeland, as their predecessors failed to do.

What reason has Mr. Churchill to maintain that the leaders of contemporary Poland can submit their country to a lordship by representatives of any country whatever? Does Mr. Churchill here libel the Russians because he has intentions of sowing the seeds of discord between Poland and the Soviet Union?

Mr. Churchill is not pleased that Poland should have turned her policy toward friendship and alliance with the USSR. There was a time when in the mutual relations between Poland and the USSR there prevailed an element of conflict and contradiction. This gave a possibility to statesmen, of the kind of Mr. Churchill, to play on these contradictions, to take Poland in hand under the guise of protection from the Russians, to frighten Russia by specters of a war between Poland and herself, and to take for themselves the role of arbiters.

But this time is past. For enmity between Poland and Russia has given place to friendship between them, and Poland, present democratic Poland, does not wish any longer to be a playing ball in the hands of foreigners. It seems to be that this is just what annoys Mr. Churchill and urges him to rude, tactless outbursts against Poland. After all, it is no laughing matter for him. He is not allowed to play for other people's stakes.

As for Mr. Churchill's attack on the Soviet Union in connection with the extending of the western boundaries of Poland, as compensation for the territories seized by the Germans in the past, there it seems to me that he quite blatantly distorts the facts.

As is known, the western frontiers of Poland were decided upon at the Berlin conference of the three powers, on the basis of Poland's demands.

The Soviet Union repeatedly declared that it considered Poland's demands just and correct. It may well be that Mr. Churchill is not pleased with this decision. But why does Mr. Churchill, not sparing his darts against the Russians in the matter, conceal from his readers the fact that the decision was taken at the Berlin conference unanimously, that not only the Russians voted for this decision but also the English and Americans?

Why did Mr. Churchill have to delude people? Mr. Churchill further maintains that the Communist parties were very insignificant in all these Eastern European countries but reached exceptional strength, exceeding their numbers by far, and are attempting to establish totalitarian control everywhere; that police government prevailed in almost all these countries, even up to now, with the exception of Czechoslovakia, and that there exists in them no real democracy.

As is known in Britain at present there is one party which rules the country—the Labor party. The rest of the parties are barred from the government of the country. This is called by Churchill a true democracy meanwhile Poland, Rumania, Yugoslavia, Bulgaria and Hungary are governed by several parties—from four to six parties. And besides, the opposition, if it is loyal, is guaranteed the right to participate in the government. This, Churchill calls totalitarian and the government of police.

On what grounds? Do you expect an answer from Churchill? Does he not understand the ridiculous situation he is putting himself in by such speeches on the basis of totalitarianism and police rule? Churchill would have liked Poland to be ruled by Sosnkowski and Anders, Yugoslavia by Mikhailovitch, Rumania by Prince Stirbey and Radescu, Hungary and Austria by some king from the House of Habsburg, and so on.

Mr. Churchill wants to assure us that these gentlemen from the Fascist servants' hall can ensure true democracy. Such is the democracy of Mr. Churchill. Mr. Churchill wanders around the truth when he speaks of the growth of the influence of the Communist parties in Eastern Europe. It should, however, be noted that he is not quite accurate. The influence of Communist parties grew not only in Eastern Europe but in almost every country of Europe where fascism has ruled before: Italy, Germany, Hungary, Bulgaria, Rumania, Finland, and in countries which have suffered German, Italian or Hungarian occupation. France, Belgium, Holland, Norway, Denmark, Poland, Czechoslovakia, Yugoslavia, Greece, the Soviet Union and so on.

The growth of the influence of communism cannot be considered accidental. It is a normal function. The influence of the Communists grew because during the hard years of the mastery of fascism in Europe, Communists showed themselves to be reliable, daring and self-sacrificing fighters against Fascist regimes for the liberty of peoples.

Mr. Churchill sometimes recalls in his speeches the common people from small houses, patting them on the shoulder in a lordly manner and pretending to be their friend. But these people are not so simple-minded as it might appear at first sight. Common people, too, have their opinions and their own politics. And they know how to stand up for themselves.

It is they, millions of these common people, who voted Mr. Churchill and his party out in England, giving their votes to the

Labor party. It is they, millions of these common people, who isolated reactionaries in Europe, collaborators with fascism, and gave preference to Left democratic parties.

It is they, millions of these common people, having tried the Communists in the fire of struggle and resistance to fascism, who decided that the Communists deserve completely the confidence of the people. Thus grew the Communists' influence in Europe. Such is the law of historical development.

Of course, Mr. Churchill does not like such a development of events. And he raised the alarm, appealing to force. But he also did not like the appearance of the Soviet regime in Russia after the First World War. Then, too, he raised the alarm and organized an armed expedition of fourteen states against Russia with the aim of turning back the wheel of history.

But history turned out to be stronger than Churchill's intervention and the quixotic antics of Churchill resulted in his complete defeat. I do not know whether Mr. Churchill and his friends will succeed in organizing after the Second World War a new military expedition against Eastern Europe. But if they succeed in this, which is not very probable, since millions of common people stand on guard over the peace, then one man confidently says that they will be beaten, just as they were beaten twenty-six years ago.


*Clark Clifford*

# AMERICAN FIRMNESS VS. SOVIET AGGRESSION

*In the summer of 1946, President Truman asked his Special Counsel Clark Clifford to prepare a report on American relations with Russia. After consulting the secretaries of state, war, and navy, the Joint Chiefs of Staff, and other high level officials, and drawing upon George F. Kennan's diplomatic cables from Moscow, Clifford wrote a lengthy memorandum (September 24, 1946). It was a summary indictment of Soviet foreign policy, listing "violations" of agreements and asserting that Marxist theory advocated military aggression against capitalist states. Many scholars have questioned his interpretation of Communist ideology, arguing instead that the theory meant war was inevi-*

*table among capitalist nations, not between Communist and capitalist countries, and that it did not advocate Communist military aggression. Clifford further urged that the United States arm for possible war, enter negotiations reluctantly, avoid compromises which might be interpreted as American weakness, and use foreign aid to build a "barrier to communism." Although Truman thought the report "too hot" to be made public, Clifford's paper reflected the steadily developing "get tough" and "containment" policies in Washington. After leaving the Truman administration in 1950, Clifford opened a successful law practice in Washington, D.C. and served as secretary of defense from 1968 to 1969.*

It is perhaps the greatest paradox of the present day that the leaders of a nation, now stronger than it has ever been before, should embark on so aggressive a course because their nation is "weak." And yet Stalin and his cohorts proclaim that "monopoly capitalism" threatens the world with war and that Russia must strengthen her defenses against the danger of foreign attacks. The USSR, according to Kremlin propaganda, is imperilled so long as it remains within a "capitalistic encirclement." This idea is absurd when adopted by so vast a country with such great natural wealth, a population of almost 200 million and no powerful or aggressive neighbors. But the process of injecting this propaganda into the minds of the Soviet people goes on with increasing intensity.

The concept of danger from the outside is deeply rooted in the Russian people's haunting sense of insecurity inherited from their past. It is maintained by their present leaders as a justification for the oppressive nature of the Soviet police state. The thesis, that the capitalist world is conspiring to attack the Soviet Union, is not based on any objective analysis of the situation beyond Russia's borders. It has little to do, indeed, with conditions outside the Soviet Union, and it has risen mainly from basic inner-Russian necessities which existed before the Second World War and which exist today. . . .

The Soviet government, in developing the theme of "encirclement," maintains continuous propaganda for domestic consumption regarding the dangerously aggressive intentions of American "atom

From pp. 428, 430–31, 468, 470, 476–79, 482 of *Memoirs* by Arthur Krock. Copyright © 1968 by Arthur Krock. Reprinted by permission of the publishers, Funk & Wagnalls, New York. The complete memorandum is available in Krock's book and in the Harry S. Truman Library, Independence, Missouri.

diplomacy" and British imperialism, designed to arouse in the Soviet people fear and suspicion of all capitalistic nations.

Despite the fact that the Soviet government believes in the inevitability of a conflict with the capitalist world and prepares for that conflict by building up its own strength and undermining that of other nations, its leaders want to postpone the conflict for many years. The Western powers are still too strong, the USSR is still too weak. Soviet officials must therefore not provoke, by their policies of expansion and aggression, too strong a reaction by other powers.

The Kremlin acknowledges no limit to the eventual power of the Soviet Union, but it is practical enough to be concerned with the actual position of the USSR today. In any matter deemed essential to the security of the Soviet Union, Soviet leaders will prove adamant in their claims and demands. In other matters they will prove grasping and opportunistic, but flexible in proportion to the degree and nature of the resistance encountered.

Recognition of the need to postpone the "inevitable" conflict is in no sense a betrayal of the Communist faith. Marx and Lenin encouraged compromise and collaboration with non-Communists for the accomplishment of ultimate communistic purposes. The USSR has followed such a course in the past. In 1939 the Kremlin signed a nonaggression pact with Germany and in 1941 a neutrality pact with Japan. Soviet leaders will continue to collaborate whenever it seems expedient, for time is needed to build up Soviet strength and weaken the opposition. Time is on the side of the Soviet Union, since population growth and economic development will, in the Soviet view, bring an increase in its relative strength. . . .

A direct threat to American security is implicit in Soviet foreign policy which is designed to prepare the Soviet Union for war with the leading capitalistic nations of the world. Soviet leaders recognize that the United States will be the Soviet Union's most powerful enemy if such a war as that predicted by Communist theory ever comes about and therefore the United States is the chief target of Soviet foreign and military policy.

A recent Soviet shift of emphasis from Great Britain to the United States as the [principal] "enemy" has been made known to the world by harsh and strident propaganda attacks upon the United States and upon American activities and interests around the globe. The

United States, as seen by radio Moscow and the Soviet press, is the [principal] architect of the "capitalistic encirclement" which now "menaces the liberty and welfare of the great Soviet masses." These verbal assaults on the United States are designed to justify to the Russian people the expense and hardships of maintaining a powerful military establishment and to insure the support of the Russian people for the aggressive actions of the Soviet government.

The most obvious Soviet threat to American security is the growing ability of the USSR to wage an offensive war against the United States. This has not hitherto been possible, in the absence of Soviet long-range strategic air power and an almost total lack of sea power. Now, however, the USSR is rapidly developing elements of her military strength which she hitherto lacked and which will give the Soviet Union great offensive capabilities. Stalin has declared his intention of sparing no effort to build up the military strength of the Soviet Union. Development of atomic weapons, guided missiles, materials for biological warfare, a strategic air force, submarines of great cruising range, naval mines and mine craft, to name the most important, are extending the effective range of Soviet military power well into areas which the United States regards as vital to its security....

Although the Soviet Union at the present moment is precluded from military aggression beyond the land mass of Eurasia, the acquisition of a strategic air force, naval forces and atomic bombs in quantity would give the USSR the capability of striking anywhere on the globe. Ability to wage aggressive warfare in any area of the world is the ultimate goal of Soviet military policy.

The primary objective of United States policy toward the Soviet Union is to convince Soviet leaders that it is in their interest to participate in a system of world cooperation, that there are no fundamental causes for war between our two nations, and that the security and prosperity of the Soviet Union, and that of the rest of the world as well, is being jeopardized by the aggressive militaristic imperialism such as that in which the Soviet Union is now engaged.

However, these same leaders with whom we hope to achieve an understanding on the principles of international peace appear to believe that a war with the United States and the other leading capitalistic nations is inevitable. They are increasing their military power and the sphere of Soviet influence in preparation for the "inevitable" conflict, and they are trying to weaken and subvert their potential opponents by every means at their disposal. So long as these men adhere to these beliefs, it is highly dangerous to conclude that hope of international peace lies only in "accord," "mutual understanding," or "solidarity" with the Soviet Union.

Adoption of such a policy would impel the United States to make sacrifices for the sake of Soviet-U.S. relations, which would only have the effect of raising Soviet hopes and increasing Soviet demands, and to ignore alternative lines of policy, which might be much more compatible with our own national and international interests.

The Soviet government will never be easy to "get along with." The American people must accustom themselves to this thought, not as a cause for despair, but as a fact to be faced objectively and courageously. If we find it impossible to enlist Soviet cooperation in the solution of world problems, we should be prepared to join with the British and other Western countries in an attempt to build up a world of our own which will pursue its own objectives and will recognize the Soviet orbit as a distinct entity with which conflict is not predestined but with which we cannot pursue common aims.

As long as the Soviet government maintains its present foreign policy, based upon the theory of an ultimate struggle between communism and capitalism, the United States must assume that the USSR might fight at any time for the two-fold purpose of expanding the territory under Communist control and weakening its potential capitalist opponents. The Soviet Union was able to flow into the political vacuum of the Balkans, Eastern Europe, the Near East, Manchuria and Korea because no other nation was both willing and able to prevent it. Soviet leaders were encouraged by easy success and they are now preparing to take over new areas in the same way. The Soviet Union, as Stalin euphemistically phrased it, is preparing "for any eventuality."

Unless the United States is willing to sacrifice its future security for the sake of "accord" with the USSR now, this government must, as a first step toward world stabilization, seek to prevent additional Soviet aggression. The greater the area controlled by the Soviet Union, the greater the military requirements of this country will be.

Our present military plans are based on the assumption that, for the next few years at least, Western Europe, the Middle East, China and Japan will remain outside the Soviet sphere. If the Soviet Union acquires control of one or more of these areas, the military forces required to hold in check those of the USSR and prevent still further acquisitions will be substantially enlarged. That will also be true if any of the naval and air bases in the Atlantic and Pacific, upon which our present plans rest, are given up. This government should be prepared, while scrupulously avoiding any act which would be an excuse for the Soviets to begin a war, to resist vigorously and successfully any efforts of the USSR to expand into areas vital to American security.

The language of military power is the only language which disciples of power politics understand. The United States must use that language in order that Soviet leaders will realize that our government is determined to uphold the interests of its citizens and the rights of small nations. Compromise and concessions are considered, by the Soviets, to be evidences of weakness and they are encouraged by our "retreats" to make new and greater demands.

The main deterrent to Soviet attack on the United States, or to attack on areas of the world which are vital to our security, will be the military power of this country. It must be made apparent to the Soviet government that our strength will be sufficient to repel any attack and sufficient to defeat the USSR decisively if a war should start. The prospect of defeat is the only sure means of deterring the Soviet Union.

The Soviet Union's vulnerability is limited due to the vast area over which its key industries and natural resources are widely dispersed, but it is vulnerable to atomic weapons, biological warfare, and long-range power. Therefore, in order to maintain our strength at a level which will be effective in restraining the Soviet Union, the United States must be prepared to wage atomic and biological warfare. A highly mechanized army, which can be moved either by sea or by air, capable of seizing and holding strategic areas, must be supported by powerful naval and air forces. A war with the USSR would be "total" in a more horrible sense than any previous war and there must be constant research for both offensive and defensive weapons.

Whether it would actually be in this country's interest to employ atomic and biological weapons against the Soviet Union in the event of hostilities is a question which would require careful consideration in the light of the circumstances prevailing at the time. The decision would probably be influenced by a number of factors, such as the Soviet Union's capacity to employ similar weapons, which can not now be estimated. But the important point is that the United States must be prepared to wage atomic and biological warfare if necessary. The mere fact of preparedness may be the only powerful deterrent to Soviet aggressive action and in this sense the only sure guaranty of peace.

The United States, with a military potential composed primarily of [highly] effective technical weapons, should entertain no proposal for disarmament or limitation of armament as long as the possibility of Soviet aggression exists. Any discussion on the limitation of armaments should be pursued slowly and carefully with the knowledge constantly in mind that proposals on outlawing atomic warfare and long-range offensive weapons would greatly limit United States strength, while only moderately affecting the Soviet Union. The Soviet Union relies primarily on a large infantry and artillery force and the result of such arms limitation would be to deprive the United States of its most effective weapons without impairing the Soviet Union's ability to wage a quick war of aggression in Western Europe, the Middle East or the Far East.

The Soviet government's rigid controls on travellers, and its internal security measures, enable it to develop military weapons and build up military forces without our knowledge. The United States should not agree to arms limitations until adequate intelligence of events in the USSR is available and, as long as this situation prevails, no effort should be spared to make our forces adequate and strong. Unification of the services and the adoption of universal military training would be strong aids in carrying out a forthright United States policy. In addition to increasing the efficiency of our armed forces, this program would have a salutary psychological effect upon Soviet ambitions.

Comparable to our caution in agreeing to arms limitation, the United States should avoid premature disclosure of scientific and technological information relating to war material until we are assured of either a change in Soviet policies or workable international controls. Any disclosure would decrease the advantage the United States now has in technological fields and diminish our strength in relation to that of the USSR.

In addition to maintaining our own strength, the United States should support and assist all democratic countries which are in any way menaced or endangered by the USSR. Providing military support in case of attack is a last resort; a more effective barrier to communism is strong economic support. Trade agreements, loans and technical missions strengthen our ties with friendly nations and are effective demonstrations that capitalism is at least the equal of communism. The United States can do much to ensure that economic opportunities, personal freedom and social equality are made possible in countries outside the Soviet sphere by generous financial assistance. Our policy on reparations should be directed toward strengthening the areas we are endeavoring to keep outside the Soviet sphere. Our efforts to break down trade barriers, open up rivers and international waterways, and bring about economic unification of countries, now divided by occupation armies, are also directed toward the reestablishment of vigorous and healthy non-Communist economies.

The Soviet Union recognizes the effectiveness of American economic assistance to small nations and denounces it bitterly by constant propaganda. The United States should realize that Soviet propaganda is dangerous (especially when American "imperialism" is emphasized) and should avoid any actions which give an appearance of truth to the Soviet charges. A determined effort should be made to expose the fallacies of such propaganda.

*            *            *

In conclusion, as long as the Soviet government adheres to its present policy, the United States should maintain military forces powerful enough to restrain the Soviet Union and to confine Soviet influence to its present area. All nations not now within the Soviet sphere should be given generous economic assistance and political support in their opposition to Soviet penetration. Economic aid may also be given to the Soviet government and private trade with the USSR permitted provided the results are beneficial to our interests and do not simply strengthen the Soviet program. We should continue to work for cultural and intellectual understanding between the United States and the Soviet Union but that does not mean that, under the guise of an exchange program, Communist subversion and infiltration in the United States will be tolerated. In order to carry out an effective policy toward the Soviet Union, the United States government should coordinate its own activities, inform and instruct the American people about the Soviet Union, and enlist their support based upon knowledge and confidence. These actions by the United States are necessary before we shall ever be able to achieve understanding and accord with the Soviet government on any terms other than its own.

Even though Soviet leaders profess to believe that the conflict between Capitalism and Communism is irreconcilable and must eventually be resolved by the triumph of the latter, it is our hope that they will change their minds and work out with us a fair and equitable settlement when they realize that we are too strong to be beaten and too determined to be frightened.

*Henry A. Wallace*
# THE AMERICAN DOUBLE STANDARD

*Disturbed by what he believed was a growing American militancy toward Russia, Secretary of Commerce Henry Wallace wrote the following letter to the president in July 1946; it was made public in September of that year. That same month Wallace was ousted from the cabinet for delivering a Madison Square Garden speech critical of American foreign policy. Truman had grown impatient with Wallace and exclaimed with reference to his critics: "The Reds, phonies and 'parlor pinks' seem to be banded together and are becoming a national danger. I am afraid they are a sabotage front for Uncle Joe Stalin." In his July letter, Wallace complained that the Truman administration applied a double standard to American actions and to those of other nations. Wallace stated too that since the United States was in no position to remove Soviet influence in Eastern Europe, recognition of the fait accompli would reduce real Soviet security fears. In essence refuting Churchill and Clifford, he told the president that the awesome American monopoly of atomic power and*

*superior economic power were major contributors to Soviet-American tension.
In 1948, Wallace ran as a presidential candidate for the Progressive party,
but his ideas and candidacy fared quite badly as most Americans endorsed
Truman's policies.*

How do American actions since V-J Day appear to other nations? I
mean by actions the concrete things like $13 billion for the War and
Navy Departments, the Bikini tests of the atomic bomb and continued production of bombs, the plan to arm Latin America with our
weapons, production of B-29s and planned production of B-36s, and
the effort to secure air bases spread over half the globe from which
the other half of the globe can be bombed. I cannot but feel that
these actions must make it look to the rest of the world as if we were
only paying lip service to peace at the conference table. These facts
rather make it appear either (1) that we are preparing ourselves to
win the war which we regard as inevitable or (2) that we are trying
to build up a predominance of force to intimidate the rest of mankind. How would it look to us if Russia had the atomic bomb and we
did not, if Russia had ten thousand-mile bombers and air bases
within a thousand miles of our coast lines and we did not?

Some of the military men and self-styled "realists" are saying:
"What's wrong with trying to build up a predominance of force? The
only way to preserve peace is for this country to be so well armed
that no one will dare attack us. We know that America will never
start a war."

The flaw in this policy is simply that it will not work. In a world
of atomic bombs and other revolutionary new weapons, such as
radioactive poison gases and biological warfare, a peace maintained
by a predominance of force is no longer possible.

Why is this so? The reasons are clear:

First. Atomic warfare is cheap and easy compared with old-
fashioned war. Within a very few years several countries can have
atomic bombs and other atomic weapons. Compared with the cost
of large armies and the manufacture of old-fashioned weapons,
atomic bombs cost very little and require only a relatively small part
of a nation's production plant and labor force.

From Henry A. Wallace, "The Path to Peace with Russia," *New Republic* 115 (September 30, 1946): 401–406.

Second. So far as winning a war is concerned, having more bombs—even many more bombs—than the other fellow is no longer a decisive advantage. If another nation had enough bombs to eliminate all of our principal cities and our heavy industry, it wouldn't help us very much if we had ten times as many bombs as we needed to do the same to them.

Third. The most important, the very fact that several nations have atomic bombs will inevitably result in a neurotic, fear-ridden, itching-trigger psychology in all the peoples of the world, and because of our wealth and vulnerability we would be among the most seriously affected. Atomic war will not require vast and time-consuming preparations, the mobilization of large armies, the conversion of a large proportion of a country's industrial plants to the manufacture of weapons. In a world armed with atomic weapons, some incident will lead to the use of those weapons.

There is a school of military thinking which recognizes these facts, recognizes that when several nations have atomic bombs, a war which will destroy modern civilization will result and that no nation or combination of nations can win such a war. This school of thought therefore advocates a "preventative war," an attack on Russia now, before Russia has atomic bombs. This scheme is not only immoral but stupid. If we should attempt to destroy all the principal Russian cities and her heavy industry, we might well succeed. But the immediate countermeasure which such an attack would call forth is the prompt occupation of all continental Europe by the Red Army. Would we be prepared to destroy the cities of all Europe in trying to finish what we had started? This idea is so contrary to all the basic instincts and principles of the American people that any such action would be possible only under a dictatorship at home.

Thus the "predominance of force" idea and the notion of a "defensive attack" are both unworkable. The only solution is the one which you have so wisely advanced and which forms the basis of the Moscow statement on atomic energy. That solution consists of mutual trust and confidence among nations, atomic disarmament and an effective system of enforcing that disarmament.

There is, however, a fatal defect in the Moscow statement, in the Acheson report, and in the American plan recently presented to the United Nations Atomic Energy Commission. That defect is the scheme, as it is generally understood, of arriving at international agreements by "easy stages," of requiring other nations to enter into binding commitments not to conduct research into the military uses of atomic energy and to disclose their uranium and thorium resources while the United States retains the right to withhold its technical knowledge of atomic energy until the international control and inspection system is working to our satisfaction. In other words, we are telling the Russians that if they are "good boys" we may eventually turn over our knowledge of atomic energy to them and to the other nations. But there is no objective standard of what will qualify them as being "good" nor any specified time for sharing our knowledge.

Is it any wonder that the Russians did not show any great enthusiasm for our plan? Would we have been enthusiastic if the Russians had a monopoly of atomic energy, and offered to share the information with us at some indefinite time in the future at their discretion if we agreed now not to try to make a bomb and give them information on our secret resources of uranium and thorium? I think we should react as the Russians appear to have done. We would have put up counterproposal for the record, but our real effort would go into trying to make a bomb so that our bargaining position would be equalized. . . .

Insistence on our part that the game must be played our way will only lead to a deadlock. The Russians will redouble their efforts to manufacture bombs, and they may also decide to expand their "security zone" in a serious way. Up to now, despite all our outcries against it, their efforts to develop a security zone in Eastern Europe and in the Middle East are small change from the point of view of military power as compared with our air bases in Greenland, Okinawa and many other places thousands of miles from our shores. We may feel very self-righteous if we refuse to budge on our plan and the Russians refuse to accept it, but that means only one thing—the atomic armament race is on in deadly earnest.

I am convinced therefore that if we are to achieve our hopes of negotiating a treaty which will result in effective international atomic disarmament we must abandon the impractical form of the "step-by-step" idea which was presented to the United Nations Atomic Energy Commission. We must be prepared to reach an agreement which will commit us to disclosing information and destroying our bombs at a specific time or on terms of specified actions by other countries, rather than at our unfettered discretion. If we are willing to negotiate on this basis, I believe the Russians will also negotiate seriously with a view to reaching an agreement.

There can be, of course, no absolute assurance the Russians will finally agree to a workable plan if we adopt this view. They may prefer to stall until they also have bombs and can negotiate on a more equal basis, not realizing the danger to themselves as well as the rest of the world in a situation in which several nations have atomic bombs. But we must make the effort to head off the atomic bomb race. We have everything to gain by doing so, and do not give up anything by adopting this policy as the fundamental basis for our negotiation. During the transition period toward full-scale international control we retain our technical know-how, and the only existing production plants for fissionable materials and bombs remain within our borders. . . .

Our basic distrust of the Russians, which has been greatly intensified in recent months by the playing up of conflict in the press, stems from differences in political and economic organizations. For the first time in our history defeatists among us have raised the fear of another system as a successful rival to democracy and free enterprise in other countries and perhaps even our own. I am convinced that we can meet that challenge as we have in the past by demonstrating that economic abundance can be achieved without sacrificing personal, political and religious liberties. We cannot meet it, as Hitler tried to, by an anti-Comintern alliance.

It is perhaps too easy to forget that despite the deep-seated differences in our culture and intensive anti-Russian propaganda of some twenty-five years' standing, the American people reversed their attitudes during the crisis of war. Today, under the pressure of seemingly insoluble international problems and continuing deadlocks, the tide of American public opinion is again turning against Russia. In this reaction lies one of the dangers to which this letter is addressed.

I should list the factors which make for Russian distrust of the United States and of the Western world as follows: The first is Russian history, which we must take into account because it is the setting in which Russians see all actions and policies of the rest of the world. Russian history for over a thousand years has been a succession of attempts, often unsuccessful, to resist invasion and conquest—by the Mongols, the Turks, the Swedes, the Germans and the Poles. The scant thirty years of the existence of the Soviet government has in Russian eyes been a continuation of their historical struggle for national existence. The first four years of the new regime, from 1917 through 1921, were spent in resisting attempts at destruction by the Japanese, British and French, with some American assistance, and by the several White Russian armies encouraged and financed by the Western powers. Then, in 1941, the Soviet state was almost conquered by the Germans after a period during which the Western European powers had apparently acquiesced in the rearming of Germany in the belief that the Nazis would seek to expand eastward rather than westward. The Russians, therefore, obviously see themselves as fighting for their existence in a hostile world.

Second, it follows that to the Russians all of the defense and security measures of the Western powers seem to have an aggressive intent. Our actions to expand our military security system—such steps as extending the Monroe Doctrine to include the arming of the Western Hemisphere nations, our present monopoly of the atomic bomb, our interest in outlying bases and our general support of the British Empire—appear to them as going far beyond the requirements of defense. I think we might feel the same if the United States were the only capitalistic country in the world and the principal socialistic countries were creating a level of armed strength far exceeding anything in their previous history. From the Russian point of view, also, the granting of a loan to Britain and the lack of tangible results on their request to borrow for rehabilitation purposes may be regarded as another evidence of strengthening of an anti-Soviet bloc.

Finally, our resistance to her attempts to obtain warm water ports and her own security system in the form of "friendly" neighboring states seems, from the Russian point of view, to clinch the case. After twenty-five years of isolation and after having achieved the status of a major power, Russia believes that she is entitled to recognition of her new status. Our interest in establishing democracy in Eastern Europe, where democracy by and large has never existed, seems to her an attempt to reestablish the encirclement of unfriendly neighbors which was created after the last war and which might serve as a springboard of still another effort to destroy her.

If this analysis is correct, and there is ample evidence to support it, the action to improve the situation is clearly indicated. The fundamental objective of such action should be to allay any reasonable Russian grounds for fear, suspicions and distrust. We must recognize that the world has changed and that today there can be no "one world" unless the United States and Russia can find some way of living together. For example, most of us are firmly convinced of the soundness of our position when we suggest the internationalization and defortification of the Danube or of the Dardanelles, but we would be horrified and angered by any Russian counterproposal that would involve also the internationalizing and disarming of Suez or Panama. We must recognize that to the Russians these seem to be identical situations.

We should ascertain from a fresh point of view what Russia believes to be essential to her own security as a prerequisite to the writing of the peace and to cooperation in the construction of a world order. We should be prepared to judge her requirements against the background of what we ourselves and the British have insisted upon as essential to our respective security. We should be prepared, even at the expense of risking epithets of appeasement to agree to reasonable Russian guarantees of security. . . .

We should also be prepared to enter into economic discussions without demanding that the Russians agree in advance to discussion of a series of what are to them difficult and somewhat unrelated political and economic concessions. Although this is the field in which my department is most directly concerned, I must say that in my opinion this aspect of the problem is not as critical as some of the others, and certainly is far less important than the question of atomic energy control. But successful negotiation in this field might help considerably to bridge the chasm that separates us. The question of a loan should be approached on economic and commercial grounds and should be dissociated as much as possible from the current misunderstandings which flow from the basic differences between their system and ours. You have already clearly dissociated yourself and the American people from the expressions of anti-Soviet support for the British loan. If we could have followed up your statement on signing the British loan bill with a loan to the USSR on a commercial basis and on similar financial terms, I believe that it would have clearly demonstrated that this country is not attempting to use its economic resources In the game of power politics. In the light of the present Export-Import Bank situation it is now of the greatest importance that we undertake general economic discussions at an early date.

It is of the greatest importance that we should discuss with the Russians in a friendly way their long-range economic problems and the future of our cooperation in matters of trade. The reconstruction program of the USSR and the plans for the full development of the Soviet Union offers tremendous opportunities for American goods and American technicians.

American products, especially machines of all kinds, are well established in the Soviet Union. For example, American equipment, practices and methods are standard in coal mining, iron and steel, oil and nonferrous metals.

Nor would this trade be one-sided. Although the Soviet Union has been an excellent credit risk in the past, eventually the goods and services exported from this country must be paid for by the Russians by exports to us and to other countries. Russian products which are either definitely needed or which are noncompetitive in this country are various nonferrous metal ores, furs, linen products, lumber products, vegetable drugs, paper and pulp and native handicrafts. . . .

Many of the problems relating to the countries bordering on Russia could more readily be solved once an atmosphere of mutual trust and confidence is established and some form of economic arrangements is worked out with Russia. These problems also might be helped by discussions of an economic nature. Russian economic penetration of the Danube area, for example, might be countered by concrete proposals for economic collaboration in the development of the resources of this area, rather than by insisting that the Russians should cease their unilateral penetration and offering no solution to the present economic chaos there.

This proposal admittedly calls for a shift in some of our thinking about international matters. It is imperative that we make this shift. We have little time to lose. Our postwar actions have not yet been adjusted to the lessons to be gained from experience of Allied cooperation during the war and the facts of the atomic age.

It is certainly desirable that, as far as possible, we achieve unity on the home front with respect to our international relations; but unity on the basis of building up conflict abroad would prove to be not only unsound but disastrous. I think there is some reason to fear that in our earnest efforts to achieve bipartisan unity in this country we may have given way too much to isolationism masquerading as tough realism in international affairs.

*Walter Lippmann*
# THE FAILURE OF THE PEACEMAKERS

*Walter Lippmann had been commenting as a respected journalist on foreign policy questions for over thirty years when he wrote this assessment of post-war disunity in late 1946. His essay invited the great powers to shift their attention from the insoluble Eastern European area and to attack the massive problem of economic reconstruction. He suggested further that Western leadership was somewhat ill-equipped to handle the postwar international crisis. By publishing* The Cold War *in 1947, Lippmann established himself as a critic of the doctrine of containment made famous by George F. Kennan's article, "The Sources of Soviet Conduct" in* Foreign Affairs *magazine (July 1947).*

Fifteen months have elapsed, as this article goes to press, since Potsdam, where the Big Three decided to approach the settlement of the world war by negotiating treaties for the European satellite states. A phase of this first chapter of the peacemaking ended with the adjournment in Paris on October 15 of the conference of the twenty-one nations. The Big Four, France having been admitted after Potsdam, are now at work in New York trying to conclude these treaties. They have fixed on the end of November as the time to begin to discuss a settlement with Germany. They have no agreement about when they will discuss Austria. They have not yet begun to discuss when they will begin to discuss the settlement with Japan.

The calendar and the agenda of the peacemaking are extraordinary, indeed astonishing. After no great war of modern times have

From Walter Lippmann, "A Year of Peacemaking," *Atlantic Monthly* 177 (December 1946): 35–40. Copyright © 1946, by The Atlantic Monthly Company, Boston, Massachusetts. Reprinted with permission.

the victors allowed so much time to pass before treating with their principal enemies. And though this is supposed to be the global settlement of a war that made this "one world," we have thus far confined our peacemaking to one region of the world.

If we ask why there has been this unusually long delay in coming to grips with the main issues of a settlement, why instead there has been this prolonged preoccupation with the satellites, the explanation would, I suppose, be that it is inordinately difficult to deal with Soviet Russia. Now there is no doubt that Mr. Truman and Mr. Byrnes, Mr. Attlee and Mr. Bevin, have found it inordinately difficult to deal with Soviet Russia. But this is not a sufficient explanation. For while it might explain a failure to reach agreement for a general settlement, which would require a settlement for Germany and Japan, it does not explain the fact that fifteen months have passed without a serious attempt to begin to negotiate a general settlement.

We must look for the explanation by asking how it happened, and why, contrary to all precedents in the making of peace, the Allies decided to postpone the settlements with the chief enemy states and to deal instead with the satellites of Germany. They took this decision at Potsdam. They took it, I believe, as the consequence of three considerations which at the time seemed of paramount importance to the Soviet Union, to Britain, and to the United States. The first was that Russia insisted on fixing de facto a new eastern frontier for Germany on the line of the Oder and the western Neisse. The second was that Britain had been given the sole control of northwestern Germany, which contains 70 percent of the prewar German heavy industry, and is the most important economic region of Europe. The third was that the United States insisted that we should have the sole control and the deciding voice in the occupation of Japan. By these three decisions each of the Big Three powers got what each of them most wanted immediately. After that a general settlement of the war, which would have had to deal with Germany and Japan, was postponed indefinitely.

Had Germany been put first on the agenda for Europe, the concession to the Soviet Union on the eastern frontier would have been reopened at once. The British control of the Ruhr and of German heavy industry would have had to be reexamined. There would have had to be negotiations about all the frontiers of Germany, not merely about the eastern. Silesia would have had to be examined along with the Ruhr, and East Prussia along with the Rhineland, and instead of the simple decision conceding the claims of Poland and the Soviet Union, there would have had to be an equal consideration of the claims of France, the Netherlands, and Belgium. It would have been necessary to strike a balance that took into account the security of all of Germany's victims, and their right to reparations, and the future of Germany itself as a viable state. It would have been necessary, in short, to negotiate, and not to postpone, a European settlement.

But the United States was inhibited from insisting upon a European settlement around Germany because the Russians would have countered by asking for a simultaneous settlement in Eastern Asia around Japan. We were as little anxious to negotiate immediately about Japan as the Russians or the British were about Germany. Russia and Britain and America would each have had to surrender the special and peculiar position it had obtained—Russia because she had played the main part in defeating Germany and was at the Elbe, Britain because Mr. Churchill had persuaded President Roosevelt to let him have the Ruhr, we because we had conquered Japan and were in possession of it.

When the Potsdam Conference had confirmed the Russian position in Eastern Germany, the British position in the Ruhr, and our position in Japan, the Allies had left on their agenda only the European satellites. And so, contrary to all precedents in settling wars, they chose to begin their peacemaking with the satellites of their principal enemy.

This meant that they would attempt to govern the moon in order to regulate the sun. For a satellite is by definition a secondary planet which revolves around a larger one. Italy, Rumania, Bulgaria, Finland, Hungary, and also Austria, were, are, and are destined to remain, secondary powers. What becomes of them, what should be done with them and for them, and what can be done, depend on the structure of Europe as a whole. Europe cannot be reconstructed around the satellites: the satellites have to be fitted into the reconstruction of Europe. For this reason no statesmen interested in a general world settlement would have considered it possible or wise to deal with the satellites until there had been a settlement among the great powers. But after Potsdam the Allied statesmen had foreclosed a general settlement.

They were confirmed in their choice of the satellites as the subject of their labors by two opposite but complementary purposes. The Soviet Union was interested in dealing with the satellites first. For this meant that the settlements would be made while the Red Army was still near its maximum power and prestige. Excepting Italy, all the satellites were under Russian military occupation, and, therefore, Russia would have the first word and the last in the negotiations. In the case of Italy the Russian and the Yugoslav claims had a better chance if they were pressed before a settlement with Germany had removed the reason for maintaining huge armies in the heart of Europe.

The British and Americans were also preoccupied with the satellites. Mr. Churchill was most particularly concerned about the strength of the Red Army and its advance to the Elbe River. Now Mr. Bevin and Mr. Byrnes were unable to force the Red Army to retire from Central Europe. But they undertook to make the Red Army retire by concentrating on the satellites. The Russians were as far west as they were because they were occupying the satellites. Mr. Byrnes and Mr. Bevin thought that if they could conclude treaties of peace with the satellites, the Russians would then have to evacuate Central and Eastern Europe. This would, they told themselves, arrest the spread of communism, would reestablish democracy and liberty behind the iron curtain, and would restore the balance of power in Germany and in Europe, which had been so radically upset by the advance of the Red Army to the Elbe River.

From the London Conference of September, 1945, through the Paris Conference which closed in October, 1946, they worked on this particular project to the exclusion of all other projects for the settlement of the world war.

The Big Three chose to begin the settlement of the world war in the eastern half of Europe. This was a gigantic blunder, made by men who had had no part in the strategic conduct of the war, and failed to take into account its strategic consequences. For it narrowed the issue between Russia and the West to the very region where the conflict was sharpest and a settlement the most difficult.

Rumania, Bulgaria, Hungary, and Finland had been occupied by the Red Army. The greater part of Venezia Giulia to the suburbs of Gorizia and Trieste was occupied by the Yugoslav Army. The Italian peninsula, up to the line to which Tito's troops were pushed back, was occupied by British and American troops. The Italian colonial empire was occupied by British troops. Given the military position at the end of the war, it would not have been possible to choose a worse theater of diplomatic negotiation in which to initiate a world settlement.

Mr. Byrnes and Mr. Bevin had set themselves an impossible task. While they held firmly for the Western powers the whole position in Africa and the Mediterranean—which they had won by defeating Italy—and the whole of Western Germany containing 46 million Germans to 18 million in the Russian zone, containing the greater part of the demobilized and disbanded veterans of the Wehrmacht and 70 percent of Germany's prewar heavy industry, they undertook by negotiation and diplomatic pressure to reduce the position in Eastern Europe—which the Soviet Union had won because the Red Army had defeated two thirds of the German Army.

I am not saying that it was not a desirable and a necessary thing to reduce the military expansion of Russia. I have no doubt that it is. But I am saying that it was an impossible thing to do immediately, and as our prime object, in the first few months after the war. Mr. Byrnes and Mr. Bevin, armed only with the Atlantic Charter and the Yalta Declaration, were attempting to take by frontal assault the main positions held by the Red Army. These positions are looked upon by all Russians as the British look upon the Low Countries, as we look upon the Caribbean region—as vital to the security of Russia against invasion. Mr. Byrnes and Mr. Bevin picked the one region of the globe where the Soviet Union was the strongest, and we most nearly impotent. In this region the Russians were in possession and could act; Mr. Byrnes and Mr. Bevin could only argue and protest.

In any other region they had power, influence, and possessions with which to bargain. They had two-thirds of Germany, much the best part of Germany. They had Japan. They had the leading position in China. They had as their close partners France and the highly civilized nations of Western and Northern and Southern Europe. They had the Mediterranean. They had the Middle East. They had the whole of Africa. They had Southern Asia. They had the whole colonial world. They had the whole democratic world. They had the whole capitalist system. They were preponderant in the organization of the United Nations. They had command of all the seas. They had command of the air. They had the atomic bomb.

The one thing they did not have was ground armies to match the Red Army in the region which the Red Army had just conquered triumphantly, and at a terrible cost of blood and treasure. Yet that was the region where they elected to put to the test their relations with the Soviet Union and the whole great business of a world settlement.

Was it not certain that here they must fail, as in fact they have failed, and in the failure to reach a settlement where it was most difficult to reach it, that they must make it infinitely difficult to make any general settlement? Let no one seek to explain away the failure by pointing out how brutal, how stubborn, how faithless, how aggressive the Russians have proved themselves to be. The worse one thinks of the Russians, the greater must be deemed the error of having elected to challenge the Russians first of all on the ground where they were most able to be, and were most certain to be, brutal, stubborn, faithless, and aggressive.

When Mr. Byrnes and Mr. Bevin decided to concentrate their efforts on Eastern Europe, they may have believed that they could not deal with Germany, with Europe as a whole, with the Mediterranean, the Middle East, the Far East, and the colonies unless they could first reduce the power of the Soviet Union. But they had no way of compelling the Soviet Union to relax its grip on Eastern Europe. There may have been as many as two hundred Soviet divisions within reach of that region of the world, whereas the British and American forces were being withdrawn and demobilized rapidly.

If, as many of Mr. Byrnes's advisers believed, the Russians wished to keep the non-Soviet world unsettled while they consolidated their own conquests behind the iron curtain, then Machiavelli himself could not have devised a plan which served better this Russian purpose. Mr. Byrnes and Mr. Bevin have spent their energies assaulting the strongest position of Russia's vital interests. Thus they have furnished the Soviet Union with reasons, with pretexts, for an iron rule behind the iron curtain, and with ground for believing what Russians are conditioned to believe: that a coalition is being organized to destroy them.

At the same time Mr. Bevin and Mr. Byrnes have subjected the small nations, which they meant to befriend, to the cruel ordeal of having to stand up publicly every day and, in the presence of Messrs. Molotov and Vishinsky, to say whether they are with the Soviet Union or with the Anglo-Americans. As a result we have compromised the political leaders and parties in Poland and elsewhere who wished to be independent of Moscow. We have sponsored them without in fact being able to support them. . . .

Poland is no more independent than it was—though we have pounded on the iron curtain for more than a year. For Poland cannot be made an independent state simply by detaching Poland from Russian domination. The fact is that Poland cannot live independently in a political vacuum. Poland can be independent only if she is attached to a European system which has settled with Germany. The same holds for Austria, for Hungary, and for Czechoslovakia. They cannot, they will not, they dare not, detach themselves from Russia unless there is something else to which they can attach themselves. That something else cannot be the waning power of Britain or the distant power of the United States. It can be only a framework for continental Europe. . . .

The answer to Russian domination in Eastern Europe was to confront them with the solidarity of the West, as an accomplished fact. Then, instead of our pushing against and picking at the Russian orbit, we should have been pulling the people of Europe away from it, pulling them not into a British-American orbit but into the orbit of Europe itself. The peoples of Eastern Europe would have had another place to go. They would have had reason for going there. But now, as we have managed the matter, we have invited them to quarrel with the Russians though we can give them only our moral support. We have not offered them the prospect of the solidarity of Europe but a choice between the Russians and ourselves—with the Continent as the appointed theater of another war.

It is most significant, I think, that in this country and in Great Britain, the men who have been trying to settle the war are a different set of men from those who conducted the war. This is most unusual. The leading figures at the Congress of Vienna and at the Paris Conference of 1919 were the leading figures of the war. But this time they have not been. Roosevelt was dead, Churchill was out of office, and Stalin had withdrawn into the recesses of the Kremlin. . . .

As the war was concluded and before it could be settled, Roosevelt and Churchill were replaced by Truman and Attlee, Byrnes and Bevin. The peacemakers for the Western world were men to whom the problems of war and the settlement of war were novel. They had experience only in the internal politics of the two democracies, where the consideration of high strategy and high diplomacy plays no part. The settlement of the war, which was integral with the conduct of the war, was abruptly transferred from the commanders in chief to civilian politicians.

Mr. Attlee and Mr. Bevin had, to be sure, been members of the War Cabinet, and had no doubt been kept reasonably well-informed by Mr. Churchill and Mr. Eden about the course of the war. But they had been immersed in domestic affairs and neither of them had, I believe, ever participated in any of the international councils of war before they took over at Potsdam. Mr. Truman had been a Senator who investigated aspects of our own mobilization. He had had no part in the direction of the war. Mr. Byrnes had been at the White House, and therefore much closer to the center of things. But until he attended the Yalta Conference, his task was to act for the President on matters that were not in the field of high policy, so that the President would be free to devote his main attention to the strategy and diplomacy of the war.

The civilian politicians, suddenly and unexpectedly charged with the settlement of the war, were unable to learn quickly the vocabulary and the grammar of diplomacy. Thus they mistook the strategical realities, and committed themselves to the task of negotiating the Soviet Union out of the sphere of its maximum interest and influence. When they found that they could not do this by arguing with M. Molotov, they fell back on the procedure and the tactics which they had learned to use against their opponents in domestic politics. . . .

But to apply the methods of domestic politics to international politics is like using the rules of checkers in a game of chess. Within a democratic state, conflicts are decided by an actual or a potential count of votes—as the saying goes, by ballots rather than bullets. But in a world of sovereign states conflicts are decided by power, actual or potential, for the ultimate arbiter is not an election but war.

To apply among sovereign states the procedures of a democratic state is, therefore, to invite trouble. The voting cannot decide the issue. But the issues are sharply defined by the voting. This causes everyone to speculate on the chances of war. Mr. Byrnes came home from Paris and deplored the amount of talk about war. But if day after day the use of public votes has advertised—the apologists say "clarified"—a conflict among armed states, and if it is demonstrated day after day that a majority of votes does not decide the issue, it is inevitable that men should think about war, which is the only arbiter that can decide an irreconcilable issue among great powers.

So what the world has seen is not the triumph of democracy but a failure of diplomacy. Yet it is only by diplomacy that the interests of sovereign nations can be modified, adjusted, and reconciled.

This failure of diplomacy is not necessarily fatal and irreparable. The first year of peacemaking may prove to have been the hardest and the worst. For while the peacemakers have not advanced towards a settlement, or even conceived in outline the form and structure of a settlement, their peoples realize it. They themselves may realize it. What they have come to is a deadlock and a stalemate. But since everywhere the hatred of war is much stronger than the willingness to fight a war, there is a margin of safety in the diplomatic failure.

Nuremberg, Germany, after bombings in 1945. *(U.S. Office of War Information)*

# II The Troublesome Issues: Security and Economic Recovery

*Gar Alperovitz*

# THE USE OF THE ATOMIC BOMB

*In 1965, Gar Alperovitz published his* Atomic Diplomacy: Hiroshima and Pots-dam, *a controversial book which challenged the traditional story of the decision to drop the atomic bomb on Japan, August 6, 1945. The atomic weapon, Alperovitz argues, was closely linked to American diplomacy. Its use was unnecessary to end the Pacific war, viable alternatives were rejected, and the bomb was exploded to frighten the Soviets into diplomatic concessions. Alperovitz updated his thinking in the following speech of December 1970 to the annual meeting of the American Association for the Advancement of Science. He is co-director of the Exploratory Project for Economic Alternatives in Washington, D.C. and is also a Fellow of The Institute for Policy Studies there, as well as co-director of the Cambridge Policy Studies Institute in Cambridge, Mass. Alperovitz has included other commentaries on atomic diplomacy in his* Cold War Essays *(1970). His ideas have stimulated vigorous debate, including Adam Ulam's critique in the next selection.*

Most historians now agree, *in retrospect*, with the conclusion of the United States Strategic Bombing Survey; namely, that the Japanese would have surrendered without the use of the atomic bomb and without an invasion. *The bombs were unnecessary.*

There is also evidence that most, if not all, key American policy makers were aware this was possible *at the time;* they urged policies —such as changing the surrender terms, describing in proclamations the precise nature of the nuclear weapons, awaiting the outcome of a Russian declaration of war—to see if surrender were possible *before* using the atomic bomb.

Although there were three months before a small landing was scheduled (on Kyushu), and six months before the "planned" invasion available to test the various options offered without losing lives in an assault, official policy makers passed up all opportunities to end the war without the atomic bomb. Winston Churchill's observation is quite accurate: "The historical fact remains, and must be

Gar Alperovitz, "The Use of the Atomic Bomb." Excerpts from a speech to the 137th Meeting of the American Association for the Advancement of Science, Chicago, Illinois, December 28, 1970. Reprinted by permission of Gar Alperovitz. Further details and references to evidence reported in the speech may be obtained in Alperovitz's *Atomic Diplomacy* (Simon and Schuster, 1965) and *Cold War Essays* (Doubleday, 1970).

judged in the after time, that the decision whether or not to use the atomic bomb ... *was never even an issue.*"

The main reason it was not an issue seems to be that a "momentum of events" took over. The *momentum*, however, even many conservative historians see is *not* easily explained by military factors but rather, to a significant extent, by *diplomatic considerations related to Russia.*

The remaining issue is not whether these considerations played a role, but precisely how significant they were. ...

As to the first point, most historians agree with Herbert Feis that

> *there cannot be a well-grounded dissent from the conclusion reached as early as 1945 by members of the U.S. Strategic Bombing Survey ...* "*that certainly prior to 31 December 1945 and in all probability prior to 1 November 1945, Japan would have surrendered even if the atomic bombs had not been dropped, even if Russia had not entered the war, and even if no invasion had been planned or contemplated.*"

Indeed, there were many options available. The first was a diplomatic one: Since intercepted Japanese cables showed that the Emperor was actively trying to open a negotiating channel through Moscow, it seemed that a minor face-saving change in the unconditional surrender formula might have ended the fighting. The second option was military, but did not involve invasion. The Navy and Air Force felt that a blockade alone, or a blockade combined with conventional bombardment, might have ended the war. The third—and most important—possibility was to await the Russian declaration of war, which was expected in early August. With Japan tottering, United States intelligence experts estimated that the shock of Russia's shift from neutrality to full-scale war might in itself end the war unconditionally. The fourth course was to test the potency of a specific advance warning of Russia's intention to declare war. The fifth was to demonstrate the atomic bomb in an unpopulated area. The sixth was a specific advance warning that an atomic bomb existed and would be used unless Japan surrendered.

The recent release of 1945 State Department documents shows that use of the bomb seemed unnecessary to many, not only in retrospect but *at the time.* The Japanese code had been broken early in the war. Until June 1945 it may have been possible to believe an invasion was inevitable. In the middle of June, however, six members of the Japanese Supreme War Council authorized Foreign Minister Togo to approach the Soviet Union "with a view to terminating the war if possible by September." At this time the Emperor himself became personally involved in the effort, and a stream of intercepted messages revealed his urgent efforts to open a negotiating channel through Moscow. During the last days of July, for instance, a message instructed the Japanese ambassador in Tokyo to arrange a Moscow visit for the Emperor's personal envoy, Prince Konoye: "The mission . . . was to ask the Soviet government to take part in mediation to end the present war and to transmit the complete Japanese case in this respect. . . . Prince Konoye was especially charged by His Majesty the Emperor to convey to the Soviet government that it was exclusively the desire of His Majesty to avoid more bloodshed. . . ."

This message was given directly to President Truman by the Russians. (The President has confirmed that at the time he also saw it and other key cables in intercepted form.) Although it was impossible to know precisely whether the messages meant what they said, they were significant evidence of the willingness of the "other side" to negotiate. Furthermore, they showed that although the Japanese sought assurances that "our form of government" would be preserved, they were prepared to surrender on the basis of the Atlantic Charter. The "difficult point," as the Japanese foreign minister stated in one intercepted cable, was the "formality of unconditional surrender."

Most historians have ignored two crucial facts: President Truman, as the private papers of both Acting Secretary of State [Joseph C.] Grew and Secretary of War [Henry L.] Stimson show, had told both men *even before the July messages* that he had no serious objection to making the alterations in favor of the Japanese imperial "form of government" which the messages revealed were the only serious obstacle to surrender. Thus the two governments had by July apparently arrived at a basis for ending the war—and the President *knew it.*

Second, Truman had several months before the proposed November landing to find out if the Japanese position was really as close to his own as the messages suggested—*if he so desired.*

Such speculation is not a matter of hindsight. The atomic bombs could easily have been held off while other courses were attempted. Not only was it known *at the time* that the Japanese were desperately trying to keep the Russians neutral, but United States officials knew that when the Red Army marched across the Manchurian border it would drive home—especially to the Japanese military—the fact that Japan was defeated. Even without a modification in the surrender terms, the Joint Chiefs believed in early May 1945 that the mere threat of Soviet entry might produce surrender; on May 21, 1945, Secretary Stimson advised of the "profound military effect" of the Soviet declaration; and by early June, the War Department Operations Division judged that a Russian declaration of war would produce *unconditional surrender,* either alone or in combination with a landing or "imminent threat of a landing. . . ." In mid-June, General [George C.] Marshall offered this advice directly to the President. By mid-July, the Joint Intelligence Committee stated explicitly: "An entry of the Soviet Union into the war would finally convince the Japanese of the inevitability of complete defeat."

Nor was it a matter of hindsight that a change in the surrender terms alone might have produced surrender. Faint Japanese peace feelers appeared as early as September 1944—almost a year before the bombing of Hiroshima. In April 1945 the Joint Staff planners advised that an invasion *"threat* in itself" might bring about *unconditional* surrender. And even before the intercepted July messages indicated that the only difficult point was the "formality" of unconditional surrender, Acting Secretary of State Grew, Secretary of the Navy [James] Forrestal, and Secretary of War Stimson all urged the President to modify the surrender terms. Again, the President chose *not* to test whether, as seemed likely, this would end the war.

Some, like the Franck Committee,[1] urged the "technical demonstration" option *at the time.* Others—particularly Assistant Secretary of War John McCloy and Undersecretary of the Navy Ralph Bard—urged that the Japanese be specifically informed about the atomic bomb. They did so, too, *at the time.*

Oddly, when one reviews the military positions, although few men

---

[1] Headed by James Franck, this independent committee of concerned nuclear scientists argued in a June 1945 report against a surprise attack on Japan which might arouse mistrust in a shocked Russia.—Ed.

actively challenged the assumption the bomb would be used, there seemed to be no driving, overwhelming military demand for its use. If it was a matter of overriding necessity, as some claim, who in the United States government not only went along with the decision but *actively pushed for it?* Who insisted that none of the options be tested? Certainly not the secretary of state for much of the period, Edward Stettinius. Stettinius urged that the Russians be included in the warning proclamation. The acting secretary of state for much of the period, Joseph Grew, urged specific assurances for the Emperor. So did Secretary of War Stimson—up to the very last minute before the President issued the Potsdam Proclamation. The Navy Department—both the secretary and the undersecretary—either seconded Grew or suggested both a compound warning and a change in the surrender formula.

As for the military, the Air Force (General [Carl A.] Spaatz, Commander of the Strategic Air Force, and General [Henry H.] Arnold, Commanding General of the U.S. Army Air Forces) did not feel that the bomb was vital. General Curtis LeMay is reported to have felt that "even without the atomic bomb and the Russian entry into the war, Japan would have surrendered in two weeks. . . . The atomic bomb had nothing to do with the end of the war." Admiral King did not think it essential.

The President's Chief of Staff, Admiral [William] Leahy (the Henry Kissinger of the period) wrote after the war:

> *In my opinion the use of this barbarous weapon at Hiroshima and Nagasaki was of no material assistance in our war against Japan. The Japanese were already defeated and ready to surrender.*

Of the key diplomatic and military departments involved, all but one can be eliminated as prime movers inflexibly unwilling to test other possibilities. The situation, then, was hardly one in which cabinet members and Joint Chiefs were lined up shoulder to shoulder, unanimously demanding that the bomb be used without considering the alternatives.

General [Dwight D.] Eisenhower, for one, actively advised *against* it. Here is Eisenhower's pre-Hiroshima response when Stimson told him that the bomb would be used:

*During his recitation of the relevant facts, I had been conscious of a feeling of depression and so I voiced to him my grave misgivings, first on the basis of my belief that Japan was already defeated and that dropping the bomb was completely unnecessary, and secondly, because I thought that our country should avoid shocking world opinion by the use of a weapon whose employment was, I thought, no longer mandatory as a measure to save American lives.*

"It wasn't necessary to hit them with that awful thing," he later recalled.

The other key Army figure was General Marshall. How strongly did he urge it? Clearly Marshall wished to prevent an invasion if possible. But he was also one of the men who advised the President as early as mid-June that a Russian declaration of war in itself might bring unconditional surrender. At other times, too, he reminded Stimson of the importance of a Russian entry, although he differed as to the timing. Marshall is on record as having favored in May a change in the unconditional surrender formula. *He seems clearly to have understood* that a Russian declaration combined with a modification of the surrender formula was likely to end the war not only before the invasion itself, but even before the proposed November landing on Kyushu. Marshall hinted as much in the one important interview he gave on this subject before his death: He remarked that the bombs shortened the war only "by months." The idea of a powerful, overriding military demand that the bomb simply had to be used dissolves upon close inspection.

In summary, there is substantial evidence that, unless one regards the President of the United States as totally ignorant, or blind to all of the information *offered at the time,* there were many possibilities he *could have tested* before risking one life in a landing, to say nothing of an invasion. Why were the options not tested?

As many now see, there was no real "decision" to use the atomic bomb. General [Leslie] Groves has underscored the point: *"There was never any question as to the use of the bomb. . . ."* Instead, the use of the bomb flowed out of the *momentum* of events, out of the locked-in quality of men (and institutions) who, once committed, saw no way to rearrange their priorities and decisions.

Most observers who recognize the point assume the momentum

was a military one, generated in the rush to end World War II. Let me stress here again that, although the word "momentum" may be helpful, the word "military" is not, since by July 1945 none of the highest *military* officials actively urged that the bomb was essential to end the war without a land invasion (although, of course, they *had* argued this view earlier in the spring of 1945).

The question is: Why did the momentum remain when the military reasons disappeared during the summer of 1945 as Japan's power crumbled? Though it is impossible with presently available materials to answer the question conclusively, it appears that the inability of American policy makers to alter their assumption that the bomb would be used can be explained, after July 1945, *only in conjunction with diplomatic plans* related to the Soviet Union. In short, a *diplomatic* momentum had by this time taken control of policy.

One may sense the relationship of the "momentum" to diplomatic considerations by asking why it was that the Secretary of State ([James F.] Byrnes) was in such a hurry to end the war—not merely before a landing, but *immediately.* Why such haste with three months available before a landing?

The use of the bomb, of course, might have made concessions to the Emperor unnecessary, but few have seriously argued that atomic bombs were used merely to protect the sanctity of the unconditional surrender formula—a matter which the President had already said was not a major issue—and which after Hiroshima did not prove to be.

The only other important reason for wanting an *immediate* surrender—as distinct from one within the period between July and the November landing—was that the Russians were expected to declare war in early August, and an *immediate* surrender might have ended the war without their entry.

P. M. S. Blackett, the British Nobel Prize-winning physicist, pointed this out twenty years ago. Since then, Secretary Byrnes has repeatedly and openly confirmed that in July 1945, after the successful Alamogordo test, he and the President hoped to end the war before Russia entered and gained control of Manchuria and North China: "We wanted to get through with the Japanese phase of the war before the Russians came in."

At Potsdam, Churchill was aware of Byrnes's objective. He told Eden: "It is quite clear that the United States do not at the present time desire Russian participation in the war." An entry dated July 28, 1945 in Secretary of the Navy Forrestal's diary records that Byrnes made no bones about that fact that "he was most anxious to get the Japanese affair over with before the Russians got in. . . ."

One must, however, read the documents of the time to understand how intimately the bomb was connected with diplomacy toward Russia. First, here is a diary entry Stimson made after a discussion of United States objectives in Asia almost three months *before* Hiroshima:

> *I thought it was premature to ask those questions; at least we were not yet in a position to answer them. . . . It may be necessary to have it out with Russia on her relations to Manchuria and Port Arthur and various other parts of North China, and also the relations of China to us. Over any such tangled weave of problems [the atomic bomb secret] would be dominant. . . . It seems a terrible thing to gamble with such stakes in diplomacy without your master card in your hand. . . .*

Second, another passage from Stimson's diary, written at Potsdam after the President received a report describing the successful atomic test:

> *[The Prime Minister] told me . . . "Now I know what happened to Truman yesterday. I couldn't understand it. When he got to the meeting after having read this report he was a changed man. He told the Russians just where they got on and off, and generally bossed the whole meeting. . . ."*

Third, Lord Alanbrooke's diary at Potsdam:

> *[The Prime Minister] . . . had absorbed all the minor American exaggerations and, as a result, was completely carried away. . . . We now had something in our hands which would redress the balance with the Russians . . . (pushing out his chin and scowling); now we could say, "If you insist on doing this or that, well. . . ." And then where are the Russians!*

Fourth, from Stimson's diary a few weeks after Hiroshima:

> *I took up the question . . . how to handle Russia with the big bomb. I found that Byrnes was very much against any attempt to cooperate with Russia. His mind is full of his problems with the coming meeting of foreign ministers and he looks to having the presence of the bomb in his pocket, so to speak, as a great weapon to get through the thing. . . .*

Truman also told Stimson during the Potsdam negotiations that the bomb gave him "an entirely new feeling of confidence." Indeed, the bomb served to toughen the United States approach to disputed Central and Eastern European issues even before it was actually used. Few recall this murky history, but it can be shown that the President, who had already experienced difficulties in dealing with Russia, by July 1945 had derived sufficient confidence from the new weapon to attempt major reversals in negotiations over Poland, Germany, Hungary, Bulgaria, and Rumania.

More important for our purposes, once the bomb had become involved in diplomatic planning, *this fact itself* began to color the approach to its use. To understand the point, the sequence of events in 1945 must be precisely recalled: During *early* 1945, *before* the Japanese began their rather frantic efforts to open negotiations, it was assumed, quite naturally, that the bomb, like any military weapon, would be used to shorten the war. As A. H. Compton[2] recalled, it was a "foregone conclusion that the bomb would be used," and the scientists were asked not *whether* but simply *how* best to use it. Having shared this natural assumption, President Truman *based a new diplomatic strategy on it,* deciding in late April 1945 to postpone diplomatic confrontations until the new weapon—"the master card"—had been demonstrated and had strengthened his hand against Russia. But *thereafter,* between mid-June and late July, mounting evidence showed that the Japanese were prepared to stop the war on acceptable terms.

It was in the *early* period, as [J. Robert] Oppenheimer[3] has recalled, that "much of the discussion revolved around the question raised by Secretary Stimson as to whether there was any hope of using the development to get less barbarous relations with Russia." Truman has written that in April Byrnes advised the bomb would permit the United States "to dictate [its] own terms at the end of the war." Inevitably, in May and June the first military assumption became freighted with the greater issue of impressing Russia. "That bomb was developed on time...," Vannevar Bush has testified; not only did it produce an immediate surrender, but "it was also de-

[2] Member of the Interim Committee appointed by President Harry S. Truman to advise him on the use of the atomic bomb and its political implications.—Ed.
[3] Director of the Los Alamos, New Mexico Laboratory which ran the test of the atomic bomb on July 16, 1945.—Ed.

livered on time so that there was no necessity for any concessions to Russia at the end of the war."

Thus it appears that the natural military assumption that the bomb would be used became intermeshed with diplomatic strategy in a way so subtle it was probably not completely understood by the participants themselves. Using the bomb became so deep an assumption that, as Churchill reminds us, "the historical fact remains, and must be judged in the after time, that the decision whether or not to use the atomic bomb . . . *was never even an issue*." After July, when it became apparent the bomb was no longer militarily essential, the evidence shows that, although other choices were offered, Secretary of State Byrnes and President Truman were unable or unwilling to test them—and they never challenged the basic assumption as did some military men (like Eisenhower) who were not involved in diplomacy. It seems that they were either blind to the implications of the changed military situation, or, more explicitly, (as Leo Szilard[4] reported after a conversation in May 1945 with Byrnes), that Byrnes at least *understood* Japan was ready to end the war, but wanted the bomb anyway to make the Russians more "manageable." Either possibility leads to the conclusion that the overriding reason for the use of the bomb was that (implicitly or explicitly) it was judged necessary to strengthen the United States's hand against Russia.

There has been much discussion recently about the Japanese military officers who were against surrender. It is true that a faction was actively opposed. Nevertheless, there was plenty of time, *had policy makers so desired*, to test the power of these groups within official circles. Some historians simply record the fact that an opposition group existed and *assume* that they were all powerful. The truth is that they were, simply, a faction which, ultimately, most intelligence experts believed, would be overcome by events. But again, the vital point is that there was *no interest whatsoever in testing whether this was so in the time available*. Instead, the civilians of Hiroshima and Nagasaki were massacred. . . .

---

[4] A scientist who worked in the Manhattan Project for atomic development at the University of Chicago and who argued against unilateral use of the bomb for fear that it would badly damage postwar international cooperation.—Ed.

## Adam B. Ulam
# THE DIPLOMATIC IMPOTENCE
# OF THE BOMB

*In his book,* Expansion and Coexistence: The History of Soviet Foreign Policy *(1968; rev. ed. 1974), Adam Ulam depicted a weak and cautious postwar Russia with no blueprint for expansion and a realistic Stalin who would not risk a military clash with the stronger United States. Ulam also wrote that the atomic bomb did not cause "either panic or undue apprehension" in the Kremlin, and hence that the American monopoly of the nuclear weapon until 1949 was not central to the Cold War. In the following selection from his book* The Rivals *(1971), Ulam challenges revisionists like Gar Alperovitz by arguing that the development and use of the atomic bomb produced little change in American diplomacy toward the Soviet Union and was not employed as a diplomatic weapon. In fact he suggests that it should have been used as a "bargaining counter" to secure diplomatic advantages. Ulam has been on the faculty of Harvard University since 1946 and is the author of* Titoism and the Cominform *(1952) and* Stalin: The Man and His Era *(1973).*

. . . The news of the successful testing of the atom bomb was conveyed, after some hesitation, to Stalin by Truman [at the Potsdam Conference]. During a break in one of the sessions, the President simply approached Stalin to say that the United States had a weapon of unusual force. It would have dearly pleased Churchill, avidly watching the scene from some distance, if Stalin had blanched or in a broken voice asked for details. But none of that. He was pleased to hear the news and hoped the Americans would use the new weapon against Japan, said Stalin. Churchill and Truman, the wish being father to the thought, concluded that this was the first Stalin had heard about the atomic bomb. Some Soviet accounts embellish the occasion. According to Marshal Zhukov's memoirs, published in 1969, which strive to rehabilitate Stalin, the dictator reported wrathfully upon his return to Russian headquarters how gleefully Churchill had watched the encounter, and ordered an immediate speedup in Soviet nuclear research. We know from more reliable sources, however, that Soviet nuclear research had begun on a modest scale in

From *The Rivals: America and Russia Since World War II* by Adam B. Ulam. Copyright © 1971 by Adam B. Ulam. Reprinted by permission of The Viking Press, Inc., New York, pp. 76–77, 81–82, 93–95, 103–107. (Footnotes edited.)

1942 and gathered momentum after January 1945, when Soviet espionage reported that the Americans were making progress on the weapon. It is unlikely that Stalin was entirely surprised and equally unlikely that he realized fully the awesome potentialities of the bomb.

Churchill's joy at the news was great. He felt that the bomb would at least neutralize the Russians' military preponderance in Europe and might yet save the Continent from Soviet domination. This excessive joy now warped his political judgment. He claims to have perceived a new air of determination and strength in Truman's behavior at the conference. He believed that the Americans no longer wished for Soviet participation in the Pacific war. This was largely wishful thinking. There had been no abrupt turnabout in American policy. It was still thought likely that a speedy end to the war might require an invasion of Japan, and hence Soviet assistance was still needed. It will be argued below that possession of the atomic bomb had in fact a debilitating effect on American foreign policy vis-à-vis Russia. For a dictator, a special advantage in military technology is a spur to action; for democracy, it is a convenient rationalization for inaction. . . .

Few historical arguments are more fallacious than the one advanced by "revisionist" historians concerning the use of the atom bomb. Its thesis is that the first bomb was dropped not in the hope of speeding Japan's surrender, but to scare the Russians and to wrest political concessions from them. As such, it cannot withstand the test of simple logic, not to mention the facts. If the bomb was used in order to rob the Russians of some political advantages, if the Americans knew that Japan would collapse without Hiroshima, why did they still require Soviet help against Japan? Why did they not cancel the whole Yalta bargain, under which Soviet help was to be paid for by substantial Chinese concessions?

In fact this would have been a most sensible as well as fair policy: You tell your ally his help is no longer needed, he no longer has to incur casualties, expenses, etc. Hardly atomic blackmail. But as we have seen, even at Potsdam *after* the new weapon had been fully tested, it was a firm decision of the American leaders that Soviet help would still be needed, and that the price for it should be paid in full.

We shall revert to the revisionist argument, since it has become an important part of the argument concerning the Cold War. As a matter [of] fact, what *is* astounding is that *no* attempt was made by the United States to exploit politically the monopoly of this weapon of unique destructiveness when it came to the peace settlement in Europe or Asia. *Even Soviet sources,* while freely accusing the United States of practicing atomic diplomacy during the Cold War, and assailing the atomic bombing of Hiroshima and Nagasaki as both unnecessary and barbarous, do not accuse the United States of threatening the Soviet Union in 1945. Indeed, the Russians would be hard put to specify what more the USSR would have gotten had the United States *not* had the bomb.

\*     \*     \*

When it comes to political disasters Americans are strangely unwilling to accept an error of judgment as an explanation. They tend to seek the answer in moral guilt. Policy mistakes are assumed to have their source in sin (a striking parallel to Stalin's Russia, where an official was seldom discharged for incompetence, administrative or political failure being attributed to treason, Trotskyism, etc.). When it soon became obvious that the peace settlement was both imperfect and precarious, the public inquest addressed itself to the question: Who is guilty? It was easy to answer by attributing moral depravity and evil designs to the rulers of the Soviet Union. Few have the patience to probe for more subtle historical explanations, and fewer still to follow such reasoning. Then the inquiry shifted inevitably to the American scene and asked: Who betrayed? The American people were unwilling to recognize themselves as having been naive and historically unsophisticated, but they were ready to accept that they had been intentionally deceived. Their officials, especially those entrusted with foreign affairs, were accused, in turn, not so much of being misinformed or unsubtle, as, in some crucial cases, being guilty of virtual treason. The United States, then, with its idealism in world affairs, was confronted with the bad will of its partners, primarily the Soviet Union, its policies constantly frustrated or betrayed not through the incompetence or unrealism of their executors but because of their Communist leanings or ties.

A reaction to these simplistic views of the late 1940s and '50s made its debut when the American people tired in turn of these undifferentiated anti-Communist policies and were frustrated in their exertions and sacrifices on behalf of what had long been known as the free world. But what the "revisionists" revise is not so much the plot as the cast of characters. The villain is no longer the Soviet Union or "godless communism," but American capitalism, or that equally murky entity, the American establishment and especially that branch referred to (the term having been spawned in a fateful moment by General Eisenhower's speech writer) as the "military-industrial complex." And as a large part of the American public had confessed to having sinned by accepting the notion of a peaceful and progressive Russia, so now the society was accused of having indulged in unpardonable "arrogance of power." Historical revisionism is thus one expression of that intellectual masochism which has colored the discussion of so many problems in American society. With this broader phenomenon we shall have to deal later. Here we must address ourselves to the immediate problem: Do the views propounded by so-called revisionist historians illuminate or obscure American policy in the period under discussion?

Some of their arguments, as we have seen in the case of the alleged practice of atomic diplomacy, fall of their own weight. But there is an extension of the atomic diplomacy argument which is sometimes used: that the mere fact of the United States' monopoly of the weapon, even if Russia was not explicitly threatened, was bound to have upsetting effects on the USSR and to make Stalin more insistent about Russia's security—hence about having his way in Eastern Europe, etc.; that the best way of disarming Russia's suspicions, of moderating her rule in East Europe, and of securing her collaboration within the U.N. would have been a generous American offer to share atomic technology. This view is, in fact, close to the one expounded after the war by Henry Wallace. What is more surprising, something similar was urged by Henry Stimson, then U.S. secretary of war, shortly before he left office in 1945. In his memorandums to Truman, the aged American statesman had never been clear as to what exactly he proposed should be done concerning the USSR and the bomb—at one time suggesting that the secrets of the bomb could not be shared until Stalin put in effect the 1936 constitution and granted democracy to the Russian people, at another time thinking of offering to trade the weapon for introduction of democratic freedoms in Russia. Finally, in a memorandum dated September 11, 1945, Stimson seemed to lean (his language is not very clear) to an outright sharing of atomic technology with Russia. The letter is full of qualifications and hypothetical cases, but in a key sentence Stimson says: "The chief lesson I have learned in a long life is that the only way you make a man trustworthy is to trust him, and the surest way to make him untrustworthy is to distrust him and show your distrust." [1] It is a heartening sentiment, especially coming from a hardheaded man of affairs, a lifelong Republican, and a lawyer. Stimson can be pardoned for not being familiar with Stalin's biography. But he ought to have remembered the consequences of Neville Chamberlain's applying the principle he recommends in dealing with Hitler.

The letter is valuable testimony to the embarrassment widely felt in some American circles about possession of the atom bomb, the feeling that somehow it was not fair for the U.S. to enjoy a monopoly of this weapon. Stimson deplored that the bomb was viewed by some "as a substantial offset to the growth of Russian influence on the continent"—that growth in influence presumably being, in contrast to the American bomb, natural and justifiable. Furthermore, we know that his views on some form of collaboration with the Russians in the nuclear field were shared by a number of high American officials. Hardly atomic diplomacy.

But the main fallacy of Stimson in 1945 and the revisionists today is to believe, as Stimson wrote, that satisfactory relations with Russia were "not merely connected with but virtually dominated by the problem of the atomic bomb." Absolutely nothing suggests that Soviet policies in 1945 were dominated by the fear of or were a reaction to America's possession of the atom bomb. Stalin's policies toward the United States were dominated by two feelings: one of great respect for the United States' vast economic and hence military potential, quite apart from the bomb; and the other of scant respect for the American capacity to translate this potential into political gains. There was thus no immediate fear, but only vague apprehension that sometime in the future America's resources *might* be mobilized and employed against the USSR. But to begin to remove these apprehensions, Russia would have had to become as strong economically as the United States. . . .

The problem of the bomb of course increasingly dominated

---

[1] Henry L. Stimson and McGeorge Bundy. *On Active Service in Peace and War* (New York, 1947), p. 644.

American thinking on world affairs, and eventually, with the develop-
met of the hydrogen bomb and intercontinental missiles, it posed a
basic challenge to the very possibility of a rational conduct of foreign
relations.

Paradoxical though it sounds, however, the early monopoly of the
new weapon debilitated rather than helped American foreign policy.
In peacetime, democracies are prone to indolence and procrastina-
tion in international affairs, and the bomb was a powerful inducement
in that direction. It encouraged, in short, a Maginot Line psychology.

We have also seen that with some representatives of the American
government, among them a man as unimpeachably conservative in
background as Stimson, possession of the atomic bomb led to a
feeling of national guilt. Push it farther and you would get arguments
that somehow it was not "fair" for the United States to have this
advantage; as long as it did, wasn't it fair for the Russians to have
Eastern Europe? Wasn't Communist distrust of the United States and
its intentions somehow justified? . . .

The bomb could not be used as a threat or as a means of pressure
(there is a difference between the two), but it might have made sense
to use it as a bargaining counter—not, to be sure, as poor Stimson
speculated to entice Stalin into democratic ways, but to secure some
concrete political advantage: genuine democratic elections for an
all-German government in 1947, a free political life for Poland, etc.
Scientists after all were warning that the American monopoly would
not last long. Even before 1950 and the apprehension of Klaus Fuchs,
it was realized that the Russians had secured valuable information
through espionage; and probabilities are that Stalin would have
spurned any bargains, so confident was he that he could wait out
the Americans and get his own bomb without paying for it. But at
least it could have been tried and the offer would have been of great
psychological value as demonstrating the *right kind* of idealism: The
Americans were willing to share the awesome secret, not to obtain
Russian signature on a sonorous declaration, not because it would
bring tears of gratitude and trust from the Soviets, but to secure real
freedom for real people. But no public figure made such a proposal,
in fact it does not seem to have occurred to anybody. Like a miser
with a treasure, so America hugged the evanescent atom monopoly
to its bosom, equally unable to exploit it or to exchange it for something useful.

The last may not seem quite fair in view of the United States' offer to give up its monopoly in favor of international control of atomic energy. This was elaborated in the Baruch Plan, the document put forward by the American government in 1946 proposing an international atomic development authority to be set up under the auspices of the United Nations and endowed with a virtual monopoly on all forms of atomic energy production. It would be armed with the power of sanctions against any state violating the agreement, which sanctions were to be imposed by a majority vote (thus the right of veto reserved to the Security Council's permanent members would be given up in this case). Once the authority was established and effectively functioning, the United States pledged, she would dispose of her stock of bombs and cease their production.

The American plan reflected several strains in American thinking at the time of its unveiling in 1946. The beginning of the Atomic Age gave rise among many, especially within the intellectual community, to the feeling epitomized by the phrase "one world or none." Time is running out on mankind, was the theme of many editorials. Cartoonists delighted in variations of the same theme with clocks set at five minutes to twelve. "It is no reflection on the [U.N.] Charter," wrote one commentator, "to say it has become a feeble and antiquated instrument for dealing with the problems of an Atomic Age. ... Time today works against peace. ... Once the nature and imminency of the peril are clearly understood by the peoples of the world their differences will not be a bar but an incentive to common government." [2] All the old complaints against the U.N. Charter's preservation of the veto power, hence of the obsolete notion of state sovereignty, were revived to nourish a myriad of new plans for world government. Understandable anxiety lay behind such agitation, and in many ways the sentiments in favor of a fundamentally new approach toward peace were commendable. Still, this burst of despair over one's own country acquiring such a decisive weapon was a remarkable phenomenon. The shock was not nearly so great nor the response so emotional at the subsequent news in 1949 of Russia's first nuclear weapon and in 1964 of China's. Time, of course, dulls sensitivity to danger.

The Baruch Plan was a carefully prepared official document, not

[2] Norman Corwin, *Modern Man Is Obsolete* (New York, 1945), pp. 41–42.

an agonized plea for mankind to repent and set up a world government. But the international authority it proposed was bound to become a sort of superstate. As such, it was simply out of the question
that the USSR would even in principle agree to the plan. They might
well, for tactical reasons, have pretended to agree, quibbled about
details, and prolonged the discussion as much as possible. But
Andrei Gromyko, then Soviet delegate to the U.N. Atomic Commission, made crystal-clear that the Soviets would never agree to a
renunciation of the veto power. All that the Soviets proposed was a
simple convention prohibiting the production or use of atomic weapons and requiring the destruction of existing ones. This position in
turn was of course unacceptable to the Americans, who would not
surrender the monopoly without what was being described as proper
safeguards: sanctions against violators, inspection, etc.

Apart from the sanctions, the mere idea of inspection ran against
the grain of the entire Soviet government. At about this time, Soviet
authorities were refusing a handful of Russian women married to
Britons and Americans during the war permission to leave the USSR.
If what those few women could tell about life in Russia was considered to be a danger justifying this extraordinary inhumanity and
pettiness, what of inspection of bomb installations and research
facilities? . . .

All the labor and ingenuity which went into the Baruch Plan were
thus wasted. From the American point of view, it must have appeared
a small price for the Soviets to pay—to waive the veto and agree on
some minimal inspection—in order to lift what must have been an
intolerable burden of anxiety about the American monopoly of the
frightful weapon. But Soviet logic was different. Apart from the considerations given above, the USSR could not possibly admit that any
agency was impartial, or more fundamentally that there *was* such a
thing as an international agency. In their eyes the United Nations
meant basically two powers: the United States and its clients, and
the USSR and its satellites. To entrust such a body with jurisdiction
over a vital aspect of national policy, to remove the one element in
the organization that nullified the West's numerical superiority—the
veto—was unthinkable, and would have been whether Stalin or any
other Communist was at the helm.

## Thomas G. Paterson
# FOREIGN AID AS A DIPLOMATIC WEAPON

*If atomic diplomacy offered one of the first stumbling blocks to a resolution of postwar differences, so too did the question of American foreign aid and Soviet economic reconstruction. In the following selection from his book* Soviet-American Confrontation *(1973), Thomas G. Paterson argues that economic recovery was a major postwar Russian goal and that the United States employed its economic power in an uncompromising way, thereby embittering Soviet-American relations. He explores the possibility of a postwar loan to Russia as peacemaker, a consideration Arthur Schlesinger, Jr. dismisses in his selection in Part 3 of this book. Paterson is a professor of history at the University of Connecticut and also the editor of* Cold War Critics *and* Containment and the Cold War. *With Les K. Adler he authored "Red Fascism," a much-debated article on the lessons Americans incorrectly drew between the 1930s and 1940s, which appeared in the* American Historical Review *(1970).*

... Ambassador to Moscow W. Averell Harriman cabled the Department of State in January, 1945, that the Soviet Union placed "high importance on a large postwar credit as a basis for the development of 'Soviet-American relations.' From his [V. M. Molotov's] statement I sensed an implication that the development of our friendly relations would depend upon a generous credit." Reconstruction was for Russia a matter of "prime importance," and Soviet leaders hoped that the United States would help finance it. In the period 1943–1945, a loan to Russia might have served as peacemaker, but by mid-1946, both nations had become increasingly uncompromising on major issues, and the usefulness of a loan to the United States, to Russia, and to amicable relations had been called into serious doubt. "Whether such a loan," Secretary of State Edward R. Stettinius, Jr., later wrote, "would have made the Soviet Union a more reasonable and cooperative nation in the postwar world will be one of the great 'if' questions of history." Some historians have simply dismissed the loan question as unimportant. The unavailability of thorough Soviet

From Thomas G. Paterson, *Soviet-American Confrontation: Postwar Reconstruction and the Origins of the Cold War* (Baltimore, 1973), pp. 33–34, 37–39, 41–44, 46–49, 51–56. Copyright © 1973 by The Johns Hopkins University Press. Reprinted by permission. This selection is a revision of Paterson's article which first appeared in the *Journal of American History* (1969). (Footnotes deleted.)

historical sources certainly makes any conclusive answer to Stet-tinius' surmise impossible. However, a considerable amount of evi-dence suggests that the United States' refusal to aid Russia's post-war reconstruction through a loan similar to that granted Britain in early 1946 may have contributed to a continuation of a low standard of living for the Russian people, with detrimental international effects; to a harsher Russian policy toward Germany and Eastern Europe; and to unsettled and inimical Soviet-American relations.

World War II had been cruel to the Russians. Coupled with the deaths of millions was the devastation of Minsk, Stalingrad, 1,710 towns, and 70,000 villages. Over 30,000 industrial plants and 40,000 miles of railroad line had been destroyed. In 1945 Soviet agricultural output was about half the 1940 level. One Department of State study reported that $16 billion in fixed capital, or one-quarter of the prewar level, had been lost, and the chief of the United Nations Relief and Rehabilitation Administration (UNRRA) mission in Byelorussia re-corded that that republic alone had suffered 800,000 dead and 1,215,000 dwellings and 4,000 bridges razed. To help repair the mas-sive war damage, the Soviet government looked eagerly to the United States. . . .

On January 3, 1945, Molotov handed Harriman the first formal request for a postwar loan. At the same time, Churchill, Stalin, and Roosevelt were settling the place and date for a Big Three meeting (Yalta), and it seemed likely that the loan question would become one of the elements in the diplomatic bargaining. Harriman was extremely annoyed by the detailed Soviet aide-mémoire and chastised Molotov for his "strange procedure" in presenting the "curiously worded document." The Soviet request was indeed bold:

> *The Soviet government accordingly wishes to state the following: Having in mind the repeated statements of American public figures concerning the desirability of receiving extensive large Soviet orders for the postwar and transition period, the Soviet government considers it possible to place or-ders on the basis of long-term credits to the amount of $6 billion. Such orders would be for manufactured goods (oil pipes, rails, railroad cars, locomotives and other products) and industrial equipment. The credit would also cover orders for locomotives, railroad cars, rails and trucks and industrial equipment placed under lend-lease but not delivered to the Soviet Union before the end of the war. The credits should run for thirty years, amortization to begin on the last day of the ninth year and to end on the last day of the thirtieth year. . . .*

Harriman implored Washington to "disregard the unconventional character of the document and the unreasonableness of its terms and chalk it up to ignorance of normal business procedures and the strange ideas of the Russians on how to get the best trade." He chided the Russians for starting "negotiations on the basis of 'twice as much for half the price.'..." Any loan, he argued, should be dependent upon Russian behavior in overall international relations. "I feel strongly," he added, "that the sooner the Soviet Union can develop a decent life for its people the more tolerant they will become." But such a concern was secondary, and he again demanded complete United States control of the funds "in order that the political advantages may be retained and that we may be satisfied that the equipment purchased is for purposes that meet our general approval."

Harriman's reaction was curious. The United States had certainly been approached before by foreign governments with detailed requests for aid; in fact, later, it was to insist that the Marshall Plan recipients draw up just such proposals. And it is diplomatic practice to ask for more than one expects to get. Harriman should not have been surprised that Russia was aware of the "repeated statements of American public figures concerning the desirability of receiving extensive large Soviet orders," for [Donald] Nelson, [Eric] Johnston, and he himself had mentioned this consideration. What perhaps disturbed him most was the boldness, thoroughness, and independent attitude expressed in the Russian request, for Russia had taken the initiative with the first detailed proposal, and Harriman seemed fearful that the United States had lost some diplomatic leverage....

In a message to the State Department on April 11, 1945, one day before Roosevelt's death, Harriman was pessimistic about any postwar economic cooperation with Russia. Although the Russians were "keen" to obtain the $6 billion credit, he believed that "it certainly should be borne in mind that our basic interests might better be served by increasing our trade with other parts of the world rather than giving preference to the Soviet Union as a source of supply." The United States should undertake a domestic conservation program and end its dependence upon Soviet imports of manganese ore by seeking supplies in Brazil, Africa, and India. Should a loan agreement ever occur, Harriman wanted strict United States control over the funds because "it is not possible to bank goodwill in Moscow. . . ." But he cautioned that "it would be inadvisable to give the Soviets the idea that we were cooling off on our desire to help . . ."; the loan still retained value as diplomatic "leverage" on the issues growing out of Eastern Europe, Turkey, and China. Ten days later, Harriman was in Washington, where he again told State Department officials that it would be quite satisfactory for loan negotiations to "drag along" because delay afforded the "greatest element in our leverage." Oscar Cox, deputy administrator of the Foreign Economic Administration, was disturbed by a conversation with Harriman at San Francisco five days later: "He seems to be trending towards an anti-Soviet position."

Truman, required suddenly to handle the difficult and growing foreign policy problems facing the nation, relied heavily upon subordinates, and Harriman was prepared and eager to advise him. In the transition from one administration to another, Harriman's views on the loan, already widely held, were reaffirmed. On April 23, 1945, Truman and Harriman, among others, met with Molotov in Washington to discuss the question of Poland's government. The exchange was acrimonious, and the blunt and impatient president addressed Molotov as though he were speaking to a rebellious Missouri ward politician. He warned that Russia's international behavior would affect United States decisions on postwar aid because "legislative appropriation was required for any economic measures in the foreign field and . . . he could not hope to get these measures through Congress unless there was public support for them." At the United Nations Conference in San Francisco following the Molotov-Truman confrontation, Senator Arthur H. Vandenberg, architect of the bipartisan foreign policy and a delegate to the conference, recorded in his diary: "Stettinius added that he explained to Molotov that future Russian aid from America depends entirely upon the temper and the mood and the conscience of the American people—and that Frisco is his last chance to *prove* that he deserves this aid. This is the best news in months." To this Vandenberg added his famous bit of hyperbole: "FDR's appeasement of Russia is over."

Truman's scruples about public opinion and congressional impediments, expressed many times by administration figures, raise a number of questions. Neither the Roosevelt and Truman administrations nor the professional diplomats in the State Department ever prepared the public or Congress for a loan to Russia in the 1943–

1946 period. In fact, public discussion was discouraged, ... and certainly there was no attempt to demonstrate to the Soviet Union that the United States considered the issue an important one for immediate negotiation. The State Department was slow to recommend that the restrictive Johnson Act be repealed and that Export-Import Bank funds be expanded. In 1944 the secretary of state received such recommendations from the interdepartmental Committee on Foreign Economic Policy, and in his budget message to Congress in January, 1945, Roosevelt repeated the suggestion, but it was not until July, 1945, that Truman specifically asked Congress to increase the lending power of the Export-Import Bank from $700 million to $3.5 billion, with the idea that $1 billion of these funds could be set aside for Russia should a loan agreement be worked out. The administration did *not* have to apologize to Congress for suggesting that funds might go to Russia, a full-scale public congressional debate never occurred, and Truman got the increase he requested as well as removal of the Johnson Act obstruction. Over a year and a half after Mikoyan and Harriman first discussed postwar aid, the impediments to a loan were finally removed.

It was not so much public opinion or Congress in 1945 which served as a restraint on loan policy—for the president had persuasive powers which often shaped or created the "public" opinion the administration wanted to hear—but rather Roosevelt, Truman, and Harriman themselves, among others, who deliberately stalled negotiations as a form of diplomatic pressure on the Soviets. The calculated delay was hardly conducive to amicable relations, and, as Oscar Cox noted, "the Soviet Union unquestionably doubts whether we really mean business on this subject."

Harriman also saw diplomatic value in the generous Lend-Lease aid to Russia. Early in 1945, for example, he suggested that Washington tell Moscow that petroleum products shipped under Lend-Lease would be curtailed unless the Russians halted their penetration of the Rumanian oil industry. He helped formulate the decision of May 11, 1945, only three days after V-E Day, to reduce drastically Lend-Lease aid to Russia, which was not yet at war with Japan. The Russians were surprised and angered by the abrupt decision; Stalin complained to Harry Hopkins on May 27 that "the manner in which it had been done had been unfortunate and even brutal. ... If the refusal to continue Lend-Lease was designed as pressure on the Rus-

sians in order to soften them up then it was a fundamental mistake."
Hopkins assured the Soviet leader that the United States did not in-
tend to use Lend-Lease as a "pressure weapon" because the United
States was "a strong power and does not go in for those methods."
Yet the Lend-Lease suspension was handled in such a way as to an-
tagonize Russia, and the Soviets considered it a hostile act.

Scholars differ in their interpretations of the decision. Some argue
that it did indeed constitute economic pressure aimed directly at the
Soviets. Others believe that the Truman administration was simply
and clumsily fulfilling the law as written by Congress (and watched
over by congressmen) that at the end of the war Lend-Lease should
terminate. There is evidence to support both interpretations because
the Truman administration proceeded with the dual intention of pres-
suring the Russians and satisfying congressional opinion. Yet for the
history of Soviet-American relations, the more important consideration was the coercion of Russia: The cutback order must be viewed
in the context of the administration's thinking about economic power
as diplomatic leverage. Although Harriman and others knew full well
that Moscow would read a sharp reduction in Lend-Lease as economic pressure, they made no effort to soften the sudden blow, and,
in fact, the administration braced itself for the Soviet cries of protest
which it expected. . . .

President Truman himself endorsed the basic premise that economic power was a valuable weapon in the growing confrontation
with the Soviet Union. In early June, he met with Colonel Bernard
Bernstein, who reported to Secretary Morgenthau that the president
"didn't seem at all pessimistic about his relations with the Russians
because he felt we held all the cards and that the Russians had to
come to us." The "cards" were a loan and technical assistance, according to Truman. The president commented further on the destruction in Russia and the threat of starvation in some areas. "That was
why he felt he had the cards in American hands," Colonel Bernstein
informed Morgenthau, "and he made very clear that he proposed to
play them as American cards. . . ."

On August 9, 1945, only three days after an atomic blast leveled
Hiroshima, Harriman informed the Russians that the Export-Import
Bank was willing to consider (in Washington) Soviet proposals for
postwar aid. On August 28 the Russians presented the bank with a
request for $1 billion, the figure Mikoyan first used in February of

the previous year, but this time at 2.375 percent interest. The drop from $6 billion was necessitated by the bank's lending power limitation of $3.5 billion. Although the bank's interest rate of 3 percent was inflexible, the National Advisory Council on International Monetary and Financial Problems, set up in July to coordinate foreign loan policy, approved a loan to Russia "in principle," and in September Truman agreed that Export-Import Bank negotiations "should go forward," but apparently to be contingent upon State Department approval. . . .

In November the House Special Committee on Postwar Economic Policy and Planning issued a report on economic reconstruction in Europe which acknowledged that the Soviet economy was in massive disarray because of the German scorched-earth policy. Economic cooperation with Russia should be effected, but certain points had to be clarified before a "sound relationship" could develop. First, Russia must assure the United States that its aid would not finance a military buildup. Second, the Russians must make a "full and frank disclosure" of their production statistics. The next three demands centered on the Soviet presence in Eastern Europe: Russia must withdraw its occupation forces, disclose its trade treaties with that area, and ensure that relief supplies were distributed on nonpolitical grounds. The remaining points reflected the "open door": protection of American property in Eastern Europe; "free entry" of American planes flying ordinary Russian air routes; protection of American copyrights in Russia; and the granting of visas in "adequate quantities."

Shortly after this report was issued, Harriman assessed the status of the loan question. United States economic policy toward Russia, he said, had "so far added to our misunderstanding and increased the Soviets [*sic*] recent tendency to take unilateral action." Moreover, our loan policy "has no doubt caused them to tighten their belts as regards improvement of the living conditions of their people and may have contributed to their avaricious policies in the countries occupied or liberated by the Red Army." He added that Russia worked under long-range plans and by this time had probably formulated its program without United States credits. Hence, any aid rendered would be over and above such a plan. He called for a review of Soviet-American economic relations, apparently with the idea of denying Russia any further UNRRA assistance, from which he believed the United States realized little diplomatic benefit. Harriman's assessment indicated that the use of economic power for diplomatic concessions had thus far failed. Russia had not been swayed. . . .

On February 21, 1946, State Department officials handed the Russian chargé a note drafted by Harriman. It explained that the $1 billion credit was "one among a number of outstanding economic questions" between Russia and the United States. The note suggested negotiations in Washington on the loan and several other issues, including a general settlement of Lend-Lease (Soviet purchase of lend-lease items in Russia); claims of American nationals against Russia; copyright protection; free navigation of rivers; civil aviation; and a treaty of friendship, commerce, and navigation. The negotiations should consider policies designed to assist "the peoples liberated from the domination of Nazi Germany and the peoples of the former Axis satellite states of Europe to solve by democratic means their pressing economic problems"—in short, the status of Eastern Europe. The note further suggested that the Soviet Union send "observers" to the first meeting of the World Bank and International Monetary Fund scheduled for March 8. The Truman administration had decided to resurrect the loan question, although some advisers like Kennan were pessimistic that important concessions could be secured, since Russia would pay only "lip service" to international economic cooperation. The published State Department documents do not show clearly why at that moment Washington reversed its policy, although the immediacy of the first [World] Bank and Fund meeting and the fact that delaying tactics had not worked probably explain the shift.

Early in March, unnamed officials in the State Department informed a *New York Times* correspondent, who reported the story on the front page, that the State Department's laxity of the previous months was due to administrative confusion: The Soviet loan request had been "lost" since August, misplaced during the transfer of the papers of the Foreign Economic Administration (overseer of the Export-Import Bank during and shortly after the war) to the State Department. What is the scholar to make of this bizarre report, which until recently went unchallenged? Arthur M. Schlesinger, Jr., accepts the story of administrative clumsiness, although he admits that the explanation "only strengthened Soviet suspicions of American purposes." George F. Kennan, on the other hand, comments that "there've been a lot of statements that we lost the paper and so forth —it was not lost. It was always there in the files." Indeed, the evidence is convincing that neither the loan request nor the topic of the loan was lost. The State Department may have feigned administrative confusion in order to explain its long silence concerning the request.

The Soviet reply of March 15 arrived about a week after a Russian observer attended the initial conference of the World Bank and Fund at Savannah, Georgia, as the United States had requested. The Soviets also agreed to discuss a long-term credit, Lend-Lease, and a treaty of friendship, commerce, and navigation, but none of the other items. On that same day, Henry A. Wallace, secretary of commerce and an advocate of a loan to Russia, urged the president to make "a new approach along economic and trade lines." Critical of the current handling of economic relations with Russia, he asked the president to appoint a "new group" to undertake negotiations. And he summarized the importance of postwar aid, "We know that much of the recent Soviet behavior which has caused us concern has been the result of their dire economic needs and their disturbed sense of security. The events of the past few months have thrown the Soviets back to their pre-1939 fears of 'capitalist encirclement' and to their erroneous belief that the Western world, including the USA, is invariably and unanimously hostile." Truman later wrote: "I ignored this letter of Wallace's. . . ."

The reply to the Soviets, dispatched on April 18, applauded them for agreeing to discuss some questions and for sending an observer to Savannah. But Byrnes insisted in his letter that a credit of $1 billion should be tied closely to "the creation of an international economic environment permitting a large volume of trade and expanding mutually beneficial economic relations among nations." The letter went on to state—without mentioning specifically the Soviet economic penetration of Eastern Europe—that "certain of the questions which might stand in the way of sound development of these relations should be freely discussed. . . ." Byrnes also noted that the discussions would be facilitated by full Soviet membership in the World Bank and Fund. One news correspondent commented, "the conditions laid down by the United States are still regarded as so rugged from the Soviet point of view that there was little expectation among informed officials that the Russians would accept them."

The Russians . . . were not eager to adopt United States trade principles and to reject the state trading practices that its economic and social system required and that had been in use since the early years of the Soviet government. They were also wary about joining the World Bank and Fund, both dominated by American dollars, economic principles, voting power, and leadership. They believed they could derive little economic benefit from membership and would have to reverse a long-time policy and divulge details about the Russian economy to the bank. Nor were they willing to accept an economic open door in Eastern Europe, for they looked upon the whole principle as a disguise for United States expansion into the area. . . .

To the State Department's dismay, the Soviets made a concession when they formally communicated with Washington again on May 17. They had earlier agreed to negotiate Lend-Lease, a treaty, and a loan. Now, however, they were "prepared to exchange in a preliminary fashion opinions" on the questions of claims, copyright protection, and Eastern Europe. The note did not refer to the World Bank or Fund but did concur with the previous American suggestion that civil aviation and river navigation be discussed in separate negotiations. The department seemed bewildered; one officer noted that the Export-Import Bank did not have enough money to meet the request and that an open debate in Congress over more funds "might well worsen our relations with the USSR." He saw two alternatives: first, "to take advantage that the Soviet reply of May 17th gives to break off gracefully loan negotiations with the Soviet Union"; second, to postpone any request to Congress until "we have a clearer picture of the likelihood of successful negotiations with the USSR."

Washington's actions came closest to the first alternative. On June 13 Byrnes informed the Soviets that the United States appreciated the Soviet willingness to "widen the scope of the negotiations. . . " but stated that Washington was "unable to agree to a merely preliminary exchange of opinions on some of the questions. . . ." Finally, he insisted that Soviet participation in the World Bank and Fund would facilitate the negotiations. In short, complete Soviet agreement with the United States agenda for negotiations was required, and the Soviet concession was virtually ignored. The loan issue appeared dead.

To salvage something, the State Department decided in September, 1946, to split the issues of Lend-Lease and a loan in the hope that at least a settlement of Lend-Lease could be effected. In October, Harriman told the National Press Club that the loan was no longer a "current issue." Indeed, the general question of assistance to Russian reconstruction was seldom mentioned again until June, 1947, when Secretary Marshall offered dollars to a European recovery program. Russia did not participate in the Marshall Plan, and that finally resolved the issue of postwar aid to Russia.

The history of the abortive Russian loan posits some provocative questions. Would the Soviet Union have sought such heavy reparations from former Axis countries in Eastern Europe had a loan been granted? Harriman suggested that the Russians would not have been so "avaricious." He also stated that the Russians might not have followed a "unilateral" course in Eastern Europe had a loan been granted. Morgenthau argued, according to his biographer, John Blum, that a postwar credit to Russia would "soften the Soviet mood on all outstanding political questions." And in June, 1945, Grenville Clark asked President Truman: "Now that Russia has regained self-confidence and military strength, is it surprising that without firm promises of aid from the United States . . . she should seek other methods of self-protection?"

As for Germany, one scholar writes that a loan might have taken "the acrimony out of the Russian attitude on reparations." Albert Z. Carr, an associate of Donald Nelson, believed it "altogether probable that these two matters, an American credit and German reparations, were closely linked in Soviet political thinking, for our attitude toward both questions profoundly affected the rate of Russia's postwar recovery." Indeed, as early as 1944, the ambassador to Great Britain, John G. Winant, linked the two issues and, according to one of his former staff members, argued that "the Russian need for material aid in repairing the vast destruction in the Soviet Union was bound to make the Soviet government particularly eager to receive reparations deliveries from Germany on a large scale." United States leaders did not doubt that there was a direct connection between Russia's reparation demands and her reconstruction needs. Edwin Pauley, American reparations ambassador, wrote in 1947, "it can be assumed . . . that Russia's intransigent position on unification and reparations is due to a desire to obtain the maximum amount of industrial and consumer goods from Germany, to meet internal political prestige needs and to help rebuild the Soviet industrial machine." Reporter Edgar Snow noted in the same year that "Ivan" was asking: "Did America offer Russia a serious alternative to reparations?"

Harriman commented that the absence of reconstruction aid probably caused the Russians "to tighten their belts as regards improvement of the living conditions. . . ." Others have noted that the demands of reconstruction and the absence of aid required heavy sacrifices from the Russian people, in part because consumer goods held a secondary priority. Gunnar Myrdal, head of the Economic Commission for Europe, is correct, however, in pointing out that a loan's "possible direct influence on economic reconstruction and development in the Soviet Union should not be exaggerated, but as an element in building up a spirit of friendly cooperation and giving a momentum to trade it would have been of great importance." Finally, what effect did the failure to grant Russia a loan have on the United States goal of multilateralism? We can suggest, as did Vera Micheles Dean in 1947, that Russia was forced to meet its needs through bilateral barter agreements—anathema to multilateralism.

At the close of the war, Stalin told Harriman: "I will not tolerate a new *cordon sanitaire.*" The hesitancy to grant a loan and the use of aid as a diplomatic weapon while Washington was granting Great Britain a handsome loan at an interest rate of less than 2 percent, Chiang Kai-shek was denying Soviet requests for joint companies in Manchuria, a Russian oil concession in Iran was refused, General Lucius Clay had halted German reparations shipments from the American zone of Germany to Russia, and France and Italy were receiving considerable aid—all fed Soviet fears that the United States was creating an international bloc and replaying the events which took place after World War I. As Wallace put it in a letter to Truman in July, 1946, "From the Russian point of view, also, the granting of a loan to Britain and the lack of tangible results on their request to borrow for rehabilitation purposes may be regarded as another evidence of strengthening of an anti-Soviet bloc."

The proposed American loan to Russia was never given the opportunity to demonstrate whether it could serve as a peace potion for easing increasingly bitter Soviet-American relations. The Truman administration—over the objections of Morgenthau, Nelson, White, and Wallace, among others—decided to employ the loan as a diplo-

matic weapon before negotiations began rather than as a diplomatic
tool at the conference table. Few nations or individuals are eager to
enter negotiations when the attitude of the other party is simply
"our way or not at all." The diplomatic use of economic power by
any nation possessing it is to be expected and may be helpful in
achieving fruitful and mutually beneficial negotiations. But if that
power thwarts negotiations or is employed to buttress demands
which alone are held to be the sine qua non for peaceful settlement,
the result is schism and conflict.

*Walt W. Rostow*

# THE COMMUNIST OFFENSIVE

*Toward the end of World War II, Russian armies marched into Eastern Europe on the heels of the retreating Germans, establishing a postwar Soviet sphere of influence. Americans were alarmed by this Soviet expansion, as well as by Moscow's brash refusal to entertain American protests. Churchill captured much of the resentment in his "Iron Curtain" speech. In other parts of the world, insurgent groups which included Communists in their number fomented revolutions and civil wars. Walt W. Rostow was an official in the Department of State (1945–46) who shared in the growing anti-Communist sentiment. During the 1950s he taught economic history at the Massachusetts Institute of Technology and from 1961 to 1966 he served as chairman of the State Department Policy Planning Council. From 1966 to 1969 he held the important post of special assistant to the president, largely handling national security questions. In the following selection from his book* Diffusion of Power *(1972), written while a professor of economics and history at the University of Texas, Rostow summarizes the comparative strength and outlook of the United States and Russia in 1945 and then discusses critically what he describes as Stalin's self-conscious, planned attempt to exploit opportunities for expansion in both Europe and Asia, leading to the Korean War. Some of Rostow's assumptions are questioned in the subsequent selections by Bernstein, Barnet, and Graebner.*

Reprinted with permission of Macmillan Publishing Co., Inc. from *The Diffusion of Power: An Essay in Recent History* by Walt W. Rostow. Copyright © 1972 by W. W. Rostow; pp. 1–6, 12–13. Also by permission of Julian Bach Literary Agency, Inc. (Footnotes deleted.)

... The course of the Second World War brought the United States to a position of unique but inherently transient preeminence. In part, this result emerged from the defeat of Germany, Italy, and Japan, and from the dependence of Nationalist China, beset with civil war, on the United States. In part, it arose from the economic enfeeblement of Great Britain, France, and the smaller allies of Western Europe under the strains of war and occupation. The war also fatally weakened the fabric of their imperial holdings. On the other hand, the United States, which had had 14.6 percent of its working force unemployed in 1940, was able to fight the war to a significant extent by bringing to bear idle men and idle industrial capacity. In constant dollars, the American GNP rose by more than 50 percent between 1940 and 1944; and there was even a slight increase—about 10 percent—in expenditures for personal consumption.

This surge in American economic strength was reinforced by two special developments of the war years. First, there was a massive and systematic harnessing of science and technology to military purposes. Beyond the military hardware produced, which included the atomic bomb, rockets, and turbines, the United States learned how to organize men and institutions to generate military innovations on a regular basis—as a flow, rather than the product of occasional inventiveness.

Second, there was a revolutionary rise in the importance of air power. Despite drastic postwar demobilization, there emerged from this experience a unique Strategic Air Command (SAC). Until intercontinental ballistics missiles emerged, the existence of SAC bombers, at instant readiness, was a minimum condition for national security and a powerful but limited force on the world scene; and it remains to this day a significant component of American military power.

In 1945, then, the United States towered over all others on its continental island, having brought its economy back to full strength at a time when the other major nations had been weakened. It commanded the seas and the air, and it alone had produced atomic weapons.

This combination of economic strength, organized technological capacity, and power to strike over long distances was reinforced by the wartime experience of sustained alliance operations. This experience began formally with Lend-Lease to Britain in 1941; before the end of hostilities, it embraced all the Allies fighting in Western Europe and included a wide range of generally less satisfactory alliance arrangements in Asia and the Pacific.

The rise in power of the Soviet Union was less glamorous than that of the United States. It did not involve a dramatic surge in economic strength, or new weaponry, but it was, nonetheless, real.

As with the United States, the rise of Soviet power stemmed, in part, from the negative fact that the power of Germany, Italy, and Japan was temporarily eliminated. Positively, it derived from the fact that the war was fought in such a way that it ended with Soviet ground forces as far west as the Elbe. Bulgaria, Romania, Hungary, Czechoslovakia, Poland, a part of Austria, and the eastern portion of Germany were under the physical control of the Soviet Union. The war yielded also a Communist government in Belgrade, initially allied with the Soviet Union. Moscow was in a diplomatic as well as a military position to accept the Japanese surrender in Manchuria and North Korea. Because of American, British, and French errors of the 1930s, the Second World War was, in George Kennan's words, "essentially and inescapably defensive . . . one in which we in the West were at first the weaker party, capable of achieving only a portion of our aim and of achieving that portion only in collaboration with a totalitarian adversary and at a price."

For Americans, not conscious of this flawed result and surveying the world scene in the wake of "unconditional surrender," there was satisfaction that the war had been won and a deep consensus that the error of not joining the League of Nations must not be repeated, that the United States must play its part, somehow, in maintaining peace. But there was little or no understanding of what would be involved in that commitment—and its price. The underlying national impulse was to get American forces home, dismantle them, and turn back to domestic life. Except for the memory of the First World War and the failure to consolidate the peace, there was little historical resonance for Americans in the panorama of destruction from London to Tokyo.

For men who were both Russian and Communist, the scene was quite different. Through their eyes and memories, the moment was incredible: All the powers that had harassed and restrained Russia over the centuries were prostrate or weak: Germany and Japan;

Poland and most of the smaller states, once part of the Austro-Hungarian Empire; Britain and France. Stalin, through the sacrifices of the Russian peoples and the exertions of their allies, was in a position to retrieve in Asia all that was lost in 1905; much that was lost in Europe after 1917; and far more than he tried to negotiate with Hitler in 1939, let alone what he achieved. There had been no moment like it in Russian history since the defeat of Napoleon. The conversation Harriman reports with Stalin at Potsdam was understandable as well as ominous:

> *The first time I saw him [Stalin] at the conference I went up to him and said that it must be very gratifying for him to be in Berlin, after all the struggle and the tragedy. He hesitated a moment and then replied, "Czar Alexander got to Paris." It didn't need much of a clairvoyant to guess what was in his mind.*

Stalin's vision went further than the ground on which the Soviet armies stood. Communist colleagues had triumphed in Yugoslavia. Communist insurgent forces had leverage in Greece. Communist parties had been greatly strengthened in France and Italy, not merely by the elimination of existing wartime rule but by their role in underground movements. There were Koreans trained in Moscow, ready to be installed in power, as well as Poles, Bulgars, Romanians, Hungarians, and Czechs. And there were the Chinese, awkward to deal with since the Soviet strategy on China had failed in 1927, but still a force in being with uncertain but considerable prospects for the future and ideological brothers of a sort. . . .

Poland . . . became the most important question in Allied diplomacy shaping the outcome of affairs in Germany and Eastern Europe.

At Yalta Roosevelt made the issue of free elections in Eastern Europe a paramount matter. He succeeded in extracting from Stalin, in the Yalta Declaration on Liberated Europe, a pledge for "the earliest possible establishment through free elections of governments responsive to the will of the people . . ."; in the parallel Declaration on Poland, Roosevelt achieved agreement that a new Provisional Government of National Unity should be formed, including Poles from abroad, which would be pledged to hold "free and unfettered elections as soon as possible on the basis of universal suffrage and secret ballot." But in his opening statement, Roosevelt made what Churchill described as the "momentous" prediction that the United

States would not keep a large army in Europe and its occupation of Germany could be envisaged for only two years.

In the weeks that followed, Stalin did not act on the Yalta agreements. He persisted, step by step, in moving to consolidate Communist power in Eastern Europe; and just before his death, Roosevelt was greatly concerned, in particular, about Stalin's course in Poland. Stalin postponed introduction into the Polish government of the London Poles, leaving the Lublin group to consolidate power in its hands.

On April 23, eleven days after Roosevelt's death, Truman put the issue of Poland hard to Molotov and despatched Hopkins, desperately ill, to Moscow a month later. Hopkins got Stalin to act on the Yalta agreement on Poland: that a government of national unity be formed, including Mikolajczyk as vice-premier, with three additional ministries granted to non-Lublin Poles acceptable to Great Britain and the United States. With this and several lesser concessions, the ground was cleared for the Big Three meeting at Potsdam.

At Potsdam the recognition of the reorganized Polish Provisional government (granted by the United States on July 5) was confirmed; and agreement was made that this interim government would hold free and unfettered elections on the basis of universal suffrage and secret ballot, with guarantees of access to the world press to report events before and during the elections.

Truman's diplomacy on Poland in the first four months of his administration appeared to have moved the Polish question forward in terms of the Yalta agreement. However, in the year and a half following Potsdam, Moscow-dominated Communists took over Poland in successive stages, climaxed by the election of February 1947, carefully rigged so as to avoid a repetition of the disastrously anti-Communist outcome of the plebiscite of June 1946; and in the autumn of 1947 Mikolajczyk, long since rendered politically impotent, fled the country to avoid arrest. . . .

Later Truman wrote of Eastern Europe in terms which lucidly reflect the dilemma he could not resolve:

> *I was trying to be extremely careful not to get us mixed up in a Balkan turmoil. The Balkans had long been a source of trouble and war. I believed that if the political situation in the Balkans could be adjusted so that Hungary, Yugoslavia, Rumania, and Bulgaria, as well as Poland and*

*Austria, could all have governments of their own people's choosing, with no outside interference, this would help us in our plans for peace.*

*I did not want to become involved in the Balkans in a way that could lead us into another world conflict. In any case, I was anxious to get the Russians into the war against Japan as soon as possible, thus saving the lives of countless Americans.*

*... I was trying to get Churchill in a frame of mind to forget the old power politics and get a United Nations organization to work.*

\*       \*       \*

Would Stalin have made the same basic decision if he knew substantial American forces would remain in Europe not two years but for a generation and beyond, that Germany would be rearmed, that Tito would defect, and that Moscow's satellites would become progressively more assertive and an increasing source of concern? We do not know; but his compulsion to exert total rather than dilute control within the Soviet Union and, where he could, outside makes an affirmative answer still likely. But if the question is put: Who is more responsible for the Cold War, the Americans or the Russians? I am still inclined to feel, as I did at the time, that unilateral American disarmament and the isolationist mood Roosevelt predicted at Yalta were primary factors in determining Stalin's choice. By 1946 there was not a single American Army division ready for combat, nor a single air group. We put Stalin under intolerable temptation. By the time Truman counterattacked in the spring of 1947 with the Truman Doctrine and the Marshall Plan, Moscow was too deeply committed to change course.

Debate on particular issues continued in the Kremlin. The door was not finally shut on a postwar agreement until Molotov left the Paris discussions on the Marshall Plan in July 1947. Stalin evidently decided he could not permit the Eastern European nations the advantages of the Marshall Plan without fatally risking their ties to Moscow. And on the primacy of his Eastern European empire, I believe Stalin had pretty well made up his mind by the time he delivered his electoral speech of February 9, 1946. Although the struggle in Washington to avoid the worst continued, the response of the West was given a month later in Churchill's "Iron Curtain" speech in Fulton, Missouri. If an operational rather than a rhetorical date for the beginning of the Cold War is to be chosen, it should probably be the breakdown of the Control Council in Berlin in May 1946.

In a manner resonant of Russian history, Stalin's effort to exploit the postwar disarray of Eurasia had two phases. He pressed first in the West and, then, when frustrated, turned to apparent opportunities in the East.

During the summer of 1946 Stalin increased Soviet pressure against Turkey by diplomacy and threat, in Greece by supporting substantial guerrilla warfare via Bulgaria and Yugoslavia, and in Italy and France by vigorous Communist party efforts to gain parliamentary power. Meanwhile, the process of stabilizing Germany as two organized entities proceeded. In 1947 Stalin was thrown on the offensive by Truman's counterattack. He responded to the Truman Doctrine and the Marshall Plan by accelerating the movement toward total control in the East, symbolized by the creation of the Cominform in September 1947. He succeeded in Prague (February 1948), but failed in Belgrade, where Tito's defection was announced in June 1948. The Communist effort in Greece then collapsed, the election in April 1948 saved Italy, and France found a group of center parties capable of governing, albeit uncertainly, and containing the domestic Communist menace. The deadlock in the Berlin Control Council, already two years old, was dramatized by the Soviet walkout on March 20, 1948, which set the stage for the blockade, which began on March 31.

This phase of Soviet consolidation in Eastern Europe ended with the effort to expel the West from Berlin, which was defeated by the airlift in the winter of 1948–1949. In the West this interacting process yielded the Brussels Pact (February 1948), NATO (March 1949), and the creation (May 1949) of a Federal Republic of Germany, including, for economic purposes, the western zones of Berlin, which symbolized and confirmed the Western intent to resist further Soviet expansion.

In the course of 1946 the negotiations for a truce in China also broke down. The Communists—strengthened with captured Japanese arms furnished by the Soviet Union, with some Soviet weapons, and with Soviet staff assistance—launched an all-out civil war. In 1946 Stalin probably advised against an all-out effort by the Communists to seize power; but once Mao was well started, he was backed by Stalin in 1947–1949, mainly through diversionary operations of the international Communist movement.

Communist policy in Asia formally changed in the course of 1947,

# Europe After World War II

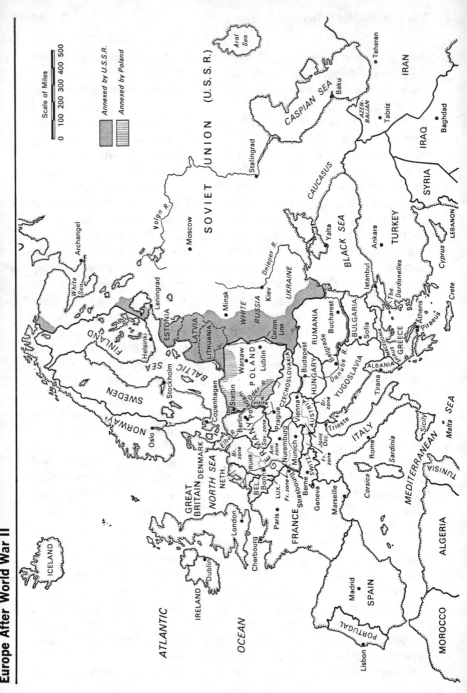

Scale of Miles
0 100 200 300 400 500

Annexed by U.S.S.R.
Annexed by Poland

ambitious new objectives being enunciated by Zhdanov at the founding meeting of the Cominform in September. Open guerrilla warfare began in Indochina as early as November 1946, in Burma in April 1948, in Malaya in June of that year, and in Indonesia and the Philippines in the autumn. The Indian and Japanese Communist parties, with less scope for guerrilla action, nevertheless sharply increased their militancy in 1948. As final victory was won in China in November 1949, Mao's political-military strategy was openly commended by the Cominform to the Communist parties in those areas where guerrilla operations were under way. Stalin and Mao met early in 1950 and confirmed the ambitious Asian strategy, planning its climax in the form of the North Korean invasion of South Korea, which took place at the end of June 1950. . . .

*Barton J. Bernstein*

# CONFRONTATION IN EASTERN EUROPE

*Barton J. Bernstein, in his edited work* Politics and Policies of the Truman Administration *(1970), challenges some traditional assumptions about the Soviet penetration of Eastern Europe in the immediate postwar years. He emphasizes the importance of wartime decisions, the mixed pattern and complexity of Soviet behavior, Poland as an early testing ground, Stalin's caution before 1947, changes between Roosevelt and Truman, and evidence of a United States double standard. Like Lippmann before him, Bernstein argues that the United States aggravated Soviet security fears. A specialist in the history of postwar America, Bernstein is a member of the Department of History at Stanford University. He is the editor of* Towards a New Past: Dissenting Essays in American History *(1968) and (with Allen Matusow)* The Truman Administration: A Documentary History *(1970), and author of numerous interpretive essays.*

Despite some dissents, most American scholars have reached a general consensus on the origins of the Cold War. As confirmed inter-

From Barton J. Bernstein, "American Foreign Policy and the Origins of the Cold War," in Barton J. Bernstein, ed., *Politics and Policies of the Truman Administration* (Chicago, 1970), pp. 15–17, 19–21, 23–30, 36–40. Copyright © 1970 Quadrangle Publications. Reprinted by permission of New Viewpoints, A Division of Franklin Watts, Inc., New York. (Footnotes deleted.)

nationalists who believe that Russia constituted a threat to America and its European allies after World War II, they have endorsed their nation's acceptance of its obligations as a world power in the forties and its desire to establish a world order of peace and prosperity. Convinced that only American efforts prevented the Soviet Union from expanding past Eastern Europe, they have generally praised the containment policies of the Truman Doctrine, the Marshall Plan, and NATO as evidence of America's acceptance of world responsibility. While chiding or condemning those on the right who opposed international involvement (or had even urged preventive war), they have also been deeply critical of those on the left who have believed that the Cold War could have been avoided, or that the United States shared substantial responsibility for the Cold War.

Whether they are devotees of the new realism or open admirers of moralism and legalism in foreign policy, most scholars have agreed that the United States moved slowly and reluctantly, in response to Soviet provocation, away from President Franklin D. Roosevelt's conciliatory policy. The Truman administration, perhaps even belatedly, they suggest, abandoned its efforts to maintain the Grand Alliance and acknowledged that Russia menaced world peace. American leaders, according to this familiar interpretation, slowly cast off the shackles of innocence and moved to courageous and necessary policies.

Despite the widespread acceptance of this interpretation, there has long been substantial evidence (and more recently a body of scholarship) which suggests that American policy was neither so innocent nor so nonideological; that American leaders sought to promote their conceptions of national interest and their values even at the conscious risk of provoking Russia's fears about her security. In 1945 these leaders apparently believed that American power would be adequate for the task of reshaping much of the world according to America's needs and standards.

By overextending policy and power and refusing to accept Soviet interests, American policy makers contributed to the Cold War. There was little understanding of any need to restrain American political efforts and desires. Though it cannot be proved that the United States could have achieved a modus vivendi with the Soviet Union in these years, there is evidence that Russian policies were reasonably cautious and conservative, and that there was at least a basis for accommodation. But this possibility slowly slipped away as President Harry S. Truman reversed Roosevelt's tactics of accommodation. As American demands for democratic governments in Eastern Europe became more vigorous, as the new administration delayed in providing economic assistance to Russia and in seeking international control of atomic energy, policy makers met with increasing Soviet suspicion and antagonism. Concluding that Soviet-American cooperation was impossible, they came to believe that the Soviet state could be halted only by force or the threat of force.

The emerging revisionist interpretation, then, does not view American actions simply as the necessary response to Soviet challenges, but instead tries to understand American ideology and interests, mutual suspicions and misunderstandings, and to investigate the failures to seek and achieve accommodation. . . .

In 1944 Roosevelt recognized the establishment of zones of influence in Europe. The Italian armistice of the year before had set the pattern for other wartime agreements on the control of affairs of liberated and defeated European nations. When Stalin requested the creation of a three-power Allied commission to deal with the problems of "countries falling away from Germany," Roosevelt and Churchill first rebuffed the Russian leader and then agreed to a joint commission for Italy which would be limited to information gathering. By excluding Russia from sharing in decision making in Italy, the United States and Great Britain, later concluded William McNeill, "prepared the way for their own exclusion from any but a marginal share in the affairs of Eastern Europe."

When Roosevelt refused to participate in an Anglo-American invasion of southeastern Europe (which seemed to be the only way of restricting Russian influence in that area), Churchill sought other ways of dealing with Russian power and of protecting British interests in Greece. In May 1944 he proposed to Stalin that they recognize Greece as a British "zone of influence" and Rumania as a Russian zone; but Stalin insisted upon seeking Roosevelt's approval and refused the offer upon learning that the United States would not warmly endorse the terms. When the Soviets liberated Rumania in September they secured temporarily the advantages that Churchill had offered. They simply followed the British-American example in Italy, retained all effective power, and announced they were "acting in the interests of all the United Nations." From the Soviet Union, W. Averell Harriman, the American ambassador, cabled, "The Russians believe, I think, that we lived up to a tacit understanding that Rumania was an area of predominant Soviet interest in which we should not interfere.... The terms of the armistice give the Soviet command unlimited control of Rumania's economic life" and effective control over political organization.

With Russian armies sweeping through the Balkans and soon in a position to impose similar terms on Hungary and Bulgaria, Churchill renewed his efforts. "Winston," wrote an associate, "never talks of Hitler these days; he is always harping on the dangers of communism. He dreams of the Red Army spreading like a cancer from one country to another. It has become an obsession, and he seems to think of little else." In October Churchill journeyed to Moscow to reach an agreement with Stalin. "Let us settle our affairs in the Balkans," Churchill told him. "Your armies are in Rumania and Bulgaria. We have interests, missions and agents there. Don't let us get at cross purposes in small ways." Great Britain received "90 percent influence" in Greece, and Russia "90 percent influence" in Rumania, "80 percent" in Bulgaria and Hungary, and "50 percent" in Yugoslavia.

In the cases of Hungary and Bulgaria the terms were soon sanctioned by armistice agreements (approved by the United States) which left effective power with the Soviets. "The Russians took it for granted," Cordell Hull, then secretary of state, wrote later, "that ... Britain and the United States had assigned them a certain portion of the Balkans, including Rumania and Bulgaria, as their spheres of influence." In December Stalin even confirmed the agreement at a considerable price: He permitted British troops to put down a rebellion in Greece. "Stalin," wrote Churchill later, "adhered strictly and faithfully to our agreement ... and during all the long weeks of fighting the Communists in the streets of Athens, not one word of reproach came from *Pravda* or *Izvestia*."

At Yalta in February 1945 Roosevelt did not seem to challenge Soviet dominance in East-Central Europe, which had been established by the Churchill-Stalin agreement and confirmed by the armistices and by British action in Greece. What Roosevelt did seek and gain at Yalta was a weak "Declaration on Liberated Europe"— that the powers would consult "where in their judgment conditions require" assistance to maintain peace or to establish democratic governments. By requiring unanimity the declaration allowed any one power to veto any proposal that seemed to threaten that power's interests. In effect, then, the declaration, despite its statements about democratic governments, did not alter the situation in Eastern Europe. The operative phrases simply affirmed the principle that the three powers had already established: They could consult together when all agreed, and they could act together when all agreed. At Yalta the broadly phrased statement provoked little discussion—only a few pages in the official proceedings. Presumably the Russians did not consider it a repudiation of spheres of influence, only as rhetoric that Roosevelt wanted for home consumption. Despite later official American suggestions, the Yalta agreement was not a product of Roosevelt's misunderstanding of the Soviet meaning of "democracy" and "free elections." Rather, it ratified earlier agreements, and the State Department probably understood this. . . .

Though Yalta has come to represent the triumph of the strategy of postponement, at the time it symbolized Allied accord. Stalin accepted a limitation of the veto power on certain quasi-judicial issues in the U.N. Security Council; Roosevelt conceded to Russia the return of the Kurile Islands, which stretched between Japan and Siberia, and special rights in Dairen and Port Arthur in Manchuria; Stalin promised to enter the Pacific war within three months of the end of the European conflict. "Stalin," as William McNeill explained, "had conceded something to the British in Yugoslavia; and Churchill had yielded a good deal in Poland."

Roosevelt's successor was less sympathetic to Russian aspirations and more responsive to those of Roosevelt's advisers, like Admiral William Leahy, chief of staff to the commander in chief; Harriman; James Forrestal, secretary of the navy; and James F. Byrnes, Truman's choice for secretary of state, who had urged that he resist Soviet efforts in Eastern Europe. As an earlier self-proclaimed foe of Russian communism, Truman mistrusted Russia. ("If we see that Germany is winning the war," advised Senator Truman after the German attack upon Russia in 1941, "we ought to help Russia, and if Russia is winning we ought to help Germany and in that way kill as many as possible.") Upon entering the White House, he did not seek to follow Roosevelt's tactics of adjustment and accommodation. Only eleven days in the presidency and virtually on the eve of the United Nations conference, Truman moved to a showdown with Russia on the issue of Poland.

Poland became the testing ground for American foreign policy, as Truman later said, "a symbol of the future development of our international relations." At Yalta the three powers had agreed that the Soviet-sponsored Lublin Committee (the temporary Polish government) should be "reorganized on a broader democratic basis with the inclusion of democratic leaders from Poland itself and from Poland abroad." The general terms were broad: There was no specific formula for the distribution of power in the reorganized government, and the procedures required consultation and presumably unanimity from the representatives of the three powers. The agreement, remarked Admiral Leahy, was "so elastic that the Russians can stretch it all the way from Yalta to Washington without ever technically breaking it." ("I know, Bill—I know it. But it's the best I can do for Poland at this time," Roosevelt replied.)

For almost two months after Yalta the great powers haggled over Poland. The Lublin Committee objected to the Polish candidates proposed by the United States and Great Britain for consultation because these Poles had criticized the Yalta accord and refused to accept the Soviet annexation of Polish territory (moving the eastern boundary to the Curzon Line). In early April Stalin had offered a compromise—that about 80 percent of the cabinet posts in the new government should be held by members of the Lublin Committee, and that he would urge the committee to accept the leading Western candidates if they would endorse the Yalta agreement (including the Curzon Line). By proposing a specific distribution of power, Stalin cut to the core of the issue that had disrupted negotiations for nearly three months, and sought to guarantee the victory he probably expected in Poland. Roosevelt died before replying, and it is not clear whether he would have accepted this four-to-one representation; but he had acknowledged that he was prepared to place "somewhat more emphasis on the Lublin Poles."

Now Truman was asked to acknowledge Soviet concern about countries on her borders and to assure her influence in many of these countries by granting her friendly (and probably nondemocratic) governments, and even by letting her squelch anti-Communist democrats in countries like Poland. To the President and his advisers the issue was (as Truman later expressed Harriman's argument) "the extension of Soviet control over neighboring states by independent action; we were faced with a barbarian invasion of Europe." The fear was not that the Soviets were about to threaten all of Europe but that they had designs on Eastern Europe, and that these designs conflicted with traditional American values of self-determination, democracy, and open markets. . . .

Having heard his advisers' arguments, Truman resolved to force the Polish question: to impose his interpretation of the Yalta agreement even if it destroyed the United Nations. He later explained that this was the test of Russian cooperation. If Stalin would not abide by his agreements, the U.N. was doomed, and, anyway, there would not be enough enthusiasm among the American electorate to let the United States join the world body. "Our agreements with the Soviet Union so far . . . [have] been a one-way street." That could not continue, Truman told his advisers. "If the Russians did not wish to join us, they could go to hell." ("FDR's appeasement of Russia is over," joyously wrote Senator Arthur Vandenberg, the Republican leader on foreign policy.) Continuing in this spirit at a private conference with Molotov, the new President warned that economic aid would depend upon Russian behavior in fulfilling the Yalta agreement. Brushing aside the diplomat's contention that the Anglo-American interpretation of the Yalta agreement was wrong, the President accused the Russians of breaking agreements and scolded the Russian foreign minister. When Molotov replied, "I have never been talked to like that in my life," Truman warned him, "Carry out your agreement and you won't get talked to like that." . . .

Presumably to patch the alliance, Truman dispatched to Moscow Harry Hopkins, Roosevelt's former adviser and a staunch advocate of Soviet-American friendship. Hopkins denied that Truman's action [in ending Lend-Lease] was an American effort to demonstrate economic power and coerce Russia ("pressure on the Russians to soften them up," as Stalin charged). Instead he emphasized that "Poland had become a symbol of our ability to work out our problems with the Soviet Union." Stalin acknowledged "the right of the United States as a world power to participate in the Polish question," but he stressed the importance of Poland to Soviet security. Within twenty-five years the "Germans had twice invaded Russia via Poland," he emphasized. "All the Soviet Union wanted was that Poland should not be in a position to open the gates to Germany," and that required a government friendly to Russia. There was "no intention," he promised, "to interfere in Poland's internal affairs" or to Sovietize Poland.

Through the Hopkins mission, Truman and Stalin reached a compromise: 70 percent of the new Polish government (fourteen of twenty ministers) should be drawn from the Lublin Committee. At the time there was reason to believe that such heavy Communist influence would not lead to Soviet control. Stalin had reaffirmed the pledge of free elections in Poland, and Stanislaw Mikolajczyk, former prime minister of the exile government in London and deputy prime minister in the new coalition government, was optimistic. He hoped (in Harriman's words) that "a reasonable degree of freedom and independence can be preserved now and that in time after conditions in Europe can become more stable and [as] Russia turns her attention to her internal development, controls will be relaxed and Poland will be able to gain for herself her independence of life as a nation even though he freely accepts that Poland's security and foreign policy must follow the lead of Moscow."

Truman compromised and soon recognized the new Polish government, but he did not lose his hopes of rolling back the Soviets from their spheres of influence in Eastern Europe. Basing most of his case on the Yalta "Declaration on Liberated Europe" (for which he relied on State Department interpretations), Truman hoped to force Russia to permit representative governments in its zones, and expected that free elections would diminish, perhaps even remove, Soviet authority. Refusing to extend diplomatic recognition to Rumania and Bulgaria, he emphasized that these governments were "neither representative of nor responsive to the will of the people."

"The opportunities for the democratic elements in Rumania and Bulgaria are not less than, say, in Italy, with which the governments of the United States and the Soviet Union have already resumed diplomatic relations," replied Stalin, who was willing to exaggerate to emphasize his case. The Russians were demanding a quid pro quo, and they would not yield. At Potsdam, in late July, when Truman demanded "immediate reorganization" of the governments of Hungary and Bulgaria to "include representatives of all significant democratic elements" and three-power assistance in "holding ... free and unfettered elections," Stalin pointed to Greece, again to remind Truman of the earlier agreements. The Russians were "not meddling in Greek affairs," he noted, adding that the Bulgarian and Rumanian governments were fulfilling the armistice agreements while in Greece "terrorism rages ... against democratic elements." (One member of the American delegation later claimed that Stalin at one point made his position clear, stating that "any freely elected government [in Eastern Europe] would be anti-Soviet and that we cannot permit.") In effect, Stalin demanded that the United States abide by his construction of earlier agreements, and that Truman acknowledge what Roosevelt had accepted as the terms of the sphere-of-influence agreements—that democratic forms and anti-Communist democrats of Eastern Europe be abandoned to the larger cause of Russian-American concord. . . .

The London conference [September 11-October 2, 1945] ended in deadlock, disbanding without even a joint communiqué. Despite American possession of the bomb, Molotov would not yield to American demands to reorganize the governments of Bulgaria and Rumania. In turn, he demanded for Russia a role in the occupation government of Japan, but Byrnes rebuffed the proposal. Unprepared for this issue, Byrnes was also unwilling or unable to understand Soviet anxieties about the security of their frontiers, and he pressed most vigorously for the reorganization of the Rumanian government. He would not acknowledge and perhaps could not understand the dilemma of his policy: that he was supporting free elections in areas (particularly in Rumania) where the resulting governments would probably be hostile to the Soviet Union, and yet he was arguing that democracy in Eastern Europe was compatible with Soviet demands for security. Unable to accept that Byrnes might be naive, Molotov questioned the secretary's sincerity and charged that he wanted governments unfriendly to the Soviet Union. From this, Byrnes could only conclude later, "It seemed that the Soviet Union was determined to dominate Europe."

While the United States in the cases of these Eastern European nations chose to support traditional democratic principles and neither to acknowledge its earlier agreements on spheres of influence nor to respect Russian fears, Byrnes would not admit the similarity between Russian behavior in Rumania and British action in Greece. As part of the terms of his agreement with Churchill,

Stalin had allowed the British to suppress a revolutionary force in Greece, and as a result the Greek government could not be accurately interpreted as broadly representative nor as a product of democratic procedures. Yet, as Molotov emphasized, the United States had not opposed British action in Greece or questioned the legitimacy of that government, nor was the United States making a reversal of British imperialism in Greece a condition for the large loan that Britain needed.

Some American observers, however, were aware of this double standard. In the northern Pacific and in Japan, America was to have the deciding voice, but in Eastern Europe, emphasized Walter Lippmann, "we invoke the principle that this is one world in which decisions must not be taken unilaterally." Most Americans did not see this paradox, and Byrnes probably expressed crystallizing national sentiment that autumn when he concluded that the dispute with Russia was a test of whether "we really believed in what we said about one world and our desire to build collective security, or whether we were willing to accept the Soviet preference for the simpler task of dividing the world into two spheres of influence."

Despite Byrnes's views, and although he could not secure a reorganization of the Rumanian government, Communist influence was weakened in other parts of Eastern Europe. In Budapest free elections were held and the Communist party was routed; and early in November, just two days after the United States recognized Hungary, the Communists lost in the national elections there. In Bulgaria elections took place in "complete order and without disturbance," and, despite American protests, a Communist-dominated single ticket (representing most of the political parties) triumphed.

While the Soviet Union would not generally permit in Eastern Europe conditions that conformed to Western ideals, Stalin was pursuing a cautious policy and seeking accommodation with the West. He was willing to allow capitalism but was suspicious of American efforts at economic penetration which could lead to political dominance. Though by the autumn of 1945 the governments in Russia's general area of influence were subservient in foreign policy, they varied in form and in degree of independence—democracy in Czechoslovakia (the only country in this area with a democratic tradition), free elections and the overthrow of the Communist party in Hungary, a Communist-formed coalition government in Bulgaria, a broadly based but Communist-dominated government in Poland, and a Soviet-imposed government in Rumania (the most anti-Russian of these nations). In all of these countries Communists controlled the ministries of interior (the police) and were able to suppress anti-Soviet groups, including anti-Communist democrats.

Those who have attributed to Russia a policy of inexorable expansion have often neglected this immediate postwar period, or they have interpreted it simply as a necessary preliminary (a cunning strategy to allay American suspicions until the American Army demobilized and left the continent) to the consolidation and extension of power in East-Central Europe. From this perspective, however, much of Stalin's behavior becomes strangely contradictory and potentially self-defeating. If he had planned to create puppets rather than an area of "friendly governments," why (as Isaac Deutscher asks) did Stalin "so stubbornly refuse to make any concessions to the Poles over their eastern frontiers?" Certainly, also, his demand for reparations from Hungary, Rumania, and Bulgaria would have been unnecessary if he had planned to take over these countries. (America's insistence upon using a loan to Russia to achieve political goals, and the nearly twenty-month delay after Russia first submitted a specific proposal for assistance, led Harriman to suggest in November that the loan policy "may have contributed to their [Russian] avaricious policies in the countries occupied or liberated by the Red Army.")

Russian sources are closed, so it is not possible to prove that Soviet intentions were conservative; nor for the same reason is it possible for those who adhere to the thesis of inexorable Soviet expansion to prove their theory. But the available evidence better supports the thesis that these years should be viewed not as a cunning preliminary to the harshness of 1947 and afterward, but as an attempt to establish a modus vivendi with the West and to protect "socialism in one country." This interpretation explains more adequately why the Russians delayed nearly three years before ending dissent and hardening policies in the countries behind their own military lines. It would also explain why the Communist parties in France and Italy were cooperating with the coalition governments until these parties were forced out of the coalitions in 1947. The American government had long hoped for the exclusion of these Communist parties, and in Italy, at least, American intimations of greater economic aid to a government without Communists was an effective lever. At the same time Stalin was seeking to prevent the revolution in Greece.

If the Russian policy was conservative and sought accommodation (as now seems likely), then its failure must be explained by looking beyond Russian actions. Historians must reexamine this period and reconsider American policies. Were they directed toward compromise? Can they be judged as having sought adjustment? Or did they demand acquiescence to the American world view, thus thwarting real negotiations?

There is considerable evidence that American actions clearly changed after Roosevelt's death. Slowly abandoning the tactics of accommodation, they became even more vigorous after Hiroshima. The insistence upon rolling back Soviet influence in Eastern Europe, the reluctance to grant a loan for Russian reconstruction, the inability to reach an agreement on Germany, the maintenance of the nuclear monopoly—all of these could have contributed to the sense of Russian insecurity. The point, then, is that in 1945 and 1946 there may still have been possibilities for negotiations and settlements, for accommodations and adjustments, if the United States had been willing to recognize Soviet fears, to accept Soviet power in her areas of influence, and to ease anxieties.

## *H. Stuart Hughes*
# THE SECOND YEAR OF THE COLD WAR

*From 1946 to 1948, H. Stuart Hughes was chief of the State Department's Division of Research for Europe. In the following "memoir," he recalls the range of ideas on Eastern European questions within the American government in an attempt to recapture the "feel and taste" of the early Cold War. Aligning himself with neither traditional nor revisionist views today, he reflects that alternatives for Soviet-American accommodation existed in that period. He suggests that Russia was largely concerned for its security in Eastern Europe and that American acceptance of the reality of Soviet domination there—in short, acceptance of a Soviet sphere of influence—would have mitigated Cold War tension and perhaps permitted some liberalization within*

*Russia's dominated neighbors. Furthermore, Hughes writes, in the light of tragic events in Czechoslovakia, America's sometimes exaggerated anticommunism seems not wholly mistaken or evil, for it rightfully stood against the harsh Soviet suppression of civil liberties. What was inappropriate—especially for the lot of Eastern European peoples—was America's military response, its armed anticommunism. Now a professor of history at Harvard University, Hughes is the author of* The United States and Italy *(1953 and 1965),* An Approach to Peace *(1962),* History as Art and as Science *(1964), and* The Obstructed Path *(1968).*

To someone who has been out of government service, as I have, for more than twenty years, the present spate of revisionist history on the origins of the Cold War makes curious reading. One's first reaction is pleasure: It seems that those of us who originally opposed the Cold War mentality have now been rehabilitated; a stand that once was branded as mistaken, quixotic, or possibly even "subversive," in the light of today's ideological temper (at least among intellectuals), looks very good indeed. The second reaction is more perplexed: the current accounts, many of them by younger historians who did not experience the events in question at first hand, strike us as just barely out of focus. The lapse of two decades, joined to the new perspective our country's colossal mistakes in Vietnam have suggested, has etched the opening stages of the Cold War in a sharper and simpler outline than they had at the time. In ceasing to be current events and becoming "history," they have acquired an unsuspected firmness of contour; today's young historians know crucial details that at the time were the closely-guarded secrets of the top policy makers. Yet there has been a corresponding loss along the way: something of the feel and taste of the late 1940s has slipped into oblivion.

Thus much of the present polemic goes far beyond the arguments characteristic of the era itself: the reasoning of the handful of civil servants in positions of middle-range responsibility who were trying to persuade their colleagues to damp down the mounting hostility to the Soviet Union was more ambiguous and nuanced than the judgments we are offered today. It was also less moralistic:

From H. Stuart Hughes, "The Second Year of the Cold War: A Memoir and an Anticipation," *Commentary* 48 (August 1969): 27–32. Reprinted from *Commentary*, by permission; Copyright © 1969 by the American Jewish Committee. (Footnotes deleted.)

what offended a number of us at the time was the self-righteous tone both of our country's public rhetoric and of the private talk of the conventional Foreign Service types. Now, twenty years later, we are faced with moralism from the other direction: It is the United States rather than Russia that currently stands accused. Still more, from the present historical vantage point the decisive American acts of hostility seem to have come very early in the game—in the months immediately following the death of President Roosevelt in April 1945. The events of the succeeding period receive lesser attention. Yet to contemporaries it did not appear that way: when I myself got into the act, in the winter of 1946, I did not have the impression that I was arriving on the spot too late; although I found the ideological atmosphere in Washington quite different from what it had been when I had reported briefly back from Europe a year earlier, I did not think that the future had been foreclosed. The range of choice might be narrowing, but alternative paths still lay open. The year and a quarter from March 1946 to July 1947 is the period of the incipient Cold War that I know the best—indeed, the only one on which I can testify with any confidence. It is also the one during which our country and the Soviet Union together reached the point of no return.

My own involvement in these events was somewhat accidental. As a former intelligence officer in the OSS, I had found my part of that organization—the scholarly, nonsecret part—reassigned to the Department of State while I was still in Germany and in uniform. Coming home, unlike most of my friends, who quickly returned to academic life, I decided to tarry on in Washington. A few months later I found myself in charge of a large, sprawling, demoralized staff of experts known as the Division of Research for Europe. I had only just turned thirty: to all outward appearances, I had fallen into a prestigious job, with responsibilities unusual for one so young. The reality was rather different: my new division floated in limbo, distrusted by the State Department professionals and seldom listened to. After two years of bureaucratic frustration, I departed in early 1948, impelled by a mixture of ideological disappointment and the lure of university teaching.

But at least I had had a ringside seat on the Cold War's shift from tentative to definitive shape and, in the slow-paced life of pre-air-conditioned Washington, a chance to reflect on what was going on.

These reflections were not all of a piece: they oscillated between weary resignation and occasional explosions of wrath at the obtuseness of the conventional judgments—explosions that in moments of particular annoyance at official complacency might sound pro-Communist. My area of expertise, of course, was Europe. In the second year of the Cold War, European concerns still dominated the international scene. China had not yet been "lost," and besides, my counterparts in the research division for the Far East were accepted by the Foreign Service people far more as equals than was true on the European side. The purge of "old China hands" which was to sweep up diplomats and professors indiscriminately was as yet only a distant menace.

My main point of opposition to the wisdom of the State Department professionals had to do with their apocalyptic outlook on Europe. In the West, where they emphasized the threat of Communist subversion and revolution, I drew attention to the conservative recovery that was already taking place and to the possibility that the United States might eventually find itself aligned with authoritarian regimes of the Right. Where they saw crisis and collapse, I detected elements of continuity with the past and viewed the danger to society less in terms of what militant Communists might do than as the result of what routine-minded governments might fail to do in alleviating the misery of populations just emerging from the trials of war. In the East, I similarly found reasons for taking Soviet domination more calmly than was considered good form at the time. In short, I discovered the outlines of a new and unfamiliar kind of stabilization on both sides of what Winston Churchill had just baptized the "iron curtain."

Churchill's address at Fulton, Missouri, delivered in Truman's presence in March 1946, marked the opening of the Cold War phase in question. Matters that the statesmen of the West had previously spoken of in diplomatic euphemisms—however blistering their language in private—had now been laid bluntly on the line. The iron curtain speech was followed almost immediately by a series of Soviet moves which suggested that Stalin in his own fashion agreed with Churchill's gloomy estimate—more particularly a strengthening of ideological curbs at home associated with the rise of Andrei Zhdanov and a shift of economic policy in Germany presaging the partition of the country. Such were the actions and the responses that sent the Soviet-American antagonism into high gear. A year later a similar cluster of events gave the Cold War in Europe its permanent configuration: in March, the enunciation of the Truman Doctrine and the launching of a "Security Loyalty Program" in the United States; in May, the departure of the Communist ministers from the governments of France and Italy, and the Soviet-inspired elimination of the democratic leader Ferenc Nagy as prime minister of Hungary; finally, on the second of July, the Russian refusal to cooperate in the Marshall Plan and the veto on Polish and Czech participation that was its inevitable sequel.

The assumptions from which I—and a small groups of friends and associates—judged this series of events differed both from the conventional Cold War stance that was then emerging and from the revisionist view that has recently become so widespread. Perhaps our standpoint was eccentric; certainly it seems forgotten today. Recalling it may help to restore to the year 1946–1947 the quality of bewilderment and moral untidiness it had at the time.

Our first assumption was that the Cold War, however distasteful we might find it, was something more than the product of inflamed American imaginations; it was based on the irrefutable realities of an unprecedented situation—the Soviet domination of the whole of East-Central Europe. I remember looking at a map in the autumn of 1944—when the Red Army, having chased the Germans from the Balkans, stood at the gates of Warsaw and Budapest—and concluding that a severe political reaction would set in at home when my countrymen awoke to what had happened. It never occurred to me that the American government could do anything to induce the Russians to "behave"; hence the subsequent controversy about Yalta struck me as largely beside the point. The Cold War, or something resembling it, I took as a fact of life, the dominant fact in the lives of the unusual breed of civil servants among whom I worked: it could be reduced or attenuated—that was the purpose of our labors— but it could not be completely avoided, as some of the revisionist historians seem to imagine.

At just about the time in late 1944 when I was taking my look at the map, Churchill went to see Stalin in Moscow. The result was the celebrated spheres-of-influence agreement which assigned to the Russians a predominant role in the Balkans, while leaving Greece under Western supervision. The United States never accepted this arrangement, and its exact status remained unclear. Nor did those at my level in the State Department know of its existence. I first learned about it a half decade later when Churchill published the concluding volume of his wartime memoirs. I also learned later still that a minority of highly-placed figures in the American government, including Henry L. Stimson, Henry A. Wallace, and George F. Kennan, at various times and with varying emphases, had pushed the spheres-of-influence line. In the second year of the Cold War, my friends and I were quite in the dark on these matters: we reached the notion of spheres of influence on our own. This became our second assumption—that the readiest way to mitigate the ravages of the incipient Cold War was for our country to keep to its side of the iron curtain in the hope that the Soviet Union would oblige us by doing the same.

Thus in our minds the real drama—and tragedy—of the Cold War was the progressive erosion or degradation of the spheres-of-influence idea. It was not within our style of thought to assign exclusive or even predominant blame for this state of affairs to one side or the other. We saw it rather as the result of a cumulative, mutually reinforcing series of mistakes and misunderstandings—an elaborate counterpoint in which our government and that of the Soviet Union seemed almost to be working hand-in-hand to simplify the ideological map at the expense of minor political forces, intermediate groups, and nuances of opinion. Our contention had been that if each side would stay out of the other's sphere, then each could tolerate substantial dissent within that sphere. Our prize exhibits were, in the East, the quasi-democratic functioning of the governments of Hungary and Czechoslovakia and, in the West, the presence of Communists in the French and Italian ministries. But as the year 1946–1947 wore on, it became increasingly apparent that all such "bridges" or way-stations were doomed. Their mere existence offered an excuse for one side to accuse its adversary of maintaining a fifth column in its midst. Virtually every move of either one—however neutral its intent—bred suspicion in the other. As Russians and Americans alike tried to shore up the governments of the countries dependent on them, each act of ideological buttressing was bound to produce a corresponding reaction in the opposing camp.

It may sound paradoxical to have believed that a de facto partitioning of Europe would have facilitated rather than hindered the building of bridges from one side to the other. But that was what eventually proved true. In the crucial year 1946–1947 the Russians were treating this partition as the legitimate consequence of their military victories and the indispensable guarantee of their national security: the Americans were speaking of it as abnormal and immoral. Such at least was their public rhetoric; in actuality our government was to accept piece by piece over the years a situation it had originally rejected in toto. The proof came a decade later, in the autumn of 1956, when the United States failed to go to the aid of the anti-Communist insurrection in Hungary. And the result was what my friends and I had predicted: once the Russians knew that the Americans would not step over the line into what they had always considerd their own sphere of influence, a thaw in the Cold War, the beginnings of liberalization in Eastern Europe, and the inauguration of East-West cultural contacts finally became possible.

But that is to get ahead of our story. In the context of the Cold War's second year, what was of prime importance was that the spheres-of-influence concept survived in the State Department's bureaucratic underground. Moreover, those of us who thought in such terms acted on the conviction, which we seldom, if ever, explicitly expressed, that our chiefs did not mean quite what they said. This was our third assumption—that neither our own country nor the Soviet Union had any serious intention of resorting to force in its dealings with the other; neither would attempt a real power play at the other's expense. Perhaps there was wishful thinking in our attitude; certainly we needed to grasp at some shred of comfort to get us through the rigors of an inordinately depressing year. Yet we were less far afield than the revisionist historians who have defined "the object of American policy" in the immediate postwar era as "not to defend Western or even Central Europe but to force the Soviet Union out of Eastern Europe." In my own experience in Washington I never found any solid evidence of such a plan. There were warlike noises aplenty—everyone from President Truman down talked tough when the occasion (ordinarily incarnate as Congress) seemed to demand it. But these pronouncements were exceedingly vague; they were far less sinister than they have appeared in retrospect. Before the Korean War the American capability in conventional arms was patently inadequate for the task of "liberating" Eastern Europe, and while atomic blackmail may always have been lurking in the wings, Stalin and Molotov, who prided themselves on their nerves of steel, were not allowing themselves to be frightened.

If a military showdown was tacitly ruled out, what remained? Was it simply a choice between preserving the close Soviet-American relationship of the period 1942–1944, and institutionalized hostility in the form of the Cold War, as revisionist historiography seems to argue? At the time, my friends and I thought otherwise—and this was our fourth and final assumption. We believed that one could find an intermediate course between armed antagonism and a cordial modus vivendi. Such a course, we recognized, was inordinately difficult to chart, and I am far from sure today what its outlines might have been. The best I can think of is some formula like wary, cautious, mutually suspicious relations handled with the "correctness" and consummate diplomatic tact that Europe's precarious situation required.

With the options thus narrowed, what was there that a middle-level official with my convictions could do? Naturally it was very little: in my division at least, we felt most of the time as though we were firing our memoranda off into a void. The atmosphere was that of Kafka's *Castle,* in which one never knew who would answer the telephone or even whether it would be answered at all. Two tasks, however, seemed possible: one was to try to explain that Soviet actions which our superiors thought outrageous would look rather less so if viewed in a spheres-of-influence context; the second was the notion of using America's economic power to build bridges between East and West.

While a whole succession of Soviet moves in the autumn and winter of 1946–1947 aroused official ire in Washington, the key event occurred in Hungary the following May. Hungary, we subsequently learned, had been treated in the original spheres-of-influence agreement in a peculiar fashion: as opposed to Bulgaria and Rumania, in which Soviet influence was to predominate, it had been assigned fifty-fifty to the Russians and to those oddly referred to as "the others." Parenthetically, it is also worth noting that Czechoslovakia and Poland were not covered by this agreement at all—hence the ramifying post-Yalta difficulties, particularly with regard to the latter. Such fine distinctions were lost on my friends and me: not knowing that any accord existed (even if unrecognized by our country), we simply assumed that the Soviet sphere should be considered coterminous with the area in which the presence or vicinity of the Red Army was the primary fact of life. Thus it seemed natural to us to lump with the two Balkan countries where Soviet influence was already entrenched, the three nations to the west of them, two of which had held relatively free elections and were struggling to maintain the basic minimum of democratic procedures.

The overthrow of democracy in the second of these, Czechoslovakia, in early 1948 has so caught the attention of historians as to dim the importance of the similar series of events that occurred in Hungary a year earlier. Yet viewed in retrospect, the destruction of Ferenc Nagy's Smallholders' party may be the more important of the two, as offering the first sign of what the Russians would and would not tolerate in the part of Europe they regarded as theirs. I am not sure today that I was right in saying as flatly as I did— I quote from a memorandum I wrote at the time—that "it was not the democratic character of the Hungarian government that brought down upon it the wrath of the Soviet Union. It was its foreign policy of cultivating the favor of the Western democracies, particularly the United States." The subsequent fate of Czechoslovakia was to suggest that with the Cold War in high gear, internal policies alone might be sufficient to arouse Russian suspicion. Yet I think I was correct in arguing that the action in Hungary was a "routine and anticipated move on the part of the USSR to plug an obvious gap in its security system." Although "whittling down the Smallholder majority ... had been going on for months, ... the enunciation of the Truman Doctrine accelerated the process," as did "the removal of the Communist ministers from the governments of France and Italy. ... Once the United States had served notice that it was beginning to organize a counterbloc," the Soviet Union was bound to tighten its grip on its own client states. And I concluded: "The coup in Hungary has really altered nothing: it has only destroyed a few illusions."

Some of the illusions, of course, were my own. On rereading after more than twenty years my note on Hungary, I find in it the tone of a rearguard action and of slightly desperate special pleading. The time was fast running out in which an effort to explain Soviet actions in East-Central Europe could find a hearing in Washington.

My second self-imposed task was more promising. Fortunately enough, my division was awarded the job of preparing preliminary studies for what later became the Marshall Plan. Besides reviving the flagging spirits of my associates, this technically challenging and ideologically congenial assignment gave me a chance to put on paper my thoughts as to the form an economic recovery program for Europe should take.

A month before Secretary Marshall gave his celebrated commencement address at Harvard, I had noted down the following:

1. The aid program should be administered by an international body....
2. Aid should be granted solely on objective economic rather than political grounds.
   a. No discrimination against Soviet satellites;
   b. No effort to give overt or tacit support to any particular political groups or parties;
   c. Reliance solely on the indirect political effect of improved standard of living, etc.

In a very general sense, the offer which Marshall made to the Europeans conformed to these criteria. I believed at the time and still believe that the plan which went by his name was the most statesmanlike action the United States took in the opening years of the Cold War—indeed the only one that held out a real chance of bridging the widening chasm in Europe. And its rejection by the Soviet Union came as the last and bitterest of the succession of disappointments that my friends and I had experienced over the previous year. There is no need to retrace here the process of gradual reinterpretation by which the Marshall Plan eventually came to be viewed by both sides in a Cold War context. What is more relevant is to recall that such had been from the start the view of a large and influential body of State Department professionals; in their eyes the extension of the offer of economic aid to Eastern Europe was always rather perfunctory. Hence the sharp, dogmatic tone of my own memorandum on the subject. I felt that I was in the minority and that I had to argue hard. I also sensed that even small changes in the manner in which the offer was made might be crucial to its acceptance or rejection—that the Russians might oblige the hardliners in my own country by confirming their predictions.

My memorandum ended on a note of warning: "Any program stated in terms of 'either the Soviet Union cooperates or ...' would almost certainly eventuate in the latter alternative being adopted; those already skeptical of the merits of a Europe-wide, undiscriminatory program would be proved right, and an outright anti-Soviet program would be the result."

Thus the curtain came down on a cruel year, during the course of which the mutually reinforcing squeeze from East and West finally left my friends and me without a standing ground. I spent my last six months in Washington in a state of mild depression, punctuated by gloomy (and exaggerated) predictions of the fate that was about to overtake the democratic Left. Nor was my conscience as clear as in retrospect might be supposed of one who had fought and lost the good fight for Soviet-American reconciliation. In the summer of 1947 I had the trial and execution of Nikola Petkov to reckon with and that I found extremely hard to bear.

If Ferenc Nagy is almost forgotten today—as opposed to Imre Nagy, of 1956 fame—his agrarian counterpart in Bulgaria, Nikola Petkov, is probably even less remembered. Yet at the time these two, along with Stanislaw Mikolajczyk, the Polish peasant spokesman, and like Nagy a fugitive abroad, were celebrated as offering a democratic middle course between Communist domination and the rightist-authoritarian, anti-Soviet type of government that had ruled most of East-Central Europe before the Second World War. It was hard not to feel sympathy for agrarian leaders who, after the briefest of respites, were finding themselves once more in the state of political persecution that had been their usual lot before the "liberation" of their countries. And among them the case of Petkov was the most compelling. As opposed to Mikolajczyk and Nagy, the Bulgarian chose the more perilous course of staying on in his own country and fighting what he must have known was a hopeless battle. Tried on trumped-up charges of collusion with the United States, he was condemned to death in August 1947 and hanged the following month.

My associates followed with anguished interest Petkov's stubborn struggle for survival. I recall a friend's showing me a report of a scene in the Bulgarian parliament and of the taunt "You are trembling, Nikola Petkov" hurled at him by a political enemy. The words struck me like a body blow—as though I were in some sense guilty of Petkov's approaching death. And, as emotional truth, my reaction was not exaggerated. In our spheres-of-influence reasoning, in our anxiety to preserve good relations with the Soviet Union, my friends and I had hardened our hearts and in effect condemned Petkov and his like, just as we had consigned the populations of East-Central Europe to Communist tyranny. We had done this with regret; we had sought to make a stand at every halting place along the way; but in the end we had bowed our shoulders and given up as lost the agrarian leaders and the electoral majorities that either had voted for them or would have voted for them if they could.

This emotional actuality is above all what gets lost in revisionist historiography on the origins of the Cold War—the doubts by which we of the bureaucratic opposition were shaken and which gave our policy recommendations so fumbling and tentative a character. The State Department professionals, the fledgling cold warriors, were troubled by no such scruples; they saw the moral issues in simple terms; their consciences were clear. Not ours—our efforts to adopt the coolly detached stance of junior statesmen were constantly undercut by a half-conscious recognition that we might be mistaken and that the policy we advocated carried with it an enormous price in human misery.

It was to be more than a decade before I recovered my equilibrium, before I was able to see clearly in what sense I had been right and in what sense the majority of American intellectuals had been wrong. Until the late 1950s the view prevailed that sympathy for the people of East-Central Europe dictated a moral anticommunism and that this sense of outrage in turn required an endorsement of the Cold War. I simplify, of course—but such I think was the tacit assumption of most of the intellectual community; hence their reluctance to engage in any far-reaching critique of the official wisdom. Nor did the events of 1956 change many people's minds: the lesson of their country's total inability to react to the Soviet occupation of Budapest was lost on most of them. Not until the 1960s, and more particularly with the replay of Budapest that occurred in Prague twelve years later, did it finally sink in that in this case armed hostility was an inappropriate and counterproductive form in which to manifest the moral indignation with which it had so long been justified.

Throughout the first eight months of 1968 I was haunted by a sense that I was back where I had come in, at first joyous as the Czech idyll took a course which was too good to be fully believed, then profoundly depressed. The familiar litany—1938, 1948, 1968— had a special personal immediacy for one who had been in State Department service two decades earlier. And this was as true of the spring of expectation as it was of the autumn of bitterness. Just as the 1948 coup in Prague had snuffed out the last flickers of the political "openness" in which my friends and I had vested our hopes, so in 1968 Alexander Dubcek suddenly materialized as the reincarnation of those hopes, as the living embodiment of the ideological synthesis—left Socialist in the West, liberal Communist in the East— that our moments of optimism had sketched out. The promised land we had glimpsed had never been very substantial. Yet this non-dogmatic, neutralist, Popular-Front type of government had been precisely what a large and distinguished part of the Resistance to Hitler had longed for. Events had seemed to doom it utterly. And then quite unexpectedly, in the early months of 1968, Dubcek and his colleagues were on their way to making it a reality.

This time the subsequent disappointment banished any thought of a Cold War solution. Those in the West who twenty years earlier had been profoundly divided on Czechoslovakia now saw eye to eye. Nearly everyone dismissed a military response as inappropriate: even the calls for a reinvigoration of NATO sounded perfunctory. It was as though it had taken two decades to realize that the Cold War and the fate of the populations under Soviet control were separable issues and that an emphasis on the one was of little help to the other. The armed standoff between the two superpowers could contribute nothing to improving the lot of the peoples of East-Central Europe—rather the contrary; a question that was at bottom one of civil liberties, or of the quality of life, could not be dealt with by military means. In this respect, the Second World War had been the great exception to the more usual human experience: in 1944 and 1945 it had in fact proved possible—at least in the West— to liberate whole populations from tyranny at a price that the liberated were willing to pay. With the Cold War and the thermonuclear nightmare which accompanied it, such surgery became too dangerous to be attempted. But the memory and example of the "crusade" that had succeeded confused men's minds—and especially those of intellectuals—for a half-generation.

It was in this sense that my friends and I had been right two decades earlier. In the late 1940s I had been as incapable as the cold warriors of separating out the military from the civil-liberties aspect of events—hence my qualms of conscience. Today, in the light of what happened in Czechoslovakia in 1968, I am happier than I was at the time about the stand I took in the year and a half preceding the first seizure of power in Prague. Yet I am by no means satisfied with how revisionist historiography treats the events of twenty years ago. I refuse to accept the notion that my countrymen's anticommunism was evil or misguided all along the line. In 1946 and 1947, as before and after, hostility to communism made sense in certain contexts and was blind and self-defeating in others. More particularly it was not until a few Communist regimes or parties began to give a minimum respect to the human decencies that liberal-minded Americans could entertain much sympathy for them. And it is perhaps well that those too young to remember the immediate postwar era should hear such a simple truth from someone who twenty years ago labored under the suspicion of being "soft on communism."

*Thomas G. Paterson*
# THE TRAGEDY OF CZECHOSLOVAKIA

*One of the tragedies of the Soviet-American confrontation in Eastern Europe was the Communist seizure of power in Czechoslovakia in February 1948. The bloodless event stunned Americans who saw it as yet another, but more dramatic, aggressive Soviet thrust. The Washington Post soon published a full-page map of Europe with the alarming caption: "Russia Moves Westward— Where Next?" Later, George F. Kennan, who never believed that Russia would move militarily across Europe, concluded that the Czech coup d'etat was a Soviet "defensive reaction" to the Marshall Plan. In any case, the coup helped ensure final passage of the Marshall Plan which was then before Congress and spurred policy makers to think more concretely of a Western European military alliance, even though Soviet troops were not stationed in*

*Czechoslovakia at that time. In the following selection, Paterson surveys American diplomacy toward Czechoslovakia in 1945–1948, pointing out how the United States attempted to use reconstruction aid to draw that precarious country toward American foreign policy. That maneuver backfired and pushed Czechoslovakia closer to Russia. He concludes that it stands as an example of the unsophisticated, undiscriminating American policy toward Eastern Europe.*

One of the few diplomatic tools available to American officials to pry Eastern Europe open to United States influence was economic assistance. Washington conducted a conscious and active diplomacy after the war through the granting or denying of loans to Eastern European nations. When that maneuver failed to move the area out of the Soviet orbit, United States aid was cut off, and Eastern Europe fell more deeply under Russian influence. Demonstrating some flexibility, Washington treated Finland and Yugoslavia as exceptions and gave them aid without "strings," thus helping to ensure their independence, but Czechoslovakia, Poland, Rumania, and Hungary were considered Soviet fiefs and members of a tight bloc. If they could not be wooed from their foreign policy alignment with Russia—and Washington soon learned that its economic diplomacy was inadequate for that task, then they had to be isolated from the benefits of American loans and trade. Aid without "strings"—given simply to preserve what was left of independence in Eastern Europe and to maintain links between that area and the United States—was not tolerated. Secretary Byrnes's simple prescription of September, 1946, merits repeating: "We must help our friends in every way and refrain from assisting those who either through helplessness or for other reasons are opposing the principles for which we stand."

Americans faced a dilemma. If Washington extended considerable aid with "strings" to Eastern Europe, the Soviets might be aroused to halt it. If the United States refused aid altogether, Eastern Europe would become more dependent on Russia. The resolution of the dilemma would have been a nonthreatening, cautious economic foreign policy without "strings." Russia would tolerate reasonable—but not exploitative or binding—Western economic relations with its

From Thomas G. Paterson, *Soviet-American Confrontation: Postwar Reconstruction and the Origins of the Cold War* (Baltimore, 1973), pp. 120–130. Copyright © 1973 by The Johns Hopkins University Press. Reprinted by permission. (Footnotes deleted.)

sphere. But the Truman administration defined "friends" and "principles for which we stand" in narrow terms and followed a conspicuous diplomacy designed to weaken the Soviet presence.

After World War II, Czechoslovakia clung precariously to a middle ground in the developing bipolar world, attempting to perpetuate its independence and interchanges with Western Europe and the United States and at the same time to build and nurture a strategically important and sincere friendship for Russia. Well before the Communist coup of February, 1948, however, American leaders defined Czechoslovakia, a democratic socialist nation, as a Soviet satellite and virtually wrote the fledgling country off as "lost." Crucial reconstruction aid was denied and the Soviet domination that Washington had prematurely imagined became stark reality.

United States foreign policy experts grappled with three troublesome questions in Czechoslovakia in 1945: removal of American and Soviet troops, the declaration by Soviet authorities that two plants claimed by the International Telephone and Telegraph Corporation (ITT) were "war trophies," and the relationship between the Czech nationalization program, loans, and United States goals in Eastern Europe. Both the Americans and the Russians refused to withdraw their troops until it was certain that the withdrawal would be simultaneous; after some hesitation both nations removed their soldiers in December, 1945. That month, too, after American protests to Moscow that the ITT factories were American-owned and important to Czech reconstruction, Russia dropped its claim to one of the plants and demanded 50 percent ownership of the other.

The third issue was more divisive. In early 1945 the United States was anxious about Czechoslovakia's postwar intentions concerning nationalization. Ambassador Laurence A. Steinhardt successfully persuaded the Department of State to defer any loan decision by the Export-Import Bank until the Czech nationalization program had been announced. In October, the non-Communist government led by the respected Eduard Beneš nationalized American-owned and controlled enterprises valued at $109 million. Such companies as Socony-Vacuum, ITT, Remington Rand, Corn Products Refining, and Standard Oil of New Jersey were affected; John Foster Dulles of Sullivan and Cromwell represented several other claimants.

At first, Steinhardt was confident that the Czechs would compensate these businesses for nationalized property, although he recognized that their shortage of dollars would make such compensation difficult. He became impatient and more demanding as the Czech government struggled with the problem. He and the State Department came more and more to see Czechoslovakia as a prime target for the diplomatic use of economic power. Loan policy under Steinhardt's and Byrnes's guidance was aimed at slowing down nationalization, securing adequate compensation for American property, and, more significant, orienting Czech foreign policy toward the United States. . . .

In the first half of 1946 Steinhardt's attitude hardened. He insisted that "a large American loan to any foreign government in which the Communist party is strongly represented will be availed of by them indirectly to entrench their position and extend their grip." He recalled the defaulting upon World War I loans, claimed that the Czechs did not need a large reconstruction loan, mentioned again UNRRA aid, and stressed the importance of compensation. He also tried, but without success, to dissuade Washington from adding another $40 million to the $10 million already offered Czechoslovakia for the purchase of surplus United States property in Europe, which the Foreign Liquidation Commission was eager to sell. In July, to Steinhardt's dismay, negotiations for a $50 million reconstruction loan were proceeding well because the Czechs promised to open talks on compensation.

Steinhardt filed a stinging dissent. Mere promises of compensation, he contended, were not enough to justify a loan. The reconstruction loan was "our last trump" in securing compensation. But his reasoning went beyond the narrow compensation issue to the question of the place of Czechoslovakia in world affairs. Earlier he had cabled the State Department that "since election of May 26 [in which the Communists polled 38 percent of the popular vote] there has been an unmistakable though indefinable tendency on part of some officials of Czech government to show increasing indifference towards Western powers." He noted that the Czechs were "self-satisfied" and not thirsting for United States aid and that the bargaining authority of a loan seemed significantly diminished. Overemphasizing the "indifference" of some political figures, he virtually ignored the eagerness of Beneš, Hubert Ripka, and Jan Masaryk—non-Communist officials—for aid.

Steinhardt's position received dramatic and surprising support

from Byrnes at the Paris Peace Conference on August 30. The
Czechs sent ten officials to the meeting, two of whom were Communists. At one point in the discussions, these two Communist delegates applauded a Soviet charge that the United States was trying
to force its will upon weaker nations through its lending power. In-
furiated, Byrnes ordered Washington to prevent the unused portion
of the surplus property credit of $40 million from being utilized and
to suspend the Czech application for a $50 million reconstruction
loan. Henceforth the United States should aid "friends," he said, and
not subsidize "the Communist control of Czechoslovakia." He would
not tolerate "vilification of the United States and distortion of our
motives and policies." A more cautious Will Clayton believed that
since the United States had already set prerequisites for the reconstruction loan, it had a "moral commitment" to proceed with the loan
if the Czechs met the conditions. Nevertheless, the Export-Import
Bank loan application was suspended and the surplus property
credit was taken back.

Byrnes's decisions, seemingly motivated by the handclapping incident at Paris, were derived from the larger question of Czech friendship for Russia: "You must bear in mind . . . that up to the very end of
this conference Czechoslovakia has consistently opposed the United
States and voted invariably with the Slav bloc on every important
issue. . . . I should wish to see much more substantial evidence of
Czechoslovak independence and friendship toward the United States
before resuming any form of economic assistance which some members of its delegation here profess to believe may lead to Czechoslovakia's 'economic enslavement.' " The secretary had expressed such
sentiments in his September 24, 1946, cable dividing the world into
"friends" and opponents. As John C. Campbell has commented:
"The answer to the accusation of dollar diplomacy apparently was
to give the accuser a real taste of it. It was a rather unprecedented
move, to which there was some opposition within the U.S. government, on the ground that Czechoslovakia was not lost and that economic aid would strengthen ties with the West."

Byrnes's decision seems curious. It was supposedly triggered and
justified by the actions of only two members of a delegation of ten.
It assumed that Czechoslovakia had a Communist-dominated government. In fact, after the May, 1946, elections, nine of the twenty-six
top-level officials of the government were Communist, and the Com-

munists held 114 of 300 seats in the Constituent National Assembly. The prime minister (Klement Gottwald) was a Communist, other critical cabinet posts such as Information and Interior were held by the same party, the Social Democrats often voted with the Communists in the majority, and Czechoslovakia did pursue a foreign policy closely attuned to that of Moscow. But to label this government, with Jan Masaryk as foreign minister and Beneš as president, "Communist," as Byrnes did, was to ignore the facts. Even Steinhardt pointed out that in the elections of 1946 "the vote recorded was the expression of the will of the people in a democratic manner." There was far more freedom in Czechoslovakia than anywhere else in Eastern Europe.

Beneš tried to explain the complex state of affairs to Steinhardt in December, 1946. He insisted that a number of the Communists in the cabinet were "good patriots" and pointed out the importance of preserving Czech independence. He asked Steinhardt to appreciate the reality of circumstances in which a small country contiguous to Russia found itself and the necessity of avoiding "reprisals" from its neighbors. Steinhardt recorded Beneš's explanation: "Under circumstances Masaryk [at Paris] had deemed it preferable to vote with Soviet Union on almost every occasion that Poland and Yugoslavia had done so, convinced that United States was not harmed thereby whereas Czechoslovakia might benefit. *He pointed out that as result of Czechoslovakia's voting record Soviets had scrupulously refrained from interfering in Czechoslovakia's internal affairs* and that in consequence moderates were making steady progress in leading country back to democratic ways." What Czechoslovakia sought to maintain was its independence; few United States leaders appreciated this effort. Instead, they demanded closer Czech ties with the United States. One Czech writer described the possible result: "The decision of the State Department may theoretically be what diplomats of the old school used to call 'a healthy lesson,' but contrary to American intentions and the aim of Czechoslovakia, it may have a much more serious consequence, namely to push Czechoslovakia even further into the orbit of Russia and make her more deeply dependent on trade with the Soviet Union and the rest of the Slav bloc." . . .

It would appear that the United States reversed its policy on aid to Eastern Europe when it issued an open call to all European nations to participate in the Marshall Plan in mid-1947. Czechoslovakia first accepted the invitation on July 8, then rejected it two days later, thus confirming many Americans in their belief that Czechoslovakia was already a Soviet satellite. Yet the Marshall Plan, presented as it was as an American-dominated program aimed against the Soviet Union, could not have been accepted by Czechoslovakia without serious disruption of its delicate balance between East and West. There is evidence to suggest that the familiar story of Czechoslovakia giving in helplessly to the USSR lacks sophistication and precision. For example, Stalin did not force a Czech delegation to depart suddenly for Moscow to hear his appeal against the Marshall Plan; a Czech-Soviet meeting on commercial questions had been planned earlier, and the Marshall Plan issue arose at the same time—which was certainly propitious for Russia. There is no question, however, that Stalin told the Czech delegation that acceptance of the invitation to participate did not jibe with Soviet wishes.

James P. Warburg, a prolific foreign affairs publicist and friend of Jan Masaryk, reports that Masaryk told him shortly after the Czech rejection of the Marshall Plan that actually it was the American interpretation of the original Czech acceptance as a rebuff to Russia that necessitated Soviet pressure and the Czech reversal. Indeed, the official Czech statement read: "Czechoslovakia's participation would be interpreted as an act directed against our friendship with the Soviet Union." The minister of foreign trade, Hubert Ripka, a member of the National Socialist party, later explained that Czechoslovakia was unwilling to risk a break with Russia for the sake of United States aid, however badly needed, because must Czechs "have constantly in mind the German danger which has threatened them since the Middle Ages" and valued close ties with Russia. Mikaly Karolyi, a Socialist Hungarian diplomat later driven into exile by the Communists, recalled that he agreed with the Communist position on the Marshall Plan: "It was inconceivable for either of our countries [Czechoslovakia or Hungary] to risk a break with the Soviets, the only safeguard against future German revival." And a Catholic People's party member of the Czech Parliament asked: "Is it worthwhile to risk the certainty of the Soviet-Czechoslovak alliance, which we need against Germany, for such an uncertainty as is a proposition by Mr. Marshall, made at some American university, which—similar to Wilson's League—may not even be approved by the U.S. Senate?" As was evident in Byrnes's earlier 1946 policy statement and in the Truman

Doctrine, the United States insisted that nations choose sides in international relations and that Czechoslovakia virtually repudiate its friendship with Russia for the sake of an ill-defined aid program.

After Czech renunciation of the Marshall Plan, but before the coup, Steinhardt was still arguing that Czech economic distress, aggravated by the withholding of American loans, would weaken the Communists within the government because they would realize that the United States, not Russia, was the valuable ally. In late 1947 he said boldly, "we have everything to gain and little to lose by standing back at this time and shutting our ears to the pleas for help that we may expect in the comparatively near future. Some of the people around this town have been playing a double game long enough. It is high time they were brought to their senses." He complained that "all that is left of our position here as far as the Communist members of the government are concerned is their hope of either an Export-Import or International Bank loan. . . . They are still hoping for a loan." But the State Department suddenly reversed its policy just before the coup, and Steinhardt announced Washington's willingness to grant $25 million to Czechoslovakia. As a former Foreign Affairs Ministry official later wrote: "It was not only too little and too late, but also ineffective in kind."

Such economic diplomacy between 1945 and 1948 did not satisfy either Washington or Prague. Most American companies received no compensation. In April, 1949, the Czechs offered compensation in exchange for a loan and the withdrawal of United States export controls, but no bargain was consummated. The British-Czech arrangement of September, whereby British companies were compensated in exchange for a trade agreement, provided a sharp contrast. Czech-American trade dwindled. The so-called Czech moderates were not strengthened. Indeed, as a former non-Communist officer of the Czech Foreign Ministry later observed: "The reaction in Czechoslovakia [to the 1946 loan suspension] was exactly that which the Communists and the Soviet government wished: shock, disappointment, a feeling that the West had failed to understand the country's problems in its struggle for independence." More important, the United States failed to achieve its major goal of orienting Czech foreign policy toward the West. Soviet-Czech economic relations improved, Russia stepped in to supply Czech needs for cotton and wheat, and granted Czechoslovakia $33 million in 1948. On December 4, 1947, Czechoslovakia and Russia entered into a five-year trade agreement, despite the ardent wish of Czechs of varying political beliefs before the coup to trade and to maintain pacific relations with the West.

Was United States foreign policy vis-à-vis Czechoslovakia really important to that country's history from 1945 to 1948? Internal crises over control of the police, Communist fears of losses in forthcoming elections, and the resignation of non-Communist cabinet officers all help explain the coup. External issues, such as the schism between Yugoslavia and Russia, the festering disputes in Germany leading to the Berlin blockade, and the Marshall Plan, also had their impact on the political turmoil in Czechoslovakia, perhaps by prompting Russia to tighten control over its sphere of influence. It is not the argument here that United States loan policy was the controlling factor in Czech affairs, but there is some evidence that it made a difference in weakening the Masaryks and Ripkas and in augmenting Soviet influence. In trying to draw Czechoslovakia from Russia to the West through economic pressure, the United States helped undermine Czech independence. American policy makers showed little understanding of the difference between an independent country influenced by the Soviet Union and housing a large Communist movement and a subjugated country with the same elements present. Facile and inaccurate labels were attached to Czech behavior, the Soviet presence in Eastern Europe was exaggerated, a heated rhetoric was used which was often wanting in careful analysis, and Russia was constantly challenged in its sphere of influence through pressure on it or on its neighbors.

In early 1948 Jan Masaryk lamented that "Washington and London have failed completely to understand my position, and they are making a serious mistake in not granting my request for funds or material assistance." He added that "with the end of UNRRA and America's insistence on refusing help except in connection with the Marshall Plan, Czechoslovakia has become completely dependent upon the 300,000 tons of grain which the Soviet Union has promised to Gottwald." In short, "this policy has completely spoiled my chances for playing Gottwald on even terms." It was a disservice to his country, he concluded, for the United States to have thought in 1946 that Czechoslovakia lay behind an "iron curtain."

Just a few months before the coup, in December, 1947, the journalist Alexander Werth interviewed Hubert Ripka. Ripka and Werth were friends and they talked frankly. "These goddam Americans," Ripka exploded when he described his appeal to Washington for wheat to help fend off a Czech famine. "And these idiots started the usual blackmail: 'Okay, you can have 200,000 or 300,000 or even 500,000 tons of wheat, but on one condition only—that you throw the Communists out of the Czechoslovak government.'" Ripka said he tried to explain that the Czech people had voted a good number of Communists into office. "But they said they didn't care. At this point Gottwald got in touch with Stalin, who immediately promised us the required wheat. . . . And now these idiots in Washington have driven us straight into the Stalinist camp."

In his book *Czechoslovakia Enslaved,* published in 1950, Ripka claimed that he had tried to establish cordial relations with both Russia and the United States and that American aid might have maintained a balance in internal Czech politics. He thought the suspension of the loan "extremely regrettable" because the assistance was "indispensable" and because the Communists reaped considerable propaganda from the decision. "We hoped that the government of the United States would reverse its decision when it came to realize that Czechoslovakia was a country basically democratic, which must be helped against the Communist danger. Unfortunately our hopes were disappointed." It is reasonable to argue, as did Warburg in the 1940s, that United States foreign policy toward Eastern Europe —particularly Czechoslovakia—helped pull down the "iron curtain" from the American side.

*Klaus Epstein*

# THE DIVISION OF GERMANY

*During World War II, the Allies decided to divide a defeated Germany into zones for the purpose of temporary military occupation. They agreed, too, to treat the country as a single economic unit, to break up large German corporations, and to demilitarize the nation. But the major powers could not decide Germany's eastern boundaries, and by 1947, as the Cold War produced more uncompromising policies, neither Russia nor the United States was*

*willing to relinquish control of its portion of Germany, and the division be-
came permanent. Eventually Britain and France added their zones to that of
the United States, and without choice the German people witnessed their
country cut into West and East Germany. Klaus Epstein explains the reasons
for the collapse of cooperation in Germany by discussing the unilateral policies of all occupants, the early disruptive posture of France, the uncertainty
of Russian policy, and the growing American practice of drawing West
Germany into the Western European economy to contribute to the Marshall
Plan. Security and recovery questions were closely interrelated in Germany.
Epstein is the author of* The Genesis of German Conservatism *(1966) and at
his death in 1967 was chairman of Brown University's Department of History.*

There were, basically, five theoretically possible solutions to the German problem in 1945: a four-power agreement on a "Carthaginian
peace"; a four-power agreement on a "neutralized" Germany standing outside existing power blocs; Soviet domination of all of Germany; Western domination of all of Germany, leading eventually to
a free united Germany allied with the West; and a partition of Germany between a Western-oriented West Germany and an Eastern-
dominated East Germany. Each of these solutions was promoted and
hindered by several factors and attitudes among both Allies and
Germans.

1. A "Carthaginian peace" was desired by strong currents of
public opinion in all the victorious powers, an entirely understandable
fact at a time when Nazi horrors were fresh in everyone's mind. Its
ingredients would have been Allied annexation of broad German territories (e.g., annexation of the country up to the Oder-Neisse line by
Russia and Poland, and of the Rhineland by France); internationalization of the Ruhr; a drastic economic policy of dismantling, reparations, and "industrial ceilings" in the spirit of the Morgenthau Plan;
and permanent Allied controls over Germany to enforce this harsh
policy upon a hungry, sullen, and rebellious "native" population.
Such a policy was "objectively" impossible—at least in the long run
—for two reasons: It could never win the support of the German
people and hence could not be permanently acceptable to governments responsive to a "civilized" public opinion; and it presupposed
permanent agreement between Russia and the United States not to

From Klaus Epstein, "The German Problem, 1945–1950," *World Politics* 20 (January
1968): 282–288, 297, 298–300. Reprinted by permission of *World Politics*. This article
is a review essay of Peter Schwarz's *Vom Reich zur Bundesrepublik* (1966).

mobilize German resources against one another. If it is accepted that the Cold War between Russia and the U.S. was "inevitable" (even apart from conflict over Germany), then it is clear that a "Carthaginian peace" was based upon a utopian premise of continued Allied harmony.

2. A four-power agreement on a neutralized, united Germany, enjoying an ever-increasing measure of self-government—in short, the solution applied to the Austrian problem in 1955—also meant that Germany would be subjected to punitive, discriminatory treatment, although the chances of winning German support obviously stood in inverse proportion to the degree of punishment and discrimination. Like the first, this solution was made virtually impossible by the mutual hostility of Russia and America in the Cold War, as well as by the incompatibility of their aims, the basic factor behind the Cold War. By 1947 these aims were made apparent in Germany by the Russians' "Sovietizing" their zone and making enormous reparations demands, while the Americans promoted democracy and free enterprise, subsidized their zone, and worked for the integration of Western Germany into the (Western) European Recovery Program.

3. The Soviet domination of all of Germany—and presumably all of Europe—was a genuine possibility if the U.S. were to relapse into isolationism, withdraw its troops from Europe, and fail to buttress the sagging Western European economy. These possibilities were taken very seriously indeed by many influential people until the Marshall Plan of 1947 and the negotiation of NATO in 1949. Thereafter Soviet domination could only be the result of victorious war.

4. The Western domination of all of Germany—and perhaps of much of Eastern Europe as well—could have been achieved only through a ruthless Western exploitation of military superiority in 1945 to impose unfavorable (though possibly "just") terms upon the Russians. Such a policy was advocated by Winston Churchill in June 1945, but it was never seriously considered by President Truman and would not have been supported by public opinion at the time.

5. The last theoretical solution was the partition of Germany at the zonal boundary of 1945, dividing a democratic West Germany from a Communist East Germany. The latter could be created and maintained only through Russian coercion; the former, though perhaps initiated originally by American pressure, could be maintained

only with the voluntary concurrence of the majority of West Germans. Such concurrence could, in fact, be achieved because the American program of a West Germany integrated into Western Europe and the Atlantic Community offered West Germans broad advantages: psychological "rehabilitation" from the pariah status created by Nazism; a democratic libertarian constitutional structure; an economic revival promoted by Marshall Plan funds; security against Communist designs, as proved by the Berlin airlift and the permanent stationing of Allied troops; defeat of the French desire for dismemberment; and Allied refusal to recognize the Polish annexation of the Eastern territories. . . .

America's German policy was marked by continuous conflict between a "vindictive" Left, which strove for a "Carthaginian peace" in cooperation with Russia, and a "realistic" Right, which wanted to enlist West German resources in the Cold War against communism. The Left believed itself to be carrying out the legacy of President Roosevelt; its program found an extreme expression in the Morgenthau Plan and a somewhat more moderate expression in the basic occupation directive, JCS 1067, of April 26, 1945. It wanted to cooperate with "our heroic Russian ally" in eliminating the triple evil of militarism, Junkerism, and big capital through a common policy administered through the Allied Control Council (the four-power authority, composed of the four Allied military commanders, set up at Berlin on July 30, 1945). Secretary of State James Byrnes and Deputy Military Commander (after 1947, Commander) Lucius Clay were initial supporters of this policy until they learned, by the late summer of 1946, that it meant economic ruin for the American zone (necessitating food imports financed by the American taxpayer) and economic ruin for Western Europe (with the opportunity for Communist takeovers) because of the traditional interdependence of the German and Western European coal and steel economy. They were also appalled by the horrors perpetrated by the Russians in their zone, the Russian-encouraged expulsion of 12 million German refugees from Eastern Europe, and the astronomic Russian reparations demands, which far exceeded Germany's ability to pay (and would, if taken from the Western zones, be paid indirectly by the American government that subsidized those zones).

General Clay and other American military officers in contact with German realities began in fact a quiet sabotage of JCS 1067 by the summer of 1946; their sensible attitude was soon strengthened when the outbreak of the Cold War between the U.S. and Russia made a viable West Germany seem desirable. Clay's "realism" was also reinforced by the declining influence of the "Carthaginian" school in Washington (following Henry Wallace's departure from the cabinet), the development of the "containment policy" with George Kennan as its articulate spokesman, the replacement of Byrnes by Marshall as secretary of state, and the Republican triumph in the congressional elections of 1946. Prominent Republicans like Herbert Hoover, and his main adviser on German policy, émigré economist Gustav Stolper, were ideologically sympathetic to German big business threatened by dismantling and above all placed "economic common sense" above vindictive passions. The result of the triumph of these new ideas of U.S. policy making was a decision in the autumn of 1947 to promote the creation of a West German state closely linked with Western Europe—a policy which the Russians were bound to oppose and which the British and French supported only as the result of considerable American pressure.

The British constituted the smallest obstacle. Though Labourite Foreign Secretary Ernest Bevin was personally very anti-German. . . , he was essentially pragmatic in his outlook and maintained a constant feud with the Labourite left wing with its demand for a distinctly "Socialist" foreign policy whose tenets included cooperation with Russia at Germany's expense. Bevin could count for support upon the bulk of the Labour party and upon the Tory opposition, especially Winston Churchill, whose advocacy of conciliation with Germany was no doubt promoted by his anticommunism. (In most ways British views paralleled those of the "realistic" American Right.) . . . Britain ceased to have an independent German policy by the autumn of 1946; at that time its inability to feed its zone (with its huge Ruhr industrial complex but inadequate agricultural hinterland) forced Britain to agree to an economic merger with the U.S. zone through the Bizonia agreement (September 4, 1946, effective January 1, 1947). The U.S. thenceforth paid the piper and called the tune in a common Anglo-American policy.

France's German policy in the first years after 1945, as formulated by General de Gaulle and implemented by Foreign Minister Georges Bidault, frankly aimed at terminating the "German danger" once and for all. It called for the permanent dismemberment of Germany, a veto upon the "central administrative bodies" contemplated by the Potsdam Conference, the internationalization of the Ruhr with a paramount voice for France, the dismantling of German industry and heavy reparations, and the long-term control of what remained of Germany by the armies of occupation. This policy could not, of course, win any indigenous German support; its implementation far exceeded France's strength in the face of American opposition; and it ignored France's dependence upon Marshall Plan aid (whose grant was implicitly made conditional upon France's cooperation in an economically "sensible" German policy). Luckily for the future of Franco-German relations, French policy shifted in 1948 (not least because of American pressure) from dismemberment in the tradition of Richelieu to conciliation in the spirit of a "new Europe" (a shift connected with Robert Schuman's replacing Bidault at the Foreign Office). The friction between civilian government and military occupation authorities (already noted in the case of Britain and the U.S.) became especially pronounced in the French case after 1948. The French zonal command under General Koenig remained stubbornly "Gaullist" in its outlook on German policy and did its (unsuccessful) best to sabotage the creation of a West German state in 1948–1949.

Russian policy toward Germany after 1945 is especially hard to analyze because revealing sources are unavailable. It is clear, however, that the Russians operated under well-nigh fatal handicaps in carrying out any policy requiring popular German support. They were burdened by the traditional Russophobia of most Germans, by memories of Goebbels' propaganda, by atrocities perpetrated by their troops in 1945, by their own understandable but impolitic desire for quick and heavy reparations, by the cession of the Oder-Neisse territories to Poland, and by their brutal expulsion of the 12 million Germans living in Eastern Europe. Additional handicaps were the hatred of communism felt by nearly all Germans. . . . The arbitrary and terroristic manner in which social reforms were imposed upon the East zone caused general revulsion even among those Germans who believed that some of these reforms, e.g., the expropriation of the Junkers, were long overdue.

These handicaps (some inevitable, some created) suggest that the Russians never had any realistic chance in establishing any policy aiming at influence in Germany beyond their zonal boundary;

this appears to have been the view of Colonel Tulpanov, the main "political officer" of the Soviet military government, and of the "radical" faction of the Moscow Politburo allegedly led by Zhdanov. Another group of Russians, however, including Ambassador Semjonov (the Foreign Office delegate at Berlin) and representing a "moderate" Moscow faction allegedly led by Beria, had some hope for the creation of centralized German institutions that they hoped either to dominate or, at least, to use to block the otherwise inevitable integration of West Germany into the anti-Soviet bloc promoted by American policy. The creation of "all-German institutions" was conspicuously advocated by Foreign Minister Molotov at the Four-Power Conference of Foreign Ministers held at Paris (July 1946) and at Moscow (April 1947); it was rejected by the Americans partly because it was accompanied by unacceptable reparation demands, partly because it flew in the face of American federalist ideas, and mostly (in 1947) because it would prevent the by then much desired integration of West Germany into the West. It should be added that the Russians proved slippery in matters of detail, perhaps because their proposals constituted more propaganda than policy. (Must the Russians not have reckoned with the probability that German central institutions would be dominated by anti-Communists?) It cannot be denied, however, that as propaganda their proposals were largely successful, not so much at the time (since objective needs drove most West Germans to support a West German state at the price of freezing partition) but for the future: they created the basis for the widely held view that the Americans were *at least* as responsible for Germany's partition as the Russians. The Russians probably felt they had nothing to lose by their proposals: if rejected, they were good propaganda; if accepted, they would block the Western integration of West Germany at least temporarily. Moreover, Russia could probably either influence or sabotage any centralized institutions established, and as a last resort it could always fall back upon its unchallenged control of its own East zone.

\*           \*           \*

The inevitable friction between West German and East German political leaders (even those who were not Russian stooges) was in fact but one aspect of the broader Cold War that became the dominant reality of world politics in 1947. It made—so at least it appears today—the partition of Germany inevitable: Russia would not renounce control of its zone and abandon the Sovietization begun in 1945; America believed by 1947 that it needed German resources to promote the economic revival of Western Europe as part of the new policy of the containment of communism. Many West Germans, including Konrad Adenauer, were willing to go along with America's desire for a West German state. . . .

There can be no question, at any rate, that West Germany's support for a West German state was not *only* the result of the Germans' love of democracy, good Europeanism, and psychological desire to be accepted as partners of the free world. It was also promoted by solid economic considerations (the inducement of the Marshall Plan and the threat of its withdrawal) and American playing upon the Germans' fear of communism (for everyone knew that the abandonment of Berlin could easily set off a chain reaction ending in the communization of West Germany). The creation of the West German state proved justified in terms of promoting democracy, encouraging economic revival, permitting Germany to rejoin the Western world, and contributing to Western European unity and military security. All these gains were purchased, however, at the expense of freezing the country's partition and thereby perpetuating a source of constant international friction.

Who, it may be asked in conclusion, was ultimately responsible for Germany's partition? As suggested earlier, the obvious answer is Adolf Hitler, who launched an unnecessary war that ruined Germany and brought both American and Russian troops to the Elbe-Werra frontier dividing the Western zones from Russia's. Why was it, however, that an administrative demarcation line froze into a permanent state frontier? It appears that responsibility must be distributed, though scarcely in equal measure, between *both* the Russians and the Western Allies—though it is perhaps wrong to speak of "responsibility" (with its inevitable moral connotations) when describing a phenomenon made well-nigh "inevitable" by the general circumstances of the Cold War and not deliberately "planned" by either side. The Cold War between Russia and the U.S. after 1945 appears to have been inescapable in view of their conflicting ideologies, social systems, and power interests. The two nations confronted each other in the heart of Europe; each was eager (despite an initial preoccupation with purely vindictive policies) to impose its social system and ideology upon all of Germany if possible but, if the larger goal proved unattainable, upon its own zone as a minimum. There was, however, a major difference between Russian and American policy: the former had to rely upon direct coercion in view of Germany's endemic hostility to communism, whereas the latter could count upon a broad basis of voluntary support since democracy and capitalism were what most Germans wanted. The application of drastic economic pressures in 1948 to induce initial German cooperation does not, of course, invalidate this generalization.

This difference gave and gives the American program a major moral and political advantage in the eyes of all believers in self-determination. By denying East Germany self-determination, a principle that presumably ought to apply in Central Europe as well as in the lands of Asia and Africa, the Russians are primarily responsible for the creation and perpetuation of Germany's partition. To justify Russia's imperialist conduct one is forced to argue that self-determination—though usually a good principle—must be overridden in this case by other arguments and considerations such as Russia's alleged security needs, the chronic untrustworthiness (and political nonage) of the German people, the necessity of coercing the Germans (for their own and the world's good) into a desirable social revolution that they have been unable to achieve for themselves, the maintenance of a European equilibrium that would probably be threatened by the unification of Germany, and "the general opinion of mankind," which rightly or wrongly does not look upon German partition as a major grievance requiring urgent remedy.

It appears significant, when looking at the development of partition in the years 1945 to 1949, that the Western powers did not consider the avoidance of partition to be a major goal of their German policy. On the contrary, they frequently opposed Russian plans (whether sincere or not) for maintaining or restoring administrative unity and promoted policies certain to lead to partition. The French vetoed all plans in 1945–1946 for creating the "centralized administrative bodies" contemplated during the Potsdam Conference and included in its final communiqué. Secretary of State Marshall showed no interest in negotiating about Molotov's detailed plan for centralized administrative bodies (to be followed by a provisional government, nationwide elections, and the drafting of a constitution) at the Moscow Conference in April 1947. The pressure of the Allied military commanders prevented the West German premiers from placing the question of German unity on the agenda of the Munich *Ministerpräsidenten* conference of June 1947, though the Russian zone premiers had made this a condition of their participation and, rightly or wrongly, left the conference when their wishes were not met. The creation of Bizonia (January 1, 1947) and the Frankfurt *Wirtschaftsrat* (June 25, 1947) were two steps on the road to ultimate partition, and the Anglo-American level-of-industries plan of August 29, 1947, though sensible and necessary, was undoubtedly a clear violation of the Allied Control Council decision of May 26, 1946 (a decision still influenced by the spirit of the Morgenthau Plan). The creation of the West German state, initiated at the London Six-Power Conference in March 1948 though completed only in September 1949, preceded in most of its phases the creation of the German Democratic Republic.

These regrettable facts, to which could be added the precipitate rejection of Russian reunification proposals in 1952–1953 without even any negotiation about their details, are not listed to "prove" primary Allied responsibility for Germany's partition. They indicate, however, that the Western Allies, then and presumably now, value other goals above Germany's reunification—a goal that is also felt to complicate other desirable objectives (for example, Western European unity and a détente with Russia).

*Joseph Marion Jones*

# CURBING COMMUNIST EXPANSION: THE TRUMAN DOCTRINE

*On March 12, 1947, President Truman went before Congress to appeal for a special aid program for Greece and Turkey. In so doing he launched the Truman Doctrine, the ill-defined containment principle which thereafter became a commanding element of American foreign policy: "I believe that it must be the policy of the United States to support free peoples who are resisting attempted subjugation by armed minorities or by outside pressures." Joseph Jones was a speechwriter in the Department of State in the early critical months of 1947 and helped prepare Truman's momentous address. In his much-applauded history of the development of the Truman Doctrine and the Marshall Plan,* The Fifteen Weeks *(1955), Jones writes that Russia was plotting to conquer the Near and Middle East (by fomenting civil war in Greece, for example) and the Truman Doctrine was a vital revolution in American foreign policy which daunted Soviet designs.*

After the devastation of World War II in Europe and Asia the power that had supported the imperial system was broken and the morality and the fact of rule by one people over another was everywhere challenged. Each day's cables, each day's newspapers and broadcasts, brought the story: From the Mediterranean eastward to the Sea of Japan nationalism was successfully asserting itself. In the very heart of the British Empire six independent states were emerging: India, Pakistan, Burma, Ceylon, Nepal, and Afghanistan. Revolutionary movements were challenging French and Dutch control in Indochina and Indonesia, with good prospects of success. The Philippines had achieved independence; Thailand had thrown off British influence. Victorious China had freed herself of Western controls. In the Middle East, colonies were moving toward self-government, mandated countries toward independence, all toward nationalistic self-assertion that weakened alliances. The Union Jack had been hauled down with great ceremony from the Cairo citadel, the green and white flag of Farouk I hoisted, and British troops concentrated at Suez, their future status under negotiation. Syria, Lebanon, Iraq, Jordan, Saudi Arabia, and Yemen had achieved (or were soon to achieve) full independence. Palestine, then ravaged by violence, was soon to make way for the new state of Israel. What was clearly happening was the sudden disappearance of the imperial system and the rise of independent, weak, nationalist states. This had happened in Europe hundreds of years earlier—and had led to centuries of bloody, nationalistic strife.

Moreover, in 1947, the prospects for strength and stability within each nationalistic unit were bleak. Effective self-government requires experience, discipline, and at least fair economic conditions. Democratic self-government requires in addition a high degree of literacy, a reasonable standard of living, and a substantial middle class—assets that are in short supply throughout Asia. Only Japan possesses all these assets; several nations have none. Underlying these deficiencies, and the political instability they cause, are poverty, ignorance, undernourishment, and disease. Improvement in these conditions depends upon the efficient use and development of resources, including human resources. This requires outside capital and technical assistance, but capital will not invest where there is not political stability. There is thus a vicious circle in Asia, with political instability causing poor economic conditions and poor economic conditions causing political instability, which frightens away investment that might improve economic conditions.

Pressing down into this weakness, into this riot of nationalist disunity and self-assertion, was the expanding power of the Soviet Union. Ever since a Russian czar had married the daughter of the last Byzantine emperor four centuries earlier, the Russians had felt a sense of mission in Asia, as a result of which Imperial Russian control was extended from European Russia throughout north and central Asia. This expansionist urge, far from being reversed by the Bolshevik revolution, was merely reinforced by it. The chief practical difference was that the tactics of infiltration and propaganda were added to the standard forms of nineteenth-century expansionism. Monolithic in power and ideology, with a fanatical historical sense of mission, the USSR hung over fragmentized Asia in 1947, as it does today, like a dark and heavy sky over a patchwork countryside. In Manchuria, North China, and North Korea, Communist rain was coming down in sheets. Over the rest of China great spattering drops were falling. In northern Indochina a Communist-led nationalist revolution was raging. Communist agents trained in Moscow were busily organizing trouble throughout Southeast Asia. Each month brought new portents of the approaching storm. . . .

The barrier to the direct and immediate extension of Soviet power and influence into the Mediterranean, North Africa, and South Asia, was the land mass extending from the borders of Afghanistan westward to the Adriatic, comprising Iran, Turkey, and Greece. It was accordingly against these three countries that, beginning in 1945 and extending through 1948, the Soviet Union persistently deployed the powerful pressures of its diplomacy, its propaganda, and its apparatus for subversion; these were reinforced in Iran by direct armed intervention and in Greece by armed intervention of an indirect variety.

If the Soviet Union could gain control of Iran, not only would it command the oil riches of the Persian Gulf, but, more important, through that country—which has been described as the "Suez Canal of revolution"—it would be able to play a direct, open, and powerful role in the political evolution of the weak, newly independent countries of the Middle East and South and Southeast Asia.

Centrally located Turkey, anchored in Europe but extending far into Asia, astride the Dardanelles and commanding the Black Sea and the eastern Mediterranean—this was the real prize. For hundreds of years every holder of power in Europe had recognized the Turkish Straits as the key to still more power in Europe and Asia and had tried to secure control of it, meaning control of Turkey on both sides of the straits. Catherine the Great had been obsessed by it, Napoleon had called it the key to world rule. Kaiser Wilhelm, Hitler, and Stalin had lusted after it. And needless to add, for a century and a half Great Britain and France had been keenly aware of it and were determined that it should not fall into hostile hands. In 1945, with British power crumbling and French power nonexistent, the Russians took a leaf from the history of the czars and began a drive to secure control of the Turkish Straits, which, if successful, would give them control of the eastern Mediterranean, dominion over the trade routes from Europe to the East, and the possibilities of infinite mischief in North Africa and the Middle East. The oil reserves of the Middle East and the uranium mines of Africa would be within grasp. And Soviet control of Greece would be a stepping-stone to this end.

The backwash of these developments on Western Europe would be devastating—psychologically, politically, economically, and militarily. The entire continent of Europe would be fatally weakened in the face of an even more powerful Communist drive.

There can be no question, on the basis of events as they unfolded from August 1946 onward, that there was a well-organized plot to bring part or all of Greece under Communist domination. The plot showed itself, in the not uncommon Communist manner, at Lake Success, New York, where the Ukrainian delegate to the

United Nations Security Council, Dmitri Manuilsky, on August 25 brought unsubstantiated charges, which were dismissed shortly by the council, that the Greeks were provoking border incidents with Albania, planning to wrest a portion of southern Albania by force, and persecuting minorities in Macedonia, Thrace, and Epirus—all these crimes aided and abetted, he charged, by British troops stationed in Greece. The plot was evident simultaneously at the peace conference in Paris, where Bulgarians pressed a claim for western Thrace, Yugoslavia demanded an independent Macedonia, and Molotov and his Balkans satellites loosed salvoes against the "monarcho-Fascist" government of Greece, charging it with border provocations, territorial designs on Greece's neighbors, and internal terror and oppression. In the Soviet Union and the Communist-dominated Balkans the press and radio opened up a virulent campaign against Greece on these same points. And in Greece itself minor disturbances in the northern regions developed in August 1946 into organized, sustained, and well-supplied guerrilla activities, which prevented economic recovery and rapidly undermined what was left of the authority of the state. The guerrillas, numbering some thirteen thousand, were armed, trained, and given border protection and guidance by the authorities in Yugoslavia, Bulgaria, and Albania. The poorly equipped and demoralized Greek Army was powerless to check their depredations.

This situation grew worse during the fall and winter. The Greek government repeatedly exposed it, the world press freely reported it, and the American Embassy in Athens kept it under close scrutiny. On December 19, 1946, following a request from the Greek government that cited chapter and verse of outside aid to Greek guerrillas, the Security Council of the United Nations appointed a Commission of Investigation and ordered it to Greece to report on the facts.

This was of course only a new phase, now with the covert help of foreign allies, of an armed effort to dominate Greece that had been carried on for several years by veteran Greek Communists. Had it not been for the understanding, farsightedness, and diplomacy of Prime Minister Winston Churchill and his intervention in Greek affairs in the face of widespread criticism, Greece's future would have been foreclosed well before the end of the war in Europe.

During the enemy occupation of Greece many guerrilla groups had been organized to harass the Germans, but bitter personal and political rivalries, which the Nazi occupiers encouraged, had led to a dissipation of much of their strength in fighting among themselves. The two groups which had finally absorbed or destroyed the weaker guerrilla organizations were the Communist-dominated EAM (National Liberation Front), with its army of about twenty thousand, known as ELAS (Peoples' National Army of Liberation), and its smaller rightist rival known as EDES, with about five thousand men, bitterly anti-Communist, under the leadership of General Zervas. For a period the two guerrilla groups had cooperated with each other, and with British agents, to carry out sabotage operations, but by the middle of 1943 they had fallen apart and, making no further significant contribution to the war effort, had resumed their fight for political power to be exercised at war's end. To Churchill it was obvious that these two contending groups of men, organized and with guns in their hands, would be in a position to move in when the Nazis retreated and that one or the other would determine the kind of government under which 7.5 million Greeks would live for a long time to come.

The only other contender for Greek power was the Greek King in London, with the royalist politicians that composed his government in exile in Cairo and his Greek Brigade assembled in Egypt. To the King, as the head and symbol of a state that had fought as Britain's ally during the war, Churchill felt a very strong obligation, though he appears to have had a thinly veiled contempt for the "royalist politicians" who surrounded him. But Churchill's foremost loyalty was to Greece and its people. . . .

The horrors perpetrated by the Communists during the civil war of 1944–45 so revolted public opinion in faction-ridden Greece that a measure of cohesiveness was brought about, not in affirmation of a positive program but at least in opposition to communism and its exponents in Greece. In the general election held on March 31, 1946, under the watchful eyes of fifteen hundred American, British, French, and South African official observers, who pronounced it on the whole a fair expression of opinion, the parties of the Right won a large majority, and on September 1, 1946, the king was recalled to Greece by a plebiscite. The EAM nevertheless remained exceedingly active and vocal, and whatever may have been its relations with Moscow before and during the civil war, as the wartime alliance of the powers disintegrated after the cessation of hostilities in Europe, it became the clearly recognized instrument of Soviet policy in Greece and the Balkans. . . .

Notwithstanding $700 million in direct foreign aid (from UNRRA, Great Britain, the United States, and organized charities), Greece in 1945 and 1946 managed merely to survive, and the country's ability to sustain itself economically was scarcely better in early 1947 than when German troops had evacuated the country in late 1944. Greece had always had a hard time making ends meet, the poverty of its natural resources being such that it had always needed more imports than could be paid for with exports. A large part of the exports had always gone to Central European markets, especially Germany, which after the war were closed. The Italian invasion, the German invasion, four years of cruel enemy occupation, and the scorched-earth policy of the retreating Germans had left Greece the most thoroughly destroyed, disorganized, and demoralized country in Europe.

In the first two years after liberation seven changes in government did little to improve things. Some progress was made in restoring emergency communications and in reviving agriculture, but industrial production and export trade had hardly done more than start a comeback. Foreign aid kept the country from starvation, but while most people were barely subsisting, profiteers, speculators, and black marketeers throve in ostentatious wealth and luxury, causing inevitable embitterment among the masses, and none of the seven Greek governments dealt effectively with the problem.

The end of the civil war in February 1945 and the nominal disarming and disbanding of the guerrillas brought a cessation of large-scale violence, but no peace and security. Widespread lawlessness and the uncertain intentions of Greece's neighbors to the north made necessary the maintenance of an army of one hundred thousand and police forces of half that number, far more than Greece had ever supported, with crushing, intolerable effects upon the budget. Notwithstanding, people lived in a perpetual state of fear. This, plus bitter social and political tensions that had grown out of civil strife, created a climate in which governments could hardly govern at all, much less engage in rational planning, develop an effective economic policy, or inaugurate and enforce the controls necessary to bring order out of economic and financial chaos. A psychology of helplessness and inertia prevailed, a feeling that individual efforts were futile, that Greece because of her sufferings was entitled, without determination and effort on the part of Greeks themselves, to be taken care of by Greece's rich allies.

This was the situation in the fall of 1946 when the heat was turned up under Greece by her Communist neighbors. Well-supplied guerrilla bands spread terror and devastation. Refugees from the rural districts streamed into Athens and other cities. Communications were disrupted. A bad psychological, administrative, and economic situation rapidly turned worse. UNRRA was scheduled to end March 31, 1947, and the flow of life-sustaining supplies was already slowing down. Foreign exchange reserves were gone, and minimum import needs could not be financed. There was a prospect for a 1947 budget *deficit,* including provision for an expanded military establishment, of nearly $300 million, or three times the currency in circulation. By February 1947 prices were moving up steadily, threatening to skyrocket, and wage demands and social discontent were accumulating at a rapid rate.

The British had been the chief stabilizing and sustaining element in this chaotic situation. Not only had they helped finance the Greek Army, but sixteen thousand British troops, landed in Greece in October 1944 to aid in taking over control from the defeated Germans, had remained to help stabilize the country and organize and equip the Greek Army and police forces. British troops were not engaged in combat against the guerrillas in the north; nevertheless, concentrated in and around Athens, they were an important factor in maintaining order. But on February 3 the British government announced that for reasons of economy it was immediately withdrawing half its troops. The British Cabinet, confronted with financial disaster, had been debating for many weeks the matter of withdrawing all its forces, had decided upon such a course, to be effected in two stages, and although no date had been set for departure of the last contingent of eight thousand, it was expected to be soon. The Greeks felt abandoned and feared the worst.

Several times in 1946 the Greek government had asked the United States for increased financial aid, and Washington had done all it could under existing appropriations and authority, which were limited. Prime Minister Constantin Tsaldaris spoke to Secretary Byrnes early in October about Greece's need for financial assistance and military equipment. He raised the question with Byrnes again in December in New York, where he had come to request the United Nations to send a commission to Greece to investigate his charges of foreign aid to the Greek guerrillas. Secretary Byrnes and President Truman took the matter up with the Export-Import Bank, but as there was no reasonable assurance of repayment nothing further could be done under the law. In conversations between Tsaldaris and Undersecretaries of State Acheson and Clayton, it became apparent that the Greek economic and financial and administrative system was in complete chaos, that the Greeks had no documented case for loans but just wanted money and arms on a large scale, and that if granted they would probably be wasted. Accordingly, it was decided to send an American Economic Mission to Greece to make a thorough survey of the situation, and Paul A. Porter was selected to head the mission. He and his party arrived in Greece, on January 18, 1947, approximately the same time as the commission appointed by the United Nations to investigate Greek frontier incidents. The United States representative on that commission was Mark Ethridge, editor and publisher of the *Louisville Courier-Journal* and the *Louisville Times.*

Porter, Ethridge, and the American ambassador in Athens, Lincoln McVeagh, operated more or less as a team. By the latter part of February it was their combined judgment that unless Greece received immediate assurance of large-scale military and financial aid, the last vestiges of the authority of the Greek government would disappear within a matter of weeks in a skyrocketing inflation, strikes, riots, and public panic, leaving the field clear for the increasingly bold and successful Communist guerrillas to take over. One thing more was clear to them: aid in the old pattern, no matter how extensive, would not save the situation. Large-scale economic aid was necessary over a period of years, but it was equally important that this should be administered on the spot by an American mission large enough, expert enough, and exercising sufficiently direct participation in and sanctions over the Greek government to bring about a thorough reorganization of the Greek economy and administrative system. Otherwise the money would be lost, the supplies wasted, the errors of the past compounded.

There was never any doubt in Washington that aid to Greece would have to be accompanied by intervention in the country's internal affairs. When on March 3, 1947, the prime minister and the foreign minister of Greece addressed another urgent, formal appeal to the United States for financial and military aid, they also asked for "the aid of experienced American administrative, economic, and technical personnel to assure the utilization in an effective and up-to-date manner of the financial and other assistance given to Greece, to help to restore a healthy condition in the domestic economy and public administration and to train the young people of Greece to assume their responsibilities in a reconstructed economy." This was no accident. The message was drafted in the State Department and suggested to the Greek government.

To Americans in 1947 intervention was an ugly word. But in the long and turbulent history of Greece since the Golden Age mere foreign intervention had been among the nicer things that had happened to the Greek people. The more usual pattern had been, for more than two thousand years, foreign invasion, occupation, and indescribable oppression and exploitation. On the other hand, it had been the concerted, armed intervention of the British, French, and Russians in 1827–32 that had saved the Greek revolution started in 1821 against the centuries-old rule of the Ottoman Turks, and had resulted in the establishment of an independent monarchy under the protection of the three powers. Thereafter throughout most of the nineteenth century all three had intervened briefly but often, singly or jointly, in Greek affairs, but the net result of their rivalry and competitive intervention had been the maintenance, as a matter of common interest, of an independent Greece. The Nazi invasion and occupation of Greece in 1940–41 and the Soviet effort in 1946–47 to seize control were throwbacks to a much earlier pattern of conquest, rule, and oppression. Both sought the disappearance of an independent Greece, previously sustained by agreement for the common good.

*          *          *

The Speaker of the House, Joseph Martin, at 12:16 p.m. on March 12, 1947, declared the House in recess subject to the call of the Chair. The House and Senate were shortly to meet in joint session to hear a special message to be delivered in person by the President of the United States, Harry S Truman. . . .

"Mr. President, Mr. Speaker, Members of the Congress of the United States, the gravity of the situation which confronts the world today necessitates my appearance before a joint session of the Congress. The foreign policy and the national security of this country are involved."

It had been just nineteen days earlier that the first in the chain of events leading to this appearance of the President before Congress had occurred, the official news that the British government could no longer aid in sustaining and strengthening Greece and Turkey. On the fourth day after Sichel's call (the four days covered a weekend) the State Department had ready a documented statement of position approved by Secretary Marshall. On the fifth day this position had been endorsed by the Secretary of War and the Secretary of the Navy and approved by the President. On the sixth day it had been laid by the President before congressional leaders of both parties, none opposing. On the seventh day a working party in the State Department had been appointed to draw up a detailed program of aid, draft a message to Congress for the President, and work up a program of public information. In the twelve following days all this had been done, the proposed program had been approved by the Cabinet and discussed again with congressional leaders, and the message had been polished and approved in the White House for final delivery. It had all gone like clockwork. No one in the government had opposed. No one had dragged his feet. Veterans in government service had never seen anything like the unanimity of view, and this on a matter recognized as a major turning point in American history. Nor had they ever before witnessed such efficiency in the government as that with which the job was done.

Now the President was displaying the end product to Congress, to the American people, to the world.

"One aspect of the present situation ... concerns Greece and Turkey ..."

President Truman described the tragic physical, financial, and economic condition of war-wrecked Greece, the threat to the very existence of the Greek state posed by the activities of the Communist-led terrorists in the north, the inadequacies of the Greek Army, the urgent appeal of the Greek government to the United States. The British government, he said, could give no further financial or economic help after March 31. The question had been considered as to how the United Nations might assist in this crisis, but the situation was an urgent one requiring immediate action, and the United Nations and its related organizations were not in a position to extend help of the kind required.

"Greece must have assistance if it is to become a self-respecting democracy.

"The United States must supply this assistance.

"There is no other country to which democratic Greece can turn.

"No other nation is willing and able to provide necessary support for a democratic Greek government."

Mr. Truman emphasized that the Greek government had asked for our assistance in utilizing effectively the financial and other aid we might give to Greece and in improving its public administration. "It is of the utmost importance that we supervise the use of any funds made available to Greece," he said—and here he was interrupted by the first applause—"in such a manner that each dollar spent will count toward making Greece self-supporting, and will help to build an economy in which a healthy democracy can flourish."

The future of Turkey as an independent and economically sound state, the President continued, was clearly no less important to the freedom-loving peoples of the world than the future of Greece. Turkey, having been spared the disasters of war, was in much better condition than Greece, but nevertheless needed our support "in order to effect that modernization necessary for the maintenance of its national integrity. That integrity is essential to the preservation of order in the Middle East." If Turkey was to have the help it needed, the President concluded, the United States would have to supply it, for we were the only country able to do so. This was brief treatment indeed, but it is all the message contained about Turkey.

Up to this point President Truman had said things that had been more or less expected as a consequence of news leaks, discussions with congressmen over the previous two weeks, and background information officially given to the press. It was unique in our history that a President should ask Congress for an appropriation in time of peace to help foreign countries maintain their "integrity and independence"—financial aid to accomplish frankly political purposes—but it was a not illogical extension of Lend-Lease. But all the President had said thus far was but prologue. Now came the main drama.

"I am fully aware of the broad implications involved if the United States extends assistance to Greece and Turkey. . . .

"One of the primary objectives of the foreign policy of the United States is the creation of conditions in which we and other nations will be able to work out a way of life free from coercion. . . . To insure the peaceful development of nations, free from coercion, the United States has taken a leading part in establishing the United Nations. The United Nations is designed to make possible lasting freedom and independence for all its members. We shall not realize our objectives, however, unless we are willing to help free peoples to maintain their free institutions and their national integrity against aggressive movements that seek to impose upon them totaliarian regimes. This is no more than a frank recognition that totalitarian regimes imposed on free peoples, by direct or indirect aggression, undermine the foundations of international peace and hence the coourity of tho Unitod Statoc. . . .

"At the present moment in world history nearly every nation must choose between alternative ways of life. The choice is too often not a free one. One way of life is based upon the will of the majority, and is distinguished by free institutions, representative government, free elections, guarantees of individual liberty, freedom of speech and religion, and freedom from political oppression. The second way of life is based upon the will of a minority forcibly imposed upon the majority. It relies upon terror and oppression, a controlled press and radio, fixed elections, and suppression of personal freedoms.

"I believe that it must be the policy of the United States to support free peoples who are resisting attempted subjugation by armed minorities or by outside pressures.

"I believe that we must assist free peoples to work out their destiny in their own way.

"I believe that our help should be primarily through economic and financial aid, which is essential to economic stability and orderly political processes."

Here, in its essence, was the Truman Doctrine. There was at this point no applause. It was as though the President's listeners were stunned, some perhaps dismayed, by the sweep, the boldness, of the President's utterance. The President went on.

"It is necessary only to glance at a map to realize that the survival and integrity of the Greek nation are of grave importance in a much wider situation. If Greece should fall under the control of an armed minority, the effect upon its neighbor, Turkey, would be immediate and serious. Confusion and disorder might well spread throughout the entire Middle East. Moreover, the disappearance of Greece as an independent state would have a profound effect upon those countries in Europe whose peoples are struggling against great difficulties to maintain their freedoms and their independence while they repair the damages of war. Collapse of free institutions and loss of independence would be disastrous not only for them but for the world. Discouragement and possibly failure would quickly be the lot of neighboring peoples striving to maintain their independence. Should we fail to aid Greece and Turkey in this fateful hour, the effect will be far reaching to the West as well as to the East. We must take immediate and resolute action."

President Truman asked Congress to appropriate $400 million for aid to Greece and Turkey and to authorize the detail of American civilian and military personnel to Greece and Turkey, at the request of those countries, to assist in the tasks of reconstruction and to supervise the use of United States aid. He also asked authorization to train selected Greek and Turkish personnel in the United States.

"This is a serious course upon which we embark. I would not recommend it except that the alternative is much more serious. . . . The seeds of totalitarian regimes are nurtured by misery and want. They spread and grow in the soil of poverty and strife. They reach their full growth when the hope of a people for a better life has died. We must keep that hope alive. The free peoples of the world look to us for support in maintaining their freedoms. If we falter in our leadership, we may endanger the peace of the world—and we shall surely endanger the welfare of our own nation. Great responsibilities have been placed upon us by the swift course of events. I am confident that the Congress will face these responsibilities squarely."

*Richard J. Barnet*

# THE MISCONCEPTIONS OF THE TRUMAN DOCTRINE

*In his study of America's response to revolutions in the Third World,* Intervention and Revolution, *Richard J. Barnet disputes the traditional account of the Truman Doctrine as expressed by Jones. Barnet suggests that the United States worked under misconceptions when it intervened in the Greek civil war. He spells out various alternative responses which he thinks might have been more realistic. Most historians now agree with him that the Soviet Union was little involved in the Greek conflict. Since 1963 Barnet has been codirector of an independent research center in Washington, D.C., The Institute for Policy Studies. He has been an official in the Department of State and the United States Arms Control and Disarmament Agency and is the author of* Who Wants Disarmament? *(1960),* The Economy of Death *(1969), and* The Roots of War *(1972).*

In the name of the Truman Doctrine the United States supplied the military and economic power to enable the Greek monarchy to defeat an army of Communist-led insurgents in 1947–49 and won a victory which has become a model for U.S. relations toward civil wars and insurgencies. Almost twenty years later the President of the United States was defending his intervention in Vietnam by pointing to his predecessor's success in Greece. The American experience in Greece not only set the pattern for subsequent interventions in internal wars but also suggested the criteria for assessing the success or failure of counterinsurgency operations. Greece was the first major police task which the United States took on in the postwar world. One of the most important consequences of the American involvement in Greece in the 1940s was the development of new bureaucracies specializing in military assistance, police administration, and economic aid, committed to an analysis of revolu-

From Richard J. Barnet, *Intervention and Revolution: America's Confrontation with Insurgent Movements Around the World* (New York, 1968), pp. 97–101, 107–112, 121, 125–127. Reprinted by permission of The World Publishing Company and The New American Library, Inc. Copyright © 1968 by Richard J. Barnet. In 1972, The New American Library published a revised and updated edition of *Intervention and Revolution,* but no changes were made in this chapter on the Truman Doctrine. (Footnotes deleted.)

tion and a set of responses for dealing with it that would be applied to many different conflicts in the next twenty years.

In this chapter we shall look into the fateful series of decisions that culminated in the Truman Doctrine and its execution in Greece. To start this inquiry, we need to ask a basic question: Why did those in charge of the national security of the United States happen to define the problem in Greece in the way they did, and why did they use the power of the United States in the ways they did? To some the answer may be so obvious that the question itself is startling. Official history, as it always does, records these decisions as more or less inevitable responses to clear-cut challenges. There was no other practical or honorable choice.

To understand this turning point in American foreign policy, however, we must attempt to reconstruct the scene as it was seen through contemporary eyes. If we turn to Winston Churchill as chronicler, we find him, a few years after these events, expressing great surprise that the American intervention turned out the way it did. Alluding to Roosevelt's strong opposition to British military activities against the Greek Communists during the war, the former prime minister wrote, "I little thought . . . that the State Department, supported by overwhelming American public opinion, would in a little more than two years not only adopt and carry on the course we had opened, but would make vehement and costly exertions, even of a military character, to bring it to fruition."

The continuation of Britain's role in Greece was a highly accurate description of the American intervention, but it was hardly an inevitable one, especially in view of the bad press accorded the British Empire in the United States. Tradition suggested other definitions of the American responsibility toward Greece. In late 1946 and early 1947 there were at least three other plausible ways for U.S. national security managers to look at the Greek crisis. Each would have dictated a form of intervention different from the Truman Doctrine. Each would have required a different definition of the American national interest. One was to continue to regard Greece primarily as a relief problem. At the end of September, 1946, the Food and Agriculture Organization reported that Greece urgently needed a minimum of $1 billion from the United States and British governments. The United States had already provided most of the $345 million spent on Greek relief in 1945 and 1946, and the Truman administration was planning to spend $60 million more, but the Republican-controlled Eightieth Congress, elected on the economy slogan "Had Enough?", appeared unwilling to support a major project of international charity. Greek officials argued that raids by insurgents, which resumed in September, 1946, were a major factor in preventing economic recovery. But a U.S. mission under Paul Porter, which arrived in January, 1947, found that the most pressing crises were due to the collapse of the Greek currency, the resultant panic over the disappearance of gold reserves, and a strike by the entire Greek civil service.

The problem of Greece might, alternatively, have been regarded as a traditional crisis of Balkan politics. The Peace Conference held in the summer and fall of 1946 dramatized the depth and bitterness of the conflict between Greece and her Balkan neighbors, particularly Bulgaria and Yugoslavia, over disputed territories. The prime minister devoted most of his opening speech to parliament in 1946 to Greece's territorial claims. When the United States refused to back Greece's demands for northern Epirus and for certain adjustments of the frontier with Bulgaria, Greek politicians from left to right called the settlement "a most cruel injustice" and an occasion for "deepest mourning." Bulgaria and Yugoslavia made no secret of their desire to annex parts of Macedonia and Thrace. In conversations with Americans, Greek officials stressed the danger that the Soviet Union might encourage the newly Communist Balkan regimes to satisfy their territorial ambitions and thereby at the same time extend the area of Soviet influence. Thus the problem might have been seen principally as one calling for international mediation. In effect, the United States, Britain, and the Soviet Union might have continued their informal agreements during the war, establishing zones of respective "responsibility" in the Balkans and jointly guaranteeing the frontiers. However, the Great Powers would have had to agree on what their respective roles in the Balkans were to be, and it was the lack of agreement on this very issue that fanned the growing East-West suspicion into the Cold War.

The third way to look at Greece in 1946–47 was as a problem of internal political collapse. The ultrarightist government of Constantine Tsaldares, established after the British army had helped put down the Communist-led ELAS rebellion in 1945, attempted to root out opposition by force. The government ousted the leadership of the Greek Federation of Labor and replaced it with government appointees. In October, 1946, the Greek government dismissed seventeen university professors and twenty-six senior civil servants on purely political grounds, although most of them were not Communists. "The internal situation is much worse than it has ever been. Law and order are nonexistent," a former Liberal premier told a group of visiting British M.P.'s. Like the Diem government in Vietnam ten years later, the Tsaldares regime conducted what the U.S. correspondents for the *Herald Tribune* and Associated Press termed "a desperate effort to halt a growing rebellion and wipe out not only Communists but all democratic, liberal, and republican elements." The government armed right-wing supporters, and often with the collaboration of the police, encouraged them to terrorize political opponents. "This tactic," a former Progressive (moderate) party minister wrote in October, 1946, "drives the people to the hills, since no Greek is willing to be beaten without reason, only because he is an opponent of the party in power." The government was rapidly polarizing the country by limiting the expression of political choices either to wholehearted support of Tsaldares' reactionary policy or to wholehearted opposition by joining Communist-led guerrilla bands in the hills. A British parliamentary delegation, made up of Labour, Conservative, and Liberal members, visiting Greece in late summer 1946, condemned the government terrorism and urged sweeping reforms, including the restoration of constitutional liberties, an amnesty, the reestablishment of an independent labor movement, the end of political deportations, and the formation of an "all-party government . . . to include all sections with the possible exception of the extreme Left." The establishment of a regime which "resembled a dictatorship," the report observed discreetly, "would have fatal consequences." As these observers saw it, the government should attempt to accommodate the mounting political opposition in Greece, not repress it.

The United States made a few modest efforts in late 1946 to persuade the Greek government to move in the direction of reform. On October 18, Ambassador Lincoln MacVeagh showed King George II a letter from the President suggesting that the United States was prepared to grant "substantial aid and supplies" but that "the Greek government should help persuade American public opinion that the rulers of Greece constituted no oligarchy of reactionaries, bent on exploiting U.S. aid in order to tyrannize their political opponents." The government should be broadened so that Americans might come to see that all Greeks, except the Communists, were united.

However, in the minds of the U.S. national security managers, the Greek crisis soon took on a very different significance. Greece was still a relief problem, still a point of tension in age-old Balkan rivalries, and more than ever, a revolution with deep domestic political roots. But more than any of these, Greece was now seen as a pawn in a global struggle. Keeping Greece non-Communist had become the central concern of the United States.

When President Truman announced the decision to help the Greek monarchy win the civil war, he stressed that the commitment was prompted by the "terrorist activities of several thousand armed men, led by Communists." The United States was to use its power to put down violence. But, clearly, violence itself was not the issue, for throughout 1946, according to correspondents of the London *Times* and other U.S. and British papers, the Greek government itself had been carrying out mass arrests, tortures, beatings, and other retaliation against those who had been on the wrong side of the earlier civil war that ended in January, 1945. The foreign minister had resigned in early 1946, charging "terrorism by state organs." In Greece, as elsewhere, the violence of constituted authorities, however oppressive their rule, was judged by one criterion and the violence of insurgents by another. President Truman alluded to the corruption and brutality of the Greek government by conceding that it was "not perfect." But while the Fascist character of the government genuinely bothered some members of the U.S. government, most national security managers shared the judgment of former Secretary of State James Byrnes: "We did not have to decide that the Turkish government and the Greek monarchy were outstanding examples of free and democratic governments."

It was enough that the guerrillas were Communists and as such constituted, according to Joseph Jones, the State Department official who drafted the original Truman Doctrine message, an "instrument" of Soviet "expansionism." What was happening in Greece was important to officials in Washington only as it affected U.S. interests, as the State Department saw them. This is, of course, the standard by which governments customarily judge internal developments in

other countries. The interesting question is why the Truman administration saw the mounting insurgency in Greece as a threat to the
American national interest.

*                    *                    *

When the resistance began in 1941–42, the Communist-led guerrillas had no contacts at all with Moscow. The prewar links between
the Greek Communist party and Moscow, "tenuous and unreliable"
as they were, had been completely cut off by the Axis occupation.
In July, 1943,[1] eight Soviet officers arrived at the ELAS headquarters
to assess the prospects of the guerrillas. The Soviet military mission
reported that ELAS was "just a rabble of armed men, not worth
supporting." Requests for Soviet aid went unanswered; Bulgarian
guerrillas operating just over the border with Soviet support also
ignored the struggle in Greece. As the Italians and then the German
occupation forces withdrew in 1944, the rival guerrilla forces began
to attack each other. The British supported EDES; ELAS captured
most of its arms from the retreating Axis armies. General Scobie,
the British commander, sought to reconcile the various guerrilla
bands and to persuade them to operate in separate areas. Meanwhile he installed a government in Athens under George Papandreou,
a monarchist politician.

The Soviet-satellite Bulgarian Army occupied parts of Macedonia
and Thrace. The Soviets, consistent with their agreement with
Churchill to leave Greece primarily to British influence, ordered the
Bulgarian troops to evacuate Greek soil. By the end of 1944 ELAS
controlled most of the countryside of Greece and occupied all cities,
towns, and villages except for Athens, Salonika, Piraeus, and a few
other centers where British troops were stationed. EAM, the political
arm of the Communist-guerrilla movement, began to administer large
areas of the country, making use of secret police and their power
over the distribution of UNRRA supplies. Openly agitating against the
Papandreou government and the government secret police, they
charged, accurately, as it turned out, that the government was killing
and imprisoning leftist partisans while protecting former Nazi collaborators. The civil war began when ELAS, still in political control
of far more of Greece than the Athens government, refused to sur-

[1] The date actually was 1944.—*Ed.*

render its arms unless EDES also agreed to disarm. The revolt which flamed over the whole peninsula required a British force of seventy-five thousand to crush it.

In February, 1945, the British arranged a cease fire at Varkiza. The guerrillas agreed to surrender their arms, provided an immediate plebiscite on the return of the king was held, to be followed by free elections. ELAS did surrender far more weapons than anyone in the British Army thought they had had, but they hid most of their small arms and automatic weapons in the mountains. The government, which had yet to condemn a single Nazi collaborator, carried out wholesale arrests and executions of former ELAS fighters. EAM charged that at least five hundred had been murdered and twenty thousand arrested in the first five months after the cease fire. The government countered with a discovery of the bodies of eighty-eight hundred hostages allegedly murdered by the ELAS during the fighting. In the civil war both sides had taken hostages and practiced terrorism. Now, with ELAS disarmed, the government and the bands of royalist guerrillas who supported it were responsible for most of the terror and political murder.

The Greek government was not only repressive but also hopelessly corrupt. Tsaldaris spent about 50 percent of the budget on the army and the police, 6 percent on reconstruction. Capital was fleeing the country. The rich knew how to escape taxation, and inflation was rampant. At the end of the war the drachma was valued at 149 to the dollar. A year later it was five thousand to the dollar. Much UNRRA aid was diverted to the black market. In 1947 an American investigating team found huge supplies rotting in warehouses at a time when 75 percent of Greek children were suffering from malnutrition. The British proceeded to reconstruct the army, which they put in the hands of monarchist officers, including, as Ernest Bevin admitted in the House of Commons, 228 former officers of the Nazi security battalions in Greece. They also strengthened the police, leaving it under the direction of the police chief, who for three years had served the Nazis.

In 1945 and 1946 the British installed, successively, a general and an admiral as prime minister of Greece. Both filled provincial administrative posts with monarchist sympathizers before the British replaced them with an aged Liberal politician, Themistokles Sophoulis. On March 31, 1946, an election was held, which resulted in a clear-cut victory for the monarchists. Although termed a fair election by numerous Allied observers, this verdict, as Howard K. Smith, the CBS correspondent who visited Greece shortly after the elections, concluded, is open to doubt:

> With all power and armed force in the hands of the right and with the countryside under the terror of ubiquitous and merciless rightist bands, the Greek peasant was in no mood to be heroic; ... I visited a village outside Athens and was told by peasants through a neutral Greek interpreter that they had been threatened with having their village burned down if they did not yield a majority monarchist vote in the elections. In this village the newspaper of the Liberal party—the party of the premier of Greece [Sophoulis]—was forbidden to be read on pain of beatings.

Meanwhile the EAM was in the throes of an internal debate between those who favored attempting a slow political route to power and those who wanted to resume the fight. As the government repression mounted, the militants in the EAM grew stronger. Non-Communist politicians from the six parties that made up the original Liberation Front resigned. Many ex-ELAS leaders, "spurred on by what would happen to them if they were arrested, took to the hills and began collecting former comrades around them." According to Major Edgar O'Ballance's recent account of the civil war, this trend was "spontaneous rather than centrally organized or inspired," although the Greek Communist party tried to keep control over these fast-moving events.

At the end of 1945 ELAS was reorganized as the "Greek Democratic Army" with the help of members of the Bulgarian and Yugoslav general staffs. In the beginning Stalin apparently approved of the cooperation, although Soviet promises of assistance were never fulfilled. The relationship between the other Balkan Communist regimes and the Greek Communists was ambivalent from the first. Relations with Albania were the best, probably because the Greek Communist party had renounced the claim still pressed by the Athens government to annex the Albanian province of northern Epirus. In 1946 a Communist government was established in Tirana which permitted the Greek Democratic Army to build camps on its soil near the border to be used as rear bases for incursions into Greece. A Radio Free Greece was set up on Albanian soil. Actual military aid, however, was small.

Tito, in Yugoslavia, was more uncertain about aiding the Greek rebels. His political plans at the time called for a Balkan federation under his own control, and particularly a Communist Slav Macedonia, which would in all events be detached from Greece. In 1946 he did offer food, use of army camps, and a few transport vehicles, but little else. The question of Yugoslav aid provoked dissension within the Greek Communist party between nationalists, who were suspicious of Tito's territorial aims, and those party leaders who put ideological solidarity above all else.

In late 1946 Bulgaria also came under the full control of a Communist government. Dimitroff, the party chief, was also a nationalist with an interest in annexing Thrace as well as the city of Salonika.

By October, 1946, the Greek Democratic Army, which had reached the level of six thousand men, was carrying on hit-and-run raids throughout northern Greece. The government, unable to deal with them either by using the thirty-thousand-man police force or by arming loyal villagers, secured British permission to use the national army, now at a strength of one hundred thousand men. The domestic political life of the country was moving toward a new crisis when Tsaldaris, against all the pressures of the British to broaden his extreme right wing government, eliminated all the opposition parties from the cabinet and closed down two Communist newspapers.

The Balkan neighbors now agreed to step up their aid to the Communist rebels, but at a price. General Markos, the commander of the Greek Democratic Army, made agreements with Albania, Yugoslavia, and Bulgaria for the detachment from Greece of its Slavic areas and for other territorial adjustments most unfavorable to Greece. By March, 1947, when the Truman Doctrine was announced, the rebel force stood at about seventeen thousand men. Making increasing use of Yugoslav territory for regrouping and medical care, the rebels carried out raids of mounting intensity, using terrorist techniques in the countryside, including the taking and executing of hostages. General Zervas, the former head of the EDES, who was appointed minister of public order in early 1947, carried out an extensive program of political murder of his own.

By the time President Truman asked Congress for military aid for Greece, the Communists had developed a political and intelligence network that included about fifty thousand active workers who were engaged in collecting information and supplies and carrying out sabotage and other acts of terrorism. An additional two hundred and fifty thousand sympathizers gave the rebels assistance from time to time.

A Yugoslav general was now attached to the headquarters of the Democratic Army at Bulkes, Yugoslavia. The Soviet Union, which had recognized the Greek government almost immediately, withdrew its ambassador in April, 1947. Stalin gave no aid to the rebels, however. The Soviets limited their involvement to a handful of military liaison officers whose function was to observe the arrangements worked out between the Yugoslavs and the Greek guerrillas. A Balkan joint staff was formed under Yugoslav domination. Tito agreed to give more weapons and supplies in return for the right to veto any changes in the high command of the Greek Democratic Army. The Greeks were unhappy about the arrangement and distrustful of the Yugoslavs, but they had nowhere else to turn. The International Brigade of Communist volunteers, of which some of the rebels had dreamed, and some had, indeed, been promised, never materialized. By 1948 about 75 percent of the rebels' small arms were coming from the Balkan neighbors, mostly Yugoslavia; none came from the Soviet Union directly, nor, so far as one can determine, did Stalin transmit weapons to the Greeks through the Balkan satellites.

\*       \*       \*

Crucial to this analysis besides the dubious use of the term "democratic" was the assumption of "Soviet direction." As we have seen, the Soviets in fact were giving neither aid nor direction. A few months later they would vainly seek to persuade Yugoslavia to cut off the substantial aid which they were giving. "What do you think," Stalin exclaimed to the Yugoslav vice-premier in early 1948, "that Great Britain and the United States—the United States, the most powerful state in the world—will permit you to break their line of communication in the Mediterranean? Nonsense. And we have no navy. The uprising in Greece must be stopped, and as quickly as possible." Indeed, the Soviet attitude toward Greece conformed perfectly to the Stalinist pattern. Since the Greek guerrillas had taken action independent of the Red Army and Stalin's direction, the Kremlin viewed them as a nuisance and a possible threat to the diplomatic relations of the Soviet Union. Stalin saw them as potential clients of the Yugoslavs, whose claims to a role of independent political leadership in the Balkans he was already attempting to crush.

During the feverish days of preparation for the Truman Doctrine speech, no one in the national security bureaucracy appears to have ventured a political analysis of the Greek rebels, their relations with Russia, Yugoslavia, or the other Balkan neighbors. The fifth-column analogy from World War II dominated official thinking. The possibility that men had taken to the hills for reasons of their own and not as agents of a foreign power was never seriously considered. "The President has determined to take a stand to 'aid' Greece, as a counter-Russia move," David Lilienthal wrote in his diary for March 9. Writing a grocery store executive in Michigan, Senator Vandenberg made it clear that he had the same understanding of the purposes behind the new policy. It was a holding action to prevent the sweep of Soviet power in a "chain reaction" from the Dardanelles to the China Sea. "I think the adventure is worth trying as an alternative to another 'Munich' and perhaps to another war. . . ."

. . . When the Truman Doctrine was launched, some members of the State Department believed that a massive infusion of American power and money could establish a stable, moderate, reasonably democratic government and that the military operations should be regarded as instruments to set up the preconditions for bringing about political and social change. But by 1943 it had become clear that the military and political goals were incompatible. In supplying weapons and characterizing the struggle primarily as a Hitler-like fifth-column operation rather than as a conflict among Greeks over the sharing of political and economic power, by stressing the external rather than the internal aspects of the problem, the United States strengthened those forces in Greece with the least interest in reform.

When the conflicts became apparent between democratization and reform, on the one hand, and military security, on the other, those in Washington genuinely interested in reform lowered their sights. Ports and railroads were repaired; the Corinth Canal was repaired. The distribution of food prevented thousands from starving. A remarkable antimalaria campaign started under UNRRA was brought to a successful conclusion. A thousand miles of good highways were built. No progress, however, was made on the basic economic and political problems that were tearing apart the country. "Even as we undertook to bolster the economy of Greece to help her combat Communist agitation," Harry Truman records ruefully in his memoirs, "we were faced with the desire of the Greek government to use our aid to further partisan political rather than national aims." By the end of 1947 the United States had transferred substantial funds earmarked for economic reconstruction to the military effort, and most of the "reconstruction" programs that remained were road and port programs for the direct support of the counterinsurgency campaign. In the year following the arrival of the U.S. economic mission, the cost of living jumped 53 percent. In March, 1948, the Greek government announced that 32 percent of the population was on relief.

With the help of substantial American military equipment—seventy-four thousand tons arrived in the last five months of 1947—including artillery, dive bombers, and stocks of napalm, the strength of the Greek National Army was brought up to one hundred and thirty-two thousand and the National Guard to about fifty thousand. They faced a guerrilla force, which, despite heavy casualities, remained at about twenty-three thousand men. The guerrillas had no armor, no aircraft, and little artillery. While the first U.S. aid was pouring into Greece, Tito stepped up his aid, including much needed artillery, but for it he extracted a price. Substantial parts of Greece were to be detached and joined to a Yugoslav federation. The other satellite countries encouraged the rebel leader General Markos to announce a Free Democratic government, but when he did on Christmas Eve, 1947, not one Communist country, including the Soviet Union, ever recognized it.

Despite the overwhelming superiority of the government forces, the guerrillas were achieving considerable successes with a series of raids throughout 1947 and the first six months of 1948. In 1948 they lost almost thirty-two thousand men under increasing air bombardment, but, remarkably, they managed to replenish their force and to maintain it at about the same level as before.

The expulsion of Tito from the Cominform in June, 1948, did not result in the immediate end of Yugoslav aid or in the closing of the border between Greece and Yugoslavia. But it did promote a split in the Greek Communist party between those, like General Markos, who thought Tito's guns were more valuable than Stalin's dubious good wishes, and the old political functionary, Zakhariadis, who believed that allegiance to Stalin could somehow be translated into something more helpful than an occasional surveillance by Soviet officers. The Stalinist faction won, and the defeat of the guerrilla movement began.

In July, 1949, Tito announced that he would close the border, but for the last six months he had already drastically curtailed his assistance. More important, Zakhariadis, growing desperate at the defections of the Communist neighbors and the mounting guerrilla casualties, took charge of the military operations himself. He gambled that he could blunt the impact of American aid by switching from insurgent raids to full-scale conventional warfare. The results were disastrous for the Communists. The rebels, in large battles for the first time, suffered major setbacks and on May 3, 1949, they broadcast an offer for a cease fire. While they had offered twenty such proposals since 1946, this one contained substantially softer terms. However, it too was ignored by Greece and the United States.

In the final six months of the war General Van Fleet initiated a campaign for "the systematic removal of whole sections of the population" in an effort to separate the guerrillas from the supporting population. In his recent analysis of the war Major Edgar O'Ballance attaches great importance to this tactic.

> *This was more far-reaching than is generally realized. It removed the people; it demarcated a "front line," it prevented "back infiltration" and it caused a blanket of silence to descend. . . . The harsh policy of displacing thousands of people was a difficult decision for a democratic government to take, even in wartime, and the Greek government hesitated for a long time. However, once this policy was put into effect it paid handsome dividends. . . .*

On October 16, 1949, with rebel resistance almost at an end, the guerrilla radio announced that the "Greek Democratic Army" had decided to "cease fire" in order "to prevent the complete annihilation of Greece." The civil war was over. . . .

*Robert H. Ferrell*

# HEADING OFF WAR: THE MARSHALL PLAN

*A little more than three months after the president's enunciation of the Tru-
man Doctrine, Secretary of State George C. Marshall, speaking to a Harvard
University commencement (June 5, 1947), invited European nations to undertake a joint economic recovery program with American assistance. As in the
Truman Doctrine, economic uplift was linked to political stability, anticommunism, and security against the Soviet Union. The plan was more than Marshall's; it had been in the making for months as American statesmen grappled with Europe's severe postwar prostration. In early 1947 Churchill found
Europe "a rubble heap, a charnel house, a breeding-ground of pestilence and
hate." Europeans needed dollars to buy from the most prosperous and pro-
ductive nation in the world, the United States, and so they eagerly applauded
America's offer of help. In a time of considerable crisis that some historians
have likened to a "war scare," Congress approved Marshall Plan aid in March
1948 (Senate, 67 to 17; House, 329 to 74), and Truman signed the bill in April.
Russia and the Eastern European nations boycotted the plan. In his laudatory
account of the Marshall Plan from 1947 to its conclusion in 1952, Robert Ferrell of Indiana University concludes that the invitation to Russia was genuine
and that the program probably prevented a new war. Ferrell is the author of*
Peace in Their Time *(1952) and* American Diplomacy in the Great Depression
*(1957).*

The speech read much better than it sounded. The secretary called
on Europe to pull itself together, with only assistance—not direction
—from the United States. He had determined that there would not
be another lend-lease in which Europeans would bring their shop-
ping lists to the United States and the American government trim
demands down to some reasonable amount, never sure that countries with the most overblown requirements came out best after
the reduction. Marshall's demand was European leadership. "It
would be neither fitting nor efficacious for this government to undertake to draw up unilaterally a program designed to place Europe on
its feet economically. This is the business of Europeans. The initiative, I think, must come from Europe. The role of this country should

From Robert H. Ferrell, *George C. Marshall* (New York, 1966), pp. 111–14, 117–23,
132–34. Volume 15 of *The American Secretaries of State and Their Diplomacy,* eds.
Robert H. Ferrell and Samuel Flagg Bemis. Reprinted by permission of Cooper
Square Publishers, Inc. (Footnotes deleted.)

consist of friendly aid in the drafting of a European program and of later support of such a program so far as it may be practical for us to do so. The program should be a joint one, agreed to by a number, if not all, European nations."

How would the Europeans react? The British government showed immense enthusiasm at the prospect of American aid under a plan, even if the Americans seemed uncertain of details. When after Marshall's speech the permanent undersecretary of state for foreign affairs, Sir William Strang, came to Ernie Bevin with the suggestion that the Washington Embassy ask for explanation of the speech, Bevin almost literally jumped into action. "Bill," said he, "we know what he *said.* If you ask questions, you'll get answers you don't want. Our problem is what *we do,* not what *he meant.*" Bevin arranged a meeting in Paris of the European foreign ministers—Britain, France, and Russia. He announced his intention to the Americans, saying he was going to Paris for preliminary talks with Premier Paul Ramadier and Foreign Minister Bidault, and would be glad to carry any message. The British ambassador in Washington, Lord Inverchapel, bringing these tidings to Secretary Marshall, expressed hope that Will Clayton would come to London soon and not delay because of Bevin's proposed foreign ministers session in Paris. Meanwhile Bevin told a member of the American Embassy in London that the United States was in the same position in 1947 where Britain had been at the end of the Napoleonic Wars. In 1815, he said, Britain held about 30 percent of the world's wealth. The United States after the Second World War held about 50 percent. Britain for eighteen years after Waterloo, Bevin ruminated, had practically given away her exports, but the result had been stability and a century of peace.

The French were apprehensive of Bevin's fast footwork, and showed both their usual postwar sensitivity to France's European prestige and a certain fear for the opinions of French Communists. Bidault told the American ambassador in Paris, Jefferson Caffery, that he was not too happy about Bevin coming over, as it looked as if Bevin were trying to steal the show after the new American *démarche.* Caffery thought privately that Bidault wanted to steal the show but Bevin had beat him by a day or two. Ramadier remarked that France and the other West European countries were heading for economic and financial disaster and would get there during the latter part of 1948 unless someone headed off Europe's troubles. The Communists had been demonstrating high glee at the prospect of chaos, and their tactics of obstruction greatly bothered him.

As soon as Bevin arrived the question arose of Soviet cooperation. Both Bevin and Bidault told Caffery, separately, that they hoped the Soviets would refuse to cooperate, and in any event they would go ahead full steam. A momentary embarrassment occurred when Bevin and Bidault were deep in their cooperative planning stage, preparing for the Soviets: The French minister of information inadvertently gave out an announcement that they were planning, before they had opportunity to communicate with the Russians, and the ministry then had to deny that the two foreign ministers were planning.

Shortly after this initial Anglo-French diplomacy in Paris, Will Clayton and Ambassador Lewis Douglas held some sessions with members of the British cabinet in London. . . .

The third London meeting, June 26, turned attention to expected Russian difficulties at the forthcoming Anglo-French-Russian conversations in Paris. Clayton said he thought there would have to be radical change in the Russian position on European recovery and other matters before the American people would approve financial assistance to Russia. Clayton thought the Russians might not need short-term assistance with the "three f's"—food, fuel, and fiber—for they had these, but might require long-term credits. Dalton said the Russians, not members of the International Bank, could not borrow, but could join the bank if they wished. An aide interjected that this course seemed unlikely because as a member of the bank the USSR would have to reveal its gold holdings. Dalton closed the session by reverting to the note that the timetable for the U.S. loan to the U.K. was so erroneous, that Britain could take on convertibility only with great trouble.

The meeting of the three foreign ministers now opened in Paris, on June 27. The United States, not present, had exact recounting of the conversations. Molotov at the outset proposed to ask the U.S. for further information, and then ran into the Franco-British opinion that the three nations should draft a plan. Bidault offered a compromise, asking clarification on the extent of U.S. willingness to help with a proposal. Jefferson Caffery obtained the notion from what he heard of the meetings that the French, in event of Soviet tactics of delay or obstruction, would let Bevin get out in front and carry the ball. Fortunately Anglo-French unity held. It proved fairly easy for Bidault and Bevin to stay together in their proposals as the meeting turned into a considerable trial for Foreign Minister Molotov: Bidault told Caffery that Molotov's "hungry satellites are smacking their lips in expectation of getting some of your money. He is obviously embarrassed."

The Russians may have tried, but if so without success, to stir trouble for the French government by encouraging the Communists. Bevin told Caffery that the 140 technical advisers and assistants, so-called, whom Molotov brought along for the conference had little if anything to do with the discussion. He believed these Russians were all agents, brought along in view of the Communist National Congress then in session at Strasbourg, all in hope of getting Communists back into cabinet positions in the government.

The Paris conference quickly came to an end. Bevin took the French proposal and reduced it to a single page, taking out the extra words, and sent this page to Bidault and Molotov on the morning of July 1. That afternoon the Russian foreign minister reiterated arguments of previous days—no infringement on sovereignty of European states, each should establish its needs and submit total dollar costs to the United States. Bidault strongly supported Bevin. One of Molotov's aides brought in a partly decoded telegram from Moscow repeating the old arguments. Bevin said to Molotov that the Russians wanted a blank check from the Americans, and what would happen if he, Bevin, went to Moscow and asked for a blank check from the Russians? The meeting of July 1 adjourned on this note. The final meeting, held next day, brought a clean break. Bevin presided. Molotov repeated his arguments, and finished by saying that any joint Anglo-French action without Russia might have very grave consequences. Bidault said the French would go with the British. Bevin said that he, like Bidault, proposed to carry on.

The following day, July 3, the British and French governments invited all European states to meet in Paris and draw up a proposal for the American government.

Despite the break at Paris the Russians still were welcome to attend. Secretary Marshall had never excluded Russia from his offer. There had been department discussion of Russian participation, with advisers taking positions pro and con, but Marshall decided to give the Soviets a chance. In reply to the secretary's questions Kennan had advised, "Play it straight." The Soviet Union and its satellites were great producers of food and raw materials that Western Europe needed and it was sensible to encourage East-West trade. The secretary could confront the Russians with their own Marxist maxim, "From each according to his ability, to each according to his need." There would have to be sharing of information on economic and financial conditions about which the Russians traditionally had been secretive. If they changed their spots and came in, so much the better. Marshall privately described his offer as including "everything up to the Urals" and he meant it. He said "if Europe was to be divided he was not going to be the person to divide it, therefore USSR should be let in on the plan."

This great opportunity Stalinist diplomacy threw away. If they had participated in the plan the Russians could have made congressional approval of Marshall Plan outlays difficult if not impossible; Congress was in a suspicious mood, unlikely to approve billions of dollars for Russia and the satellites. Or if by some minor miracle the plan with Russian participation passed Congress, the Soviets could have ruined economic planning for Europe by sabotaging it—delaying, evading, all the devices of which they were masters. Staying out of the plan, they ensured its success.

Unfortunately for the apparent unity of the Eastern block they did not stay out of the Marshall Plan quickly enough—a confusion of signals between Moscow and the satellites led to an open Russian veto of participation by the Czechoslovak and Polish governments. Those two regimes gave tentative indication of desire to join the plan. They took pains to say that, although they wished to send delegates to the organizing meeting in Paris which was to open on July 12, final acceptance depended on the scope of the plan. Then came the belated advice from Moscow. The Polish government backed water immediately. Foreign Minister Modzelewski had some trouble informing Ambassador Griffis that his country was not sending a representative to Paris, talked continuously and refused to look Griffis in the face. Modzelewski had told Griffis a few days before that the Poles would go to Paris. But the Czechoslovak government got into the worst trouble. President Eduard Beneš told an American diplomat on July 9 that he did not anticipate a Soviet veto on Czechoslovak membership in the plan, but that in event of a veto a showdown would occur in the Prague government, forcing a choice between East and West. That very afternoon a telephone message arrived in the Czechoslovak capital from the delegation, including Prime Minister Klement Gottwald, which had gone to Moscow for consultation. The message, of course, told of a Soviet veto. The Russians had said the Americans were trying to buy up Europe, that Czechoslovak membership in the Marshall Plan would be an act of hostility against the USSR. Stalin advised the Prague regime to withdraw its acceptance and justify this action by pointing to the fact that nonparticipation of the other Slav nations and the other East European states had created a new situation. The Czechoslovaks had had two interviews, first Gottwald alone with Stalin, then a reception of the entire delegation by Stalin and Molotov. The second session was fairly relaxed, although the Russians made their points clearly and categorically. The first meeting à deux, Gottwald and Stalin, was the business meeting, and not so pleasant: Gottwald had returned to his hotel almost scared, and said he had never seen Stalin so angry.

Lacking Russian and satellite attendance, representatives of the sixteen nations met in Paris on July 12: Austria, Belgium, Denmark, France, Greece, Iceland, Ireland, Italy, Luxembourg, the Netherlands, Norway, Portugal, Sweden, Switzerland, Turkey, and the United Kingdom. Under chairmanship of Sir Oliver Franks the Europeans set up an interim Committee of European Economic Cooperation (CEEC), drew up a report, and presented it to the United States on September 22.

The Russians meanwhile organized a meeting at Warsaw where the satellites received from Moscow their own bogus economic plan, known as the Molotov Plan. The Russians announced a revived Comintern, the Communist Information Bureau ("Cominform"), on July 6, 1947. . . .

On March 15, 1948, the interim Committee of European Economic Cooperation (CEEC) representing sixteen countries and the zones of Western Germany gathered in Paris to form the Organization for European Economic Cooperation (OEEC). To OEEC the ECA (and its successor at the end of 1951, the Mutual Security Administration) between April 3, 1948 and June 30, 1952 gave $13,348,800,000. Three nations took over half this sum: The United Kingdom obtained $3,189,800,000; France $2,713,600,000; Italy (including Trieste)

"Put Me In, Coach! Put Me In!" (March 1947). *(From* The Herblock Book *[Beacon Press, 1952])*

French child's cartoon illustrating American relief aid under the Marshall Plan. *(From U.S. Dept. of State,* Third Report to Congress on the Foreign Relief Program *[1948], p. 17)*

"U.S. Assistance or . . . The Trojan Horse?" Polish depiction of the Marshall Plan. *(From* U.N. World, *October 1947, p. 57)*

Russian cartoon of Europe collapsing under the Marshall Plan. *(From* Krokodil, *1949)*

$1,508,800,000. West Germany received $1,390,600,000. The Netherlands received $982,100,000 under the Marshall Plan. Other states tapered off with lesser sums, down to Iceland with $29,300,000.

The program ended on June 30, 1952, as Marshall insisted it should. In a private meeting at the State Department in 1949 after he had left the secretaryship he said that "it ought to be terminated in 1952. Part of the reason why they imply it cannot be terminated then comes from the opponents of the present appropriations, and part comes from the foreign fellows who naturally would like to see it prolonged beyond 1952, but you have got to stop somewhere." By its end the plan had turned from an economic to a military arrangement. Prior to June, 1950, there had been stipulation that no Marshall Plan aid should go into military supplies. This did not prohibit European nations from shifting budget appropriations, and American administrators had hoped the plan would ease pressure to cut military appropriations. Early in 1951 with the Korean War at a crucial stage the United States informed the Europeans that aid under the plan would have to go for defense. By 1952 80 percent of aid was in weapons, the other 20 percent in defense support.

Contrary to some feeling expressed at the plan's inauguration, it did not disrupt the American economy. Far from bankrupting the country, it stimulated production and probably braked a fall in demand for American food and industrial products, for the initially large postwar domestic demand had slowed down. The money involved in the plan, $13,348,800,000, was a stupendous sum. But inquiry into the peculiar statistics of American consumption showed a domestic liquor bill of more than $13 billions, an athletic bill of far more than $13 billions, a tobacco bill of more. The economy had plenty of slack. It is true that the Marshall Plan added large budget deficits to the national debt—moving beyond $250 billion by 1952. The Korean War added far more. Americans could congratulate themselves that because of the Marshall Plan they did not have to spend even more in an enormous war in Europe.

Thomas G. Paterson
# THE MARSHALL PLAN REVISITED

*In this reevaluation of the development and impact of the Marshall Plan,
Paterson stresses its anti-Soviet character by studying the intent of the fram-
ers and Russia's response to the secretary of state's invitation. He discusses
the manner in which it was proposed and explains why Russia rejected participation. The Marshall Plan enjoyed the short-run success of European recovery but in the long run helped to divide Europe even further. He questions
whether the European Recovery Program prevented Europe from succumbing
to either war or communism.*

Many prominent Americans were dismayed in March of 1947 that the
president had delivered an alarmist speech filled with warnings of
imminent crisis and global confrontation, but mentioning aid only
for Greece and Turkey, a speech which appeared to be both negative and hastily prepared. Even before Truman handed a somewhat
resentful Congress his fait accompli, administration figures had
begun to discuss long-range coordinated aid to other countries.
After the addess, publicists Walter Lippmann and Marquis Childs,
congressmen, and Dean Acheson, among others, demanded to "see
the whole picture at once." They wanted a comprehensive aid program to meet the world's reconstruction needs, especially to allevi-
ate economic disorder and political unrest in countries like Italy and
France, the homes of large Communist parties. Americans became
confident that a unified aid program closely supervised by Washington would achieve peace and prosperity—economic recovery, political stability, weakened Communist parties, healthy multilateral world
trade, and American economic well being and security. By 1947 they
had come to realize that the foreign aid (in excess of $9 billion) fur-
nished to Western Europe by the United States since the end of the
war had been too haphazardly given in a variety of emergency loans,
grants, surplus sales, and international assistance, and had not fulfilled its goals. But the European Recovery Program (ERP) or Mar-

From Thomas G. Paterson, *Soviet-American Confrontation: Postwar Reconstruction
and the Origins of the Cold War* (Baltimore, 1973), pp. 207–208, 214–16, 218–19,
231–34. Copyright © 1973 by The Johns Hopkins University Press. Reprinted by
permission. (Footnotes deleted.)

shall Plan would be different; it would also be the "Truman Doctrine in Action."

Less than three months after the dramatic Truman Doctrine speech, on June 5, 1947, Secretary of State George C. Marshall stood before a Harvard commencement audience and asked for a new foreign aid plan for Europe. After the address, which lacked specifics, United States and Western European committees formulated the European Recovery Program (ERP), a four-year, United States-directed program of grants and loans under a new agency of the United States government called the Economic Cooperation Administration (ECA). With West German but without Soviet or Eastern European participation and outside the United Nations Economic Commission for Europe (ECE), the ERP helped shape and reflect the Cold War schism. This format grew from the deliberate manner in which the United States presented and shaped the Marshall Plan and ignored the ECE and from an uncompromising Russia which read the ERP as an aggressive anti-Soviet undertaking. As one commentator has noted, "with the Marshall Plan the Cold War assumes the character of position warfare. Both sides become frozen in mutual unfriendliness." Both Russia and the United States attempted to forge mutually exclusive recovery programs for their spheres; the confrontation seemed to be institutionalized by the Marshall and Molotov Plans. . . .

The Marshall speech and the invitation must have deeply troubled Soviet leaders, although the lack of Soviet documents makes an assessment difficult. Certainly, the apparent openendedness of the Marshall proposal and the ever-present suspicions of a capitalist trap must have produced vigorous discussions, at a time when the Soviets had hardly completed their diatribes against the Truman Doctrine and the developing Anglo-American cooperation. *Pravda*'s comments less than two weeks after the Harvard speech were not friendly: "Mr. Marshall's plan is, notwithstanding its apparent novelty, only a repetition of the Truman plan for political pressure with the help of dollars, a plan for interference in the domestic affairs of other countries." *Pravda* argued perceptively that it would be contradictory for the United States to include Eastern Europe in an American undertaking, in the light of its hostile policy toward that area, and that Marshall was attempting to make it appear that Russia and Eastern Europe "are excluding themselves. . . ." *Tass* added on June 19 that it was reasonable to think that the Bevin-Bidault talks were "nothing less than an attempt to make a deal behind the back of the Soviet Union and other European countries," and "what are the political considerations involved?" Yet Russia surprised many by announcing on June 22 that it would send a delegation to a Paris meeting with France and Great Britain. . . .

Molotov arrived in Paris for talks with Bevin and Bidault on June 27, and it is an open question whether he came with predetermined orders to obstruct a cohesive European program. On the eve of the conference *Pravda*'s columns were more conciliatory and complimentary than they had been, and nobody knew what to expect from the Soviets except suspicion and hard bargaining. Indeed, almost immediately upon his arrival, Molotov asked Bidault what the British and French "had done behind his back." Ambassador to Russia Walter Bedell Smith was convinced that the Russians were going to Paris for "destructive" purposes, and Bevin believed that the one hundred advisers in the Soviet delegation were really spies sent to agitate among French Communists. Yet, as Bevin recalled to Acheson, it was not until well into the discussions that Molotov was handed a note which, from the change in his tone and pained expression, probably consisted of Moscow's rejection of a joint program. . . .

The expected, and on the part of some, the desired, had happened. The answer to the question of whether there ever was any chance of Soviet participation lies partly in Soviet fears about American intentions, especially after the abortive American loan, the curtailment of UNRRA, the Truman Doctrine, numerous anti-Soviet statements by leaders like Acheson, and the obvious British and French coldness toward Soviet participation. Russia also read an integrated program as a return to the status quo ante bellum; that is, Western Europe would be the industrial center and Eastern Europe the supplier of raw materials, especially grains and coal. The Russians feared this subordination of the agricultural East to the industrial West. Eastern European countries, with Russian prodding, had developed plans for industrialization. They were essentially undeveloped nations, and their economic difficulties had been augmented by the destruction of the war. As Vera Michales Dean noted in 1948, "experts on Eastern Europe believe that only through industrialization accompanied by modernization of agriculture can the countries

of this region solve their rural overpopulation problems, and ultimately raise their standards of living." A student of the area has
added: "It is also understandable that the new regimes would wish,
from a general feeling of patriotism, to diminish their countries' dependence on foreign countries." Indeed, United States diplomats did
expect the Russian participation to provide raw materials to help
recovery in the West. Finally, Soviet influence in or control over Eastern Europe was not firm or decided in mid-1947, and a massive influx
of American dollars into the region would certainly have challenged
the Soviet position. Hence Russia put considerable pressure on Poland and Czechoslovakia, which were both eager to join, to reject
participation. Kennan and other State Department officials have suggested that the Czech coup of February, 1948, in part represented
the Soviet "defensive reaction" to the Marshall Plan. It would have
been difficult for Russia to accept a place in a program so conspicuously dominated by the United States and geared more toward
Western than Eastern Europe. One can only wonder, with Arnold
Toynbee, whether, if the Marshall Plan had preceded the Truman
Doctrine, Russia would have accepted membership.

Perhaps the invitation to Russia to join a European recovery program was not terribly critical anyway. It would have been the utmost
of illogic and contradiction for Congress to approve funds for the
Soviet Union so shortly after it had been persuaded to pass the anti-
Soviet Truman Doctrine. James P. Warburg was frank in asking
whether people could "really assume that President Truman believed
that the Congress, which he himself had indoctrinated with the spirit
of an anti-Soviet crusade, would consent to a plan which made
American dollars available to the Soviet Union and its satellites."
Then, too, some congressmen were still resentful about UNRRA,
while others were calling for restrictions on Soviet-American trade.

Kennan had said "play it straight," so Marshall agreed to let the
answer come from Moscow—an answer he and most State Department officials expected to be in the negative. It may have been Henry
Wallace who prompted the State Department not to exclude Russia.
Both State Department staffman Joseph Jones and Ambassador to
Great Britain Lewis Douglas have mentioned as a relevant factor
Wallace's early 1947 speeches advocating a massive European reconstruction plan with substantial assistance going to Russia. Yet
there was really no gamble in offering Russia access to a recovery

program. Russia would shun any American-dominated program directed in large part against it, and the United States would not compromise on control. The invitation, then, was a diplomatic gesture intended to place the burden of rejection of the Marshall Plan and of the division of Europe on the Soviet Union. Its propaganda value was immense: Americans and growing numbers of Europeans became all the more convinced that Russia was the obstructionist in Europe. Furthermore, as Kennan told Marshall, the Soviet position had strained Soviet relations with Eastern Europe and with Communist parties in the West. "Events of past weeks the greatest blow to European communism since termination of hostilities," read Kennan's notes.

\* \* \*

The Marshall Plan gave the United States its coordinated foreign aid program and a more cohesive sphere of influence, toward which Washington had been working since World War II, and the ERP revived the Western European economy. Truman himself boldly concluded in 1956 that "without the Marshall Plan it would have been difficult for Western Europe to remain free from the tyranny of communism," and Robert H. Ferrell agrees: "Americans could congratulate themselves that because of the Marshall Plan they did not have to spend even more in an enormous war in Europe." Indeed, it is a popular conviction that the Marshall Plan prevented an aggressive Russia from sweeping over Western Europe, either through revolution or overt military action. The basic premise that Russia intended to seize Western Europe has never been substantiated and is increasingly being questioned by scholars. Certainly Western Europe benefited immensely from the ERP, but it is quite doubtful that that region was saved from an "enormous war" or the "tyranny of communism" by it.

When the European Recovery Program ended in mid-1952, the United States had dispensed $13 billion to the member countries, as well as several billions more to the members of NATO. These expenditures shored up both its own and the Western European economy and created a sense of military security. The Korean War shifted the emphasis to military assistance, and by 1952 80 percent of United States aid to Western Europe consisted of weapons. At the close of the Marshall Plan, industrial production in the ERP countries had risen 35 percent above the prewar figure, agricultural production 10 percent. The dollar gap had been reduced, West Germany had been rebuilt and partially integrated into the Western European economy, and the goal of currency stabilization was partially achieved. The percentage of American exports going to the ERP countries was maintained at about 33 percent, with over half of United States exports to Western Europe financed with ECA funds by the second quarter of 1949. A guarantee program for investments allowed United States businessmen to convert profits in local currencies into dollars, and, in part because of this protection, companies like Ford, General Motors, Standard Oil, and Goodyear expanded their plants and investments in Europe. Under the ECA the American stockpiling program accelerated, as the United States gave special attention to scarce raw materials from ERP sources. By 1950, almost $57 million in rubber, platinum, industrial diamonds, bauxite, and graphite had been acquired under the ECA. On the whole, the Marshall Plan helped avert economic depression in both Western Europe and the United States, and thereby, in the American mind, contributed to more pacific international relations by curbing communism and the Soviet Union.

But contemporaries did point out some shortcomings which commentators more distant from the actual events have tended to overlook. Washington was not pleased with the Marshall Plan's meager contribution to European economic integration and stable, nonsubsidized, multilateral, nondiscriminatory trade. In 1950 the White House expressed alarm over the continued "dollar gap" in Europe, and noted that ERP's termination "will create tremendous economic problems at home and abroad unless vigorous steps are taken both by the United States and foreign countries." "Vigorous steps" were not taken, and United States trade with Europe depended for many years upon foreign aid. Will Clayton complained to Walter Lippmann in early 1952 that "economic nationalism" persisted and that Western Europe appeared to be living "on the bounty of the United States." He added that "Russia tells her satellites over and over that all Western Europe lives by United States charity.... There is just enough truth here to put us squarely on the defensive." William Draper, United States special representative in Europe, told the president in 1952 that "the existing 'dollar gap' threatens not only our own export trade, but if not reduced may unfavorably affect the mutual defense effort as well." In 1954, in his *A Foreign Economic Policy for the United States,* Clarence B. Randall reported that world trade was approaching "a shaky balance, but this equilibrium is more apparent than real" because of restrictions on East-West trade and heavy American expenditures for defense. By 1952, Harry B. Price concludes, "the continent was far more healthy than in 1948, but it had not yet acquired the dynamism needed for accelerated growth independent of external aid." Nor had economic integration—which some Americans believed to be crucial to economic stability—succeeded.

There was little restructuring of European industry or economic and social institutions. American aid tended to perpetuate the status quo, and the objective of non-Communist political stability through economic recovery was not achieved. Deflationary money policies and high unemployment rates undermined American goals. *Fortune* editorialized in 1951: "Thus the standard of living of French industrial workers . . . remained as low or lower than before the war, and they have little more stake in France's economic present or future than they had in 1788." The Marshall Plan did not eliminate communism from Western Europe, Hans Morgenthau has noted. The seed of communism continued to fall on fertile ground because the plan left the Western European "economic, social, and political structure by and large intact. The dangers to the stability and strength of Western Europe which have grown in the past from the defects of that structure have continued to grow because those defects were not repaired. The Marshall Plan almost completely lost sight of those roots of instability and unrest which antedated the emergency and were bound to operate after it was over." The United States probably could not and should not have made political and social reform a condition for aid—reform was always a secondary concern in the Marshall Plan— but there is no doubt that the goals of economic stability and anticommunism were only partially fulfilled at its close.

The thirst for raw materials represented in the Marshall Plan also contributed to European exploitation of colonial areas and nourished instability in the nondeveloped world. Belgium, for example, used some of its ERP aid to expand Congolese production of raw materials, and by mid-1951 France had spent $287 million in ECA funds for the purchase of equipment for its foreign territories. In 1950 Europe's dependent areas had provided the United States with, among other materials, 82 percent of its bauxite, 68 percent of its cobalt (critical to the manufacture of jet engines), 51 percent of its tin, and 23 percent of its manganese ore. This exploitation, with few important economic returns to colonial peoples, helped to perpetuate the conditions of social and political unrest which the peace and prosperity theme was dedicated to eliminating. The Marshall Plan, then, in the long run, produced neither world stability nor world prosperity, especially as the Soviet-American confrontation moved into developing regions in the 1950s.

The exertion of American economic power through the ERP was successful in that the immediate recovery of Europe was achieved, but it created a deeper rift between the United States and Russia. When Moscow could not accept American conditions for aid, Washington put the blame for heightened Cold War tension almost solely on it. Its Molotov Plan was read as another plot to disrupt peace rather than as a defensive move to shore up its own sphere of influence. The Marshall Plan knitted together as never before the American sphere of influence in Western Europe and was partially responsible for dividing the world in other ways. It encouraged restrictions on East-West trade, as export controls were instituted to direct products away from Eastern Europe to Western Europe. By drawing Western Germany . . . into the Western European economy, it aroused profound Soviet fears of a revived German power. The ERP, presented and formulated as an American offensive in the Cold War, was interpreted by the Soviets in 1947–1948 as a threat to their tenuous position in Eastern Europe. The coup in Czechoslovakia may be evidence of that perceived threat, as the Soviets decided to consolidate their sphere of influence in the most repressive manner. It may be true, as Adam Ulam has suggested, that Stalin feared the Marshall Plan more than the United States monopoly of the atomic bomb. Certainly Moscow was alarmed at the plan's rehabilitation of its nemesis, Western Germany.

Stephen E. Ambrose

# THE MILITARY DIMENSION: BERLIN, NATO, AND NSC-68

*After launching the Marshall Plan, the United States increasingly turned to
the containment of Russia by military means. As Stephen E. Ambrose spells
out in this selection from his* Rise to Globalism *(1971), the Soviet-American
confrontation in 1948–49 centered on a serious crisis over Berlin and the
creation of a Western military alliance (NATO), and generated a significant
review of American defense policy (National Security Council Paper No. 68).
These three issues are considered important bench marks in the Cold War.
Ambrose explains their background and underlying assumptions, pointing
out that the United States held a world-wide perspective by the outbreak
of the Korean War. Ambrose is a professor of history at Louisiana State Uni-
versity-New Orleans and the author of* Duty, Honor, Country: A History of
West Point *(1966),* Eisenhower and Berlin, 1945 *(1967),* The Supreme Commander *(1970), and with James Barber,* The Military and American Society
*(1971).*

At the beginning of the summer of 1948, the Soviets were . . . faced
with a whole series of what they considered threatening developments. The Marshall Plan was beginning to draw the Western European nations closer together. France, Britain, and the Benelux had
signed a military pact which the United States had officially welcomed and had indicated it intended to join. Americans were already beginning to talk of bringing others into the proposed organization, among them Canada, Portugal, Denmark, Iceland, Norway,
and Italy. Since these countries could contribute little or nothing to
ground defense, the Soviets judged—rightly—that the Americans
wanted them included in order to use their territory for air and sea
bases. The United States was even dickering with Fascist Spain for
bases. Equally ominous was the Western determination to give independence to West Germany. In the long run, this could only mean
that the West intended to merge West Germany into the proposed
anti-Soviet military organization.

Adding to Stalin's difficulties, his strongest satellite, Yugoslavia,

From Stephen E. Ambrose, *Rise to Globalism: American Foreign Policy, 1938–1970*
(Baltimore, Md.: Penguin Books Inc., 1971), Vol. 8 of *The Pelican History of the
United States,* ed. Robert A. Divine. Copyright Stephen E. Ambrose, © 1971. Re-
printed by permission of Penguin Books, Inc., pp. 171–81, 188–91.

refused to play the role Russia had assigned to it and struck out on an independent course. Stalin tried to topple Tito, failed, and in despair expelled Yugoslavia from the Cominform. The example Tito had set, however, could not be so easily dismissed.

Soviet foreign policy, based on an occupied and divided Germany, a weakened Western Europe, and tight control of East Europe, faced total collapse. Whether Stalin had expansive plans is unclear and at least doubtful, but what had happened made him shake, for the security of the Soviet Union itself now seemed threatened. As Kennan put it, in a grand understatement, "There can be no doubt that, coming as it did on top of the European recovery program and the final elaboration and acceptance of the Atlantic alliance, the move toward establishment of a separate government in Western Germany aroused keen alarm among the Soviet leaders." The victor in the war was being hemmed in by the West, with the vanquished playing a key role in the new coalition. Worst of all was the Western listening-post and outpost in the heart of the Soviet security belt, the Western sector in Berlin.

On 23 June 1948, Clay introduced the new currency into Western Berlin. Stalin responded immediately. He argued that since the West had abandoned the idea of German reunification, there was no longer any point to maintaining Berlin as the future capital of all Germany. The Western powers, through the logic of their own acts, ought to retire to their own zones. The Russians clamped down a total blockade on all ground and water traffic to Berlin. The British joined the Americans in a counterblockade on the movement of goods from the East into Western Germany.

In the West, there was sentiment to abandon Berlin. For many, it seemed foolish to risk World War III for the sake of a prestige objective, and there was force to Stalin's argument that if the West was going to create a West German nation it had no business staying in East Germany. Clay and Truman quickly scotched such talk. As Clay told the War Department, "We have lost Czechoslovakia. Norway is threatened. We retreat from Berlin. When Berlin falls, Western Germany will be next." Then Europe would go Communist. The frontiers of freedom, it seemed, were not on the Elbe, but beyond it. Like Stalin, the Americans felt they could not give an inch. Marshall declared, "We had the alternative of following a firm policy in Berlin or accepting the consequences of failure of the rest of our European policy," a statement that described equally well Stalin's feelings. Truman provided the last word in a succinct, simple declaration: "We are going to stay period."

Clay wanted to shoot his way through the Russian blockade. He thought the United States might just as well find out immediately whether the Russians wanted war or not. Given the ten to one disparity of ground strength in Europe, Army Chief of Staff Omar Bradley was able to convince Truman that there must be a better way. It was found with air transport, which soon began flying round-the-clock missions into Berlin, supplying up to thirteen thousand tons of goods per day. . . .

Truman, triumphant after his reelection (foreign policy had not been an issue between the major parties in the 1948 campaign), pledged in his inaugural address aid to the European nations willing to defend themselves, while the new secretary of state, Dean Acheson, pushed forward a treaty with the Europeans. On 4 April 1949 the North Atlantic Treaty was signed in Washington; Britain, France, Belgium, the Netherlands, Italy, Portugal, Denmark, Iceland, Norway, Canada, and the United States pledged themselves to mutual assistance in case of aggression against any of the signatories.

The NATO treaty signified the beginning of a new era. In the nineteenth century America had broken the bonds of a colonial, extractive economy and became a great industrial power thanks in large part to private European loans. In the first forty-five years of the twentieth century, the United States had gradually achieved a position of equality with Europe. The Marshall Plan, followed by NATO, began in earnest the era of American military, political, and economic dominance over Europe. . . .

In the spring of 1949 Truman enjoyed success after success. NATO and Point Four were followed by a victory in Berlin; on 12 May the Russians lifted the blockade. They had decided—as Clay had felt they would—that the counterblockade was hurting them more than they were injuring the West, and they realized there was no longer any hope of stopping the movement toward a West German government.[1] The Soviets still retained flickering hopes of getting something out of the Ruhr. During sporadic discussion between the Soviets and the Americans over Berlin "the Russians mentioned the

---

[1] The Bonn Republic came into being on 23 May 1949.

Ruhr repeatedly" and as the immediate price for lifting the blockade they got the West to agree to another foreign ministers' conference on Germany (it began in Paris on 23 May and was abortive).

It had been a good spring for Truman, but trouble lay ahead. The removal of the war scare, combined with the fear that NATO was going to cost a good deal of money, began to put an end to bipartisanship in foreign policy. The old issues, buried since Truman's dramatic speech on Greece, reemerged. Should the United States be a world policeman? Should it commit itself in advance to the defense of any anti-Communist government? How extensive a world role should America play? How much should it pay to play the role? And, at bottom, what was the nature and extent of the Soviet threat and how should it be met? Thoughtful Republicans, led by Senator Taft, began to question the wisdom of provoking the Soviets thousands of miles from America's shores. In the committee meetings to consider ratification of the NATO treaty, congressmen began to ask embarrassing questions about the purpose of NATO.

Senator Henry Cabot Lodge wanted to know if NATO was the beginning of a series of regional organizations designed to hem in the Russians. Acheson reassured him by stressing that no one in the administration contemplated following NATO with "a Mediterranean pact, and then a Pacific pact, and so forth." Other senators wondered why the United States did not rely upon the United Nations, where America controlled a majority of the votes. One reason was the Russian veto; another that the Europeans required some sort of special guarantee. Harriman warned that if NATO was not carried through, "there would be a reorientation" in Europe, a "restrengthening of those that believe in appeasement and neutrality." Acheson explained that "unity in Europe requires the continuing association and support of the United States. Without it free Europe would split apart." Or, as Senator Tom Connally declared, "the Atlantic Pact is but the logical extension of the principle of the Monroe Doctrine."

NATO, in other words, would speed the movement toward Western European unity while simultaneously allowing the United States to assume a new posture vis-à-vis Europe. What that posture would be was adequately, if somewhat crudely, summed up in the frequent references to the extension of the Monroe Doctrine. Europe would become, for the American businessman, soldier, and foreign policy maker, another Latin America.

All this obviously had great appeal, but serious questions remained. Could not as much be accomplished through the Marshall Plan? Why permanently split Europe, thereby abandoning all hope of ever reopening the East European market? What was the substance of the military guarantees that Americans were making or supporting? . . .

On 23 July 1949, Truman signed the North Atlantic Treaty. It marked the high point of bipartisanship and of containment in Europe. It also completed one phase of the revolution in American foreign policy. America had entered an entangling alliance. American security thereafter could be immediately and drastically affected by changes in the overseas balance of power over which the United States could not exercise much effective control. It meant that the United States was guaranteeing the maintenance of foreign social structures and governments for the next twenty years. It committed the United States to close peacetime military collaboration with the armed services of foreign nations. It signified the extent both of America's break with her past and of her determination to halt Communist expansion.

The presence among the members of Italy (and later Greece and Turkey) made a mockery of the words North Atlantic in the title; Portugal's presence made the assertion that it was an alliance in defense of democracy a hollow claim. So was the concept that NATO represented a pact between equals, for the United States had no intention of sharing the control of its atomic weapons with its NATO partners, and the bomb was the only weapon that gave NATO's military pretensions any validity at all. Acheson's denials to the contrary notwithstanding, the treaty paved the way for German rearmament. It also underscored the Europe-first orientation of Truman's foreign policy, an orientation for which he would soon have to pay a price.

First, however, it was the Senate's turn to pay. On the very day that Truman signed the NATO treaty, he presented the bill to Congress. All the assurances by administration witnesses before the Senate Foreign Relations Committee that the treaty would not inaugurate an arms race or cost the United States anything were brushed aside. Truman sent to the Congress a Mutual Defense Assistance Bill asking for $1.5 billion for European military aid. The President described the object in modest terms: "The military assistance which we propose for these countries will be limited to that which is necessary to help them create mobile defensive forces"; in other words, to equip and bring up to strength Europe's twelve or so divisions.

There was immediate opposition. Such a limited program would hardly give a "tangible assurance" to the peoples of Western Europe that they would be protected from the Red Army. Suspicious congressmen asked how long the program would last and how much it would cost. General Bradley gave a partial answer: "Our whole contention is that it is going to take time . . . it may take five years, ten years, for these countries to build up their defenses to the point where they can stop an aggressor." The Military Assistance Program of 1949 was, in short, only a small down-payment on a large, long-term investment. Senator Taft and other skeptics said this would never do, for the military assistance would be large enough only to provoke the Russians and precipitate an arms race without being adequate to halt the Red Army. Taft charged that the administration was committing the United States to a futile, obsolete, and bankrupt strategy of defending Europe by large-scale land warfare. He much preferred a unilateral American defense of Europe through building up the American Air Force and stepping up the production of atomic bombs.

This got to the heart of the matter, for despite all the intricate committee systems NATO eventually created to handle the multinational forces-in-being, and despite all the "goals" for ground strength NATO commanders continued to put forward, in point of fact the meaning of NATO was that the United States promised to use the bomb to deter a Russian attack. Bradley and most Navy officers doubted that such a strategy was realistic. They argued that if the Soviets wanted West Europe badly enough, they would march and accept the fairly limited damage the atomic bombs of that time could render. They were outvoted, however, for the good reason that if they were right the only alternative was to build up Western ground strength to match the Red Army, a politically impossible task.

The United States' promise to use the bomb to deter Russian aggression made sense only if the Americans had bases in Europe from which to deliver the bombs and if the Americans retained their monopoly. The great need was bases for the American bombers, which was the first and most important accomplishment of NATO. As Osgood wrote, "The United States backed up its guarantee to come to the defense of Europe by, in effect, extending the protective umbrella of the Strategic Air Command with the atomic bomb. In return, Europe provided the bases that the United States needed in order to strike effectively at the heart of Russia." This, however, could have been accomplished through bilateral agreements and did not require a multinational treaty; it also did not require military aid to the NATO countries. Opposition to Truman's military assistance program continued.

Then, on 22 September 1949, Truman announced that the Soviets had exploded an atomic bomb. "This is now a different world," Vandenberg painfully recorded. It was indeed. The urge to do something, anything, was irrepressible. Six days later Congress sent the NATO appropriations to the President for his approval. Truman ordered the development of the hydrogen bomb accelerated. Nothing, however, could change the fact that America's promise to defend Europe with the bomb had been dissipated almost before it had been given. If the Russians could make the bomb, they surely could develop the means to deliver it, first to Western European targets and then to the United States itself. The Soviets now had two trumps, the bomb and the Red Army, to the West's one. . . .

On 30 January 1950, Truman had authorized the State and Defense Departments "to make an overall review and reassessment of American foreign and defense policy in the light of the loss of China, the Soviet mastery of atomic energy and the prospect of the fusion bomb." Through February, March, and early April, as events whirled around it, a State-Defense committee met. By 12 April it had a report ready, which Truman sent to the National Security Council. It came back as an NSC paper, number 68; it was, as Walter LaFeber says, "one of the key historical documents of the Cold War." NSC 68, Senator Henry Jackson declared, was "the first comprehensive statement of a national strategy."

NSC 68 began by listing the four alternatives of American policy as: (1) continuation of the present course of action without strengthening American capabilities or reducing American commitments; (2) preventive war; (3) withdrawal to the Western Hemisphere, a Fortress America policy; and (4) the development of free-world military capabilities. In the light of the Russian bomb, the Communist victory in China, and McCarthy, the first was not a viable alternative; the second was probably beyond American capacities and in any case would have meant the sacrifice of West Europe to the Red Army; the third had no appeal whatsoever to the leading figures in the administration. The fourth alternative was the only logical choice.

As one of the principal authors stated, NSC 68 advocated "an immediate and large-scale buildup in our military and general strength and that of our allies with the intention of righting the power balance and in the hope that through means other than all-out war we could induce a change in the nature of the Soviet system." The statement became the basis for American foreign policy over the next twenty years. How the change was to be brought about was unclear, except that it would not be through war. NSC 68 postulated that while the West waited for the Soviets to mellow, the United States should rearm and thereby prevent any Russian expansion. The program did not look to the liberation of China or of Eastern Europe, but it did call on the United States to assume unilaterally the defense of the non-Communist world.

NSC 68 represented the practical extension of the Truman Doctrine, which had been world-wide in its implications but limited to Europe in its application. The document provided the justification for America's assuming the role of world policeman. It did so on the basis of an analysis of the Soviet Union shared by the top officials in State, Defense, and the NSC, which held that the Soviets were dedicated not only to preserving their own power and ideology but to extending and consolidating power by absorbing new satellites and weakening any "competing system of power." Implicit in the analysis was the idea that whenever the West lost a position of strength, whether it be a military base or a colony undergoing a war of national liberation, the Kremlin or the Chinese Communists, or both, were behind it. This came close to saying that all change was directed by the Communists and should be resisted. The analysis also assumed that if America were willing to try, it could stop change. This was satisfying to the McCarthyites, but the willingness to abandon East Europe, China, and Russia to communism was not. The McCarthyites, however, had no very clear idea on how to liberate the enslaved peoples either.

If the assumptions of NSC 68 were granted, it seemed to be a rational statement of international goals. A rearmed America would turn back the Communists whenever and wherever they tried to thrust outward. The concept of unlimited American power guided policy makers through the fifties and sixties; it was called into serious question only with American failures in South Vietnam. The concept of an international Communist conspiracy directing all social and political change in the world always had its critics, especially in the American intellectual and liberal communities, but even at the height of the Vietnamese struggle the Secretary of State could maintain that the historic, complex civil war raging there was the result of Communist China's machinations. And not even bloodshed along the Russo-Chinese frontier could convince some Americans that the monolithic Communist bloc was a thing of the past. At the beginning of the seventies, millions of Americans still accepted the basic assumptions of NSC 68.

NSC 68 was realistic in assessing what it would cost America to become the world policeman. The Joint Chiefs' representative on the State-Defense committee that drew up the program had come to the meetings believing that the most money that could be gotten from Congress was around $17 billion a year. He quickly learned that the State representatives were thinking in much bigger terms, and he adjusted. In the end, although NSC 68 did not include any specific figures, the State Department officials estimated that defense expenditures of $35 billion a year would be required to implement the program of rearming America and NATO. Eventually, more could be spent, for NSC 68 declared that the United States was so rich it could use 20 percent of its gross national product for arms without suffering national bankruptcy. In 1950, this would have been $50 billion.

That was a great deal of money, even for Americans. It was necessary, however, because the danger was so great. The document foresaw "an indefinite period of tension and danger" and warned that by 1954 the Soviet Union would have the nuclear capability to destroy the United States. America had to undertake "a bold and massive program" of rebuilding the West until it far surpassed the Soviet bloc; only thus could it stand at the "political and material center with other free nations in variable orbits around it." The United States could no longer ask, "How much security can we afford?" nor should it attempt to "distinguish between national and global security."

Truman recognized, as he later wrote, the NSC 68 "meant a great military effort in time of peace. It meant doubling or tripling the budget, increasing taxes heavily, and imposing various kinds of economic controls. It meant a great change in our normal peacetime way of doing things." He refused to allow publication of NSC 68 and indicated that he would do nothing about revising the budget until after the congressional elections. He realized that without a major crisis there was little chance of selling the program to the Congress or the public. He himself had only two and a half years to serve, while NSC 68 contemplated a long-term program. If the Republicans entered the White House, the chances were that their main concern would be to lower the budget, in which case the nation would have to wait for the return of the Democrats to really get NSC 68 rolling. Thus when Truman received NSC 68 in its final form in early June 1950 he made no commitment. What he would have done with it had not other events intruded is problematical.

While Truman was studying the paper, he may have noted a sentence that declared it should be American policy to meet "each fresh challenge promptly and unequivocally." If so, he was about to have an opportunity to put it into practice. The crisis that would allow him to implement NSC 68 was at hand.

*Norman A. Graebner*

# THE EXTENSION OF THE COLD WAR TO ASIA

*The Cold War originated in Europe and was later thrust upon developing nations in Latin America, Africa, and Asia. Norman A. Graebner of the University of Virginia accounts for the transfer to Asia of ideas formed in the European context, especially after the rise of the People's Republic of China in 1949. Ignoring complexities, Americans interpreted Mao Tse-tung's Communist government as an appendage of Soviet foreign policy. Similarly, the civil war in Indochina (Vietnam) and nationalist leader Ho Chi Minh were viewed as part of an international Communist plan. Indeed, the containment doctrine had become global, presenting the United States with some serious foreign policy dilemmas. Graebner's works include* Ideas and Diplomacy *(1964),* Cold War Diplomacy, 1945–1960 *(1962), and* The New Isolationism *(1956).*

From Norman A. Graebner, "Global Containment: The Truman Years," *Current His-*

# Asia After World War II

GREECE
Crete
Ankara
TURKEY
Cyprus
BLACK SEA
CAUCASUS
MEDITERRANEAN SEA
Tel Aviv
Cairo
ISRAEL
LEB.
SYRIA
JORDAN
Suez Canal
EGYPT
Nile
Baghdad
IRAQ
KUWAIT
SAUDI ARABIA
Riyadh
RED SEA
SUDAN
YEMEN
ETHIOPIA
Addis Ababa
BR. SOMALILAND
SOMALILAND
ADEN
Persian Gulf
OMAN

Volga R.
SOVIET UNION (U.S.S.R.)
Omsk
Ob R.
CASPIAN SEA
Baku
Tabriz
Teheran
IRAN
ARABIAN SEA
Tashkent
AFGHANISTAN
Kabul
PAKISTAN
Karachi
Bombay
New Delhi
INDIA
Madras
Ganges R.
Calcutta
Ceylon
INDIAN OCEAN

Scale of Miles
0   300   600   900

Ulan Bator
MONGOLIA
SINKIANG
TIBET
NEPAL
BHUTAN
KASHMIR
PAKISTAN
Dacca
CHINA
Yenan
Chungking
Yangtze R.
BURMA
Rangoon
BAY OF BENGAL
Mekong R.
THAILAND
Bangkok
LAOS
Hanoi
VIETNAM
CAMBODIA
Phnom Penh
Saigon
MALAYA
Kuala Lumpur
Singapore
Sumatra
INDONESIA
Java
Djakarta
Borneo

MANCHURIA
Vladivostok
Mukden
Peking
Pyongyang
Seoul
KOREA 38th parallel
Pusan
SEA OF JAPAN
Hokkaido
Honshu
Tokyo
JAPAN
Hiroshima
Nagasaki
Kyushu
Okinawa
Nanking
Shanghai
Hangchow
Foochow
Canton
Hong Kong
Taipei
Formosa (Taiwan)
SOUTH CHINA SEA
Luzon
Manila
PHILIPPINES
Mindanao
Celebes
Caroline Islands
New Guinea
AUSTRALIA
PACIFIC OCEAN

United States involvements in East Asia during the immediate post-war years, extensive as they were, had not brought the United States into any direct conflict with Soviet purpose. The Truman Doctrine of March, 1947, had announced a sweeping United States commitment to intervene everywhere in the world where governments might be threatened by communism regardless of the security interests involved or the prospects of success for any American effort. In practice, however, the Truman Doctrine had been limited to Greece and Turkey, and Secretary of State George C. Marshall had pointedly refused in 1948 to extend it to China. The emerging Cold War, whatever its demands on American emotions and resources, remained a European phenomenon.

Perhaps the comparative complacency with which Americans viewed the Far East was natural enough. For two long generations Japan had been the major, if not the exclusive, threat to a balanced and stable Orient. But the Japan of the late 1940s was an occupied nation, its military power broken. The continuing collapse of European colonialism in South and Southeast Asia threatened that region's historic stability.

But, nevertheless, to Americans generally even the Communist-led revolution in Indochina represented the ideal of self-determination far better than did French colonial policy. No aggressor had appeared anywhere on the scene to challenge the independence of the new Asian states, whatever their internal weakness.

China was the critical problem of the Far East. But even as Chiang Kai-shek slowly went down before Mao Tse-tung and his Chinese Communists in 1948 and 1949, the United States government did not recognize in this transferal of power in China any threat of aggression or danger to the United States. Indeed, until 1949 the United States did not reject the possibility of establishing normal and satisfactory relations with the new regime. To the extent that numerous Americans and potential critics of United States policy anticipated the Communist victory in China with deep regret, they regarded the new leadership as dangerous to Chinese traditions and to China's historic relations with the United States. They feared above all that Mao might slam shut the Open Door and thus deprive American

*tory* 57 (August 1969): 77–83, 115–16. Reprinted by permission of *Current History* and the author.

scholars, missionaries, travelers, officials and merchants of their former access to a country which was for them a region of immense charm. But even for the friends of China and of Chiang the closing of the Open Door and the subsequent mistreatment of American officials in China were not necessarily indications of Mao's aggressive intent toward China's neighbors. Communist influence and behavior in China might be tragic but did not automatically comprise a threat to United States security interests.

Still, there existed in 1949 a marked ambivalence in American attitudes toward the impending retreat of Chiang Kai-shek to the Island of Formosa. Some Americans recalled Lenin's blueprint for Russian expansion: "First we will take Eastern Europe, then the masses of Asia. Then we will surround America, the last citadel of capitalism." The Western world could not ignore the fact that soon 900 million people would be living under Communist-led governments. Indeed, with the collapse of Nationalist China late in 1949, the United States entered a period of deep intellectual crisis. What mattered during these critical months of decision was the role which American officials, editors and political leaders—the creators of public opinion—chose to assign to the USSR in the triumph of Communist power in China. The State Department's White Paper on China, published in August, 1949, publicly viewed the impending Communist victory in China as a legitimate expression of popular approval and thus no real challenge to Asian stability. But what had once appeared indigenous was beginning to loom as possibly the initial triumph of Soviet aggression as it moved into the Asian sphere.

After mid-1949, United States officials were no longer ruling out the possibility that China was being induced "to accept a disguised form of foreign rule"—as George F. Kennan expressed it in a radio program. Even in the China White Paper the new secretary of state, Dean Acheson, had called attention to the danger of Soviet imperialism in the Far East and reaffirmed United States opposition

> to the subjugation of China by any foreign power, to any regime acting in the interest of a foreign power, and to the dismemberment of China by any foreign power, whether by open or clandestine means.....

That the Chinese had indeed become puppets of the Soviet Politburo appeared to pass beyond any shadow of doubt when, in February, 1950, the world read the terms of the new Sino-Soviet Treaty of Friendship, Alliance and Mutual Assistance. By its terms the Soviets promised China considerable financial and technical aid. Acheson admitted that the Chinese people might welcome such promises but, he added,

> they will not fail, in time, to see where they fall short of China's real needs and desires. And they will wonder about the points upon which the agreements remain silent.

Acheson warned the Chinese that, whatever China's internal development, they would bring grave trouble on themselves and the rest of Asia "if they are led by their new rulers into aggressive or subversive adventures beyond their borders."

The concept of a single conspiracy, global in its pretensions and centering in Moscow, had not won universal acceptance. Indeed, many American scholars at mid-century rejected the notion completely. Journalist Walter Lippmann, speaking before the Chicago Council on Foreign Relations on February 22, 1950, reminded his audience:

> While it is true that we have lost our power and for the time being most of our influence in China, it by no means follows that Russia has won control of China or has achieved an enduring alliance with China.

Most writers on Far Eastern subjects agreed with Acheson's warning of January that the United States should not introduce the use of military force into Asia. But the final Communist victory in China, added to the interpretation of the Sino-Soviet Pact which official Washington ascribed to it, propelled the administration logically toward the extension of the containment principle to include the Far East. By March, 1950, the Chinese revolution alone seemed sufficient to demonstrate Soviet expansionist tendencies toward Asia.

\*       \*       \*

Much of the fear of further Soviet aggression eventually centered on Indochina where the French, as late as 1949, continued the struggle for their Asian empire against the determined opposition of Vietnamese nationalist Ho Chi Minh. At one time the United States had supported Ho and as late as 1949 it had revealed no official interest in his defeat. Within the context of global containment, however, the fact that Ho was a Marxist and Moscow-trained made him sufficiently suspect as an agent of Soviet imperialism to bring the full weight of United States policy against him. What embarrassed United States containment policy in Indochina at mid-century was the French reluctance to grant the region its independence.

The French promised independence for Indochina in the Elysée Agreements of March, 1949. In June, the State Department welcomed the creation of the new state of Vietnam and expressed the hope that the March agreements would "form the basis for the progressive realization of the legitimate aspirations of the Vietnamese people." The United States accepted the new Vietnamese leader, Bao Dai, with enthusiasm as the nationalist answer to Ho Chi Minh. Meanwhile the French, conscious of the growing United States fear of Soviet expansion into Asia, insisted that they were fighting for Western security in the Far East and therefore deserved United States military aid. Only the refusal of the French National Assembly to ratify the Elysée Agreements stalled the French request for United States military support in Asia in late 1949.

The events of January and February, 1950, finally rendered Ho Chi Minh a mortal enemy of the United States. On January 14, to meet the challenge of Bao Dai and French policy, Ho declared the establishment of the Democratic Republic of Vietnam, under his control, as the only lawful government representative of the Vietnamese people. At the same time Ho announced that his country would

> consolidate her friendly relations with the Soviet Union, China and other People's Democracies, actively to support the national liberation movements of colonial and semicolonial countries. . . .

Before the end of the month both China and the USSR had recognized the Democratic Republic. In a press release, Acheson declared that this

> should remove any illusion as to the "nationalist" character of Ho Chi Minh's aims and reveals Ho in his true colors as the mortal enemy of native independence in Indochina.

Eventually, the French Assembly ratified the agreements which established the new state of Vietnam, the kingdom of Laos and the kingdom of Cambodia as independent states within the French Union. On February 6, 1950, Ambassador Jessup declared in Singapore that the United States would view any armed Communist aggression against the new states of Indochina as a matter of grave concern. On the following day, the United States and Great Britain extended de jure recognition to the three Associated States of Laos, Vietnam and Cambodia, and sent a note of congratulations to Bao Dai, the chief of the new Vietnam state. The notion that Bao Dai had better claims to Vietnamese leadership than Ho and that he would ultimately triumph became official doctrine in Washington. Loy Henderson expressed it well when he said

> *The United States is convinced that the Bao Dai government of Vietnam reflects more accurately than any rival claimants to power in Vietnam the nationalist aspirations of the people of that country. It hopes by its policies with regard to Vietnam, to contribute to the peaceful progress of Vietnamese people toward the realization of the fruits of self-government. . . . My government is convinced that any movement headed by a Moscow-recognized Communist such as Ho Chi Minh must be in the direction of subservience to a foreign state, not in that of independence and self-government.*

Still the United States faced a dilemma in Indochina which belied its stated faith in either Bao Dai or the French. To give military aid to the French would lend additional credence to the charge that United States policy in Asia was primarily military and strategic with little or no genuine concern for the political advancement of the Vietnamese people. To channel aid to the government in Saigon, with Bao Dai spending his time at Dalat far removed from the activities of his government, gave no promise of effective utilization at all. Finally on May 8, 1950, Acheson, with French Foreign Minister Robert Schuman, negotiated an arrangement whereby France and the governments of Indochina together would carry the responsibility for Indochinese security and development. United States aid would simply contribute to that objective.

Again the motives of containment were clear.

> *The United States government [wrote Acheson] convinced that neither national independence nor democratic evolution exists in any area dominated by Soviet imperialism, considers the situation to be such as to warrant its according economic aid and military equipment to the Associated*

*States of Indochina and to France in order to assist them in restoring stability and permitting these states to pursue their peaceful and democratic development.*

In his request to Congress for military assistance funds in June, President Truman acknowledged the nation's determination "to preserve the freedom and integrity of Indochina from the Communist forces of Ho Chi Minh." In December, 1950, the United States signed a Mutual Defense Assistance Agreement with France, Vietnam, Cambodia and Laos for indirect United States military aid to the three states of Indochina.

\*        \*        \*

With the outbreak of the Korean War, Washington officials pushed United States rearmament in Europe and Asia with a greater sense of urgency under the assumption that the non-Soviet world had entered a period of great peril and had only a short time to prepare before the enemy reached the peak of its power. In the President's budget message of 1951, military aid became an established policy of the United States. The first Mutual Security Act, adopted that year, implied that thereafter economic aid would be used primarily to expand the military base of the recipient countries.

During 1952, military assistance to Asia grew in importance relative to Europe. The bulk of the military aid channeled into Asia went to four countries regarded as especially vulnerable to Soviet-Chinese aggression: the Republic of China on Formosa, the Republic of Korea, the Republic of Vietnam and Japan. In Korea, the United States supported one of the largest non-Communist armies in the world at a cost of almost $1 billion per year. In Indochina, the United States eventually underwrote 80 percent of the financial cost of the French effort.

That the globalization of containment would produce diminishing returns was evident even as the policy unfolded. Containment in Europe had promised success because the threat was purely military —the danger of a Red Army marching westward. The region guaranteed by NATO, moreover, comprised the seat of an ancient civilization with a tradition of political, economic and military efficiency. In Asia and the Middle East, the danger was less that of marching armies than of guerrilla warfare and subversion. This reduced containment to a matter of political, not military, effectiveness. For no government that failed to establish a broad governing base would long remain in power whatever moral and physical support it received from the United States.

Even as a venture in power, containment in Asia was prejudiced from the start. Unlike the nations of Europe, the Asian nations lacked the skilled manpower and industrial bases to develop self-sustaining military strength. Whereas the military structures of such countries would never be strong enough to resist aggression, they would always exceed in cost what the Asian economies could support. Thus they threatened the United States with an endless financial drain without contributing much useful defense.

It was essentially the absence of political stability that rendered the borderlands along the Asian periphery of Russia and China an unfortunate area in which to establish the barriers against Communist expansion. Such an effort at containment, warned Walter Lippmann in *The Cold War* (1947), would compel the United States to stake its policies

> upon satellites, puppets, clients, agents about whom we know very little. Frequently they will act . . . on their own judgments, presenting us with accomplished facts that we did not intend, and with crises for which we are unready. The "unassailable barriers" will present us with an unending series of insoluble dilemmas. We shall have either to disown our puppets, which would be tantamount to appeasement and defeat and the loss of face, or must support them at an incalculable cost on an unintended, unforeseen and perhaps undesirable issue.

From such dilemmas there would be no escape, for through the critical years of 1949 to 1951 United States officials had created an image of Asia which would not die, an image calculated to introduce the element of fear on a massive scale into the American conceptualization of the challenges which the United States faced. Global containment, responding to the challenge of an insatiable Soviet-based Communist monolith, elevated every Communist-led maneuver to first-level importance even where United States security interests were unclear and strategic conditions unfavorable. The policy would ultimately exact its toll in costly military involvements and a deeply divided nation.

*Athan Theoharis*

# THE ROAD TO McCARTHYISM: TRUMAN'S ANTI-COMMUNIST RHETORIC

*In 1950, Senator Joseph McCarthy charged that the Truman administration's foreign policy had been greatly influenced by Communists in high government places. Many historians date McCarthyism (1950–54) from that time and explain it as a cumulative but exaggerated reaction to reprehensible Soviet behavior or as the handiwork of an extremely ambitious politician with a conspiratorial mind. Athan Theoharis of Marquette University does not think it is that simple. He argues that Truman's intensification of the Cold War and his alarmist anti-Communist rhetoric in the 1945–50 period prepared the way for McCarthyism. Both Truman and the McCarthyites were militant anti-Communists who differed in means and emphasis but not in their common goal of a victory over communism. McCarthyites perceived an internal Communist threat, whereas Truman thought it external, although he himself initiated a federal employee loyalty program in March 1947, the same month he launched the Truman Doctrine. By 1950 Truman's policies could not deliver what his rhetoric had promised: victory in the Cold War. Truman was caught in his own rhetorical trap, and McCarthy and his followers easily exploited the president's loss of credibility. Importantly for the Cold War, Theoharis concludes, Truman distorted Soviet motives, cast the struggle in simple moral terms, placed undue emphasis on military might, and foreclosed rational discussion of policy alternatives. Theoharis is the author of* Seeds of Repression *(1971), from which this selection is taken, and* The Yalta Myths: An Issue in U.S. Politics, 1945–1955 *(1970).*

Ascribing the nation's problems (both domestic and international) to the existence of "Communists in government," McCarthyites simultaneously stimulated and derived support from the popular belief that national security was truly being threatened—and would continue to be threatened—unless a more resourceful approach than the Truman administration's was adopted. Indeed, by 1950 many Americans had come to believe that: (1) the Soviet Union had a definite strategy for the eventual communization of the world; (2) Soviet actions directly threatened the security of the United States; (3) that threat could assume the form of direct aggression or internal sub-version; (4) the basic impetus to any revolutionary or radical political change was a Moscow-directed Communist conspiracy; (5) superior military power was essential to achieving peace and security; (6) a diplomacy of compromise and concession was in effect a form of appeasement and betrayal; (7) American objectives were altruistic and humanitarian; (8) the United States—because omnipotent—could shape the world to conform to American ideals and principles; (9) the God-fearing United States had to triumph over godless communism; (10) international options were clear-cut and definable in terms of good versus evil; (11) the U.S. confrontation with the Soviet Union demanded not only the containment of Soviet expansion but the liberation of "enslaved peoples"; and (12) Communist leaders, whether in the Soviet Union, Eastern Europe, or China, lacked a popular base of support and were thus able to remain in power only through terror and subversion.

By 1950 these beliefs had strengthened popular demands for vic-tory over communism at home and abroad. Many Americans also believed that foreign policy could not be effective unless Communist infiltration of the government was prevented by a strong internal se-curity program. Thus the themes of "Communists in government" and "softness toward communism," though they reflected different concerns and fears, were directly linked in the public mind: victory abroad could not be secured without victory at home; a dynamic foreign policy necessitated a rigorous internal-security program.

Popular fears about threats to American national security were far indeed from being endemic in the United States at the end of World War II. In 1945, according to opinion polls, most Americans believed that a durable peace required the continuation of Allied cooperation; thus they welcomed the Yalta Conference as a means of achieving that objective. Majority opinion supported Roosevelt's efforts to promote mutual trust and understanding with the Soviet Union; it recognized the necessity for compromise and appreciated the in-evitable differences in purposes between the "democracies" of the United States, the Soviet Union, and Great Britain. In 1945 most Amer-icans considered the Soviet Union to be not the antichrist but a great power having legitimate security aims which sometimes con-flicted with those of the United States. Most differences between the United States and the Soviet Union were considered resolvable through international conferences—particularly conferences involving the Big Three—and required diplomatic compromise, not military confrontation.

In line with these views, a popular distrust of the military prevailed. This distrust was reflected in support for limiting the role of the military in the control and development of atomic energy. demands for immediate demobilization of troops, and opposition to peacetime conscription. While appreciating the limits of American military power, many citizens also recognized the important role that anti-Nazi resistance forces and British and Soviet troops had played in the ultimate Allied victory over the Axis powers.

In short, majority opinion in America believed in neither the omniscience nor the omnipotence of the United States; peace and security depended on continued American cooperation with other nations, whether major or minor powers. Finally, most Americans demanded that the administration pursue an internationalist foreign policy—multilaterally rather than unilaterally run. They considered economic problems the basis of threats to world peace, and felt that these could be settled through aid and negotiation.

By 1950 a dramatic shift in this outlook had taken place, and it contributed to the emergence of McCarthyism. It was a reaction that differed considerably from the conservative reaction following World War I. The earlier Red Scare had been a direct product of the passions and fears wrought by American involvement in the war, and represented a distinct domestic political conservatism. In contrast, McCarthyism was not directly a product of the war, since it appeared not in 1945 but in 1950, nor was its thrust overtly anti-progressive. Instead it was the product of the Cold War confrontation between the United States and the Soviet Union and the resulting obsession on the part of Americans with national security. Because this confrontation was viewed not in terms of power politics but in distinctly moralistic terms, it led to no less than an oversimplified belief in the possibility of, indeed demand for, victory over the Soviet antichrist.

This change in national opinion was in great part shaped by the rhetoric of the Truman administration. In the period 1945–1949—that is, before Senator McCarthy's Wheeling speech—the Truman administration conducted foreign policy debate along narrowly anti-Communist lines. To secure support for its containment policy, from

1947 through 1949 administration rhetoric vastly oversimplified the choices confronting the nation; it also characterized international change in terms of crisis and national security. Indeed, the administration's anti-Communist rhetoric, the thrust of its appeals both before and after McCarthy's Wheeling speech, did not differ substantively from that of McCarthy and his conservative congressional supporters.

After 1945 the Truman administration had gradually, yet distinctly, renounced the priorities of the Roosevelt administration. The bases for this shift are to be found in two dominant strains of Truman's thought: a deep distrust of Soviet objectives, and a belief in the importance of military superiority. In contrast to Roosevelt's sophisticated international approach, which relied on negotiation and détente, Truman's outlook—an outlook shaped by his World War I experience, his active participation in the American Legion, and his antipathy to the isolationism and antimilitarism of the 1930s—was based on the primacy of power in international politics. Although an avowed internationalist and advocate of peace, Truman believed that peace could best be secured through military deterrence and alliances. Unlike Roosevelt, whose distrust of the Soviet Union was mitigated by an expediential wartime alliance and an appreciation that Soviet involvement in Eastern Europe was as legitimate a security objective as United States involvement in Latin America, Truman felt that Soviet expansion merely confirmed the Soviet leaders' perfidy and imperialistic intentions, and thus must be averted.

Accordingly, Truman's "internationalism" assumed a unilateral form in which American national interests became the sole foundation for cooperation and peace. More importantly, in 1945, and increasingly after 1948, the administration tended to subordinate traditional diplomatic or economic options to its overriding commitment to attaining superior military power. In contrast to Roosevelt's view that disagreement, even conflict, between the United States and the Soviet Union was inevitable—and possibly even salutary, insuring a diverse world order—Truman made his administration's long-term goal the achievement of "freedom" and "democracy" for the peoples of Eastern Europe, the Soviet Union, China, and the underdeveloped world. He characterized the U.S.-Soviet conflict in moralistic terms, seeing America's role as a "mission," and redefining "appeasement" to mean the failure of the United States to confront revolutionary or disruptive change head on. A sense of American omnipotence, the belief that the United States could impose its will on the postwar world, was behind the Truman administration's rhetoric on foreign policy.

Yet this shift away from Roosevelt's foreign policy developed gradually. The 1952 priorities of the Truman administration differed radically from its 1945 priorities. This shift resulted in part from Soviet actions in Eastern Europe and the United Nations, in part from the administration's reassessment of basic foreign policy questions. What would have been politically feasible in 1945 had become politically impossible by 1952, for by then the administration, trapped in its own rhetoric, could no longer even suggest that any Soviet interest in peace or negotiation was valid.....

By 1949 Truman disparaged any suggestion of further summit diplomacy or indeed compromise on U.S.-Soviet differences. He contended that to engage in either would be to ignore international realities. In order for such negotiations tangibly to minimize U.S.-Soviet differences, Truman claimed, the United States would have to "give" Berlin, Korea, Germany, Japan, and East Asia to the Russians. On the other hand, he confidently predicted that the administration's confrontation approach (which he described as a "war of nerves"), relying on military strength and refusing concessions in the interest simply of reaching agreement, would finally result in "surrender" and peace. He would "raise the Iron Curtain by peaceful means." During the early 1950s Truman continued to oppose convening a conference to work out U.S.-Soviet differences or initiate discussions on disarmament by again impugning Soviet objectives; he added that the timing for such a conference was not propitious. A significant solution could be reached, he maintained, only through the deterrent force of superior American power, which had not yet been attained, and the Soviet Union's realization that her aggressive aims could not be achieved.

By 1950 the thrust of administration rhetoric expressed the need to confront the Communist threat directly; it depicted the Soviet-American conflict in moralistic terms, refusing to concede either the legitimacy of Soviet objectives or the self-seeking strategy of American ones. While the administration justified the American military build-up as self-defense, it deplored the Soviet build-up as aggressive and belligerent. It criticized Stalin's efforts to extend the

Soviet sphere of influence in Asia and Europe, but it proclaimed that such American efforts as lifting "the Iron Curtain by peaceful means" or protesting the Yugoslavian government's failure to adhere to American constitutional guarantees in its judicial proceedings were purely disinterested, noninterventionist, and internationalist. The effect of this rhetoric was cumulative; by the late 1940s the administration had managed to circumvent popular aversion to the confrontation course, which was essentially one of relying on military strength to limit Soviet influence. More importantly, by successfully discrediting the value of negotiations, the possibility of a rational discussion of policy alternatives was foreclosed. . . .

Although the basis for Truman's 1947 remarks had been the State Department's recommended economic approach to foreign affairs, by mid-1948 the administration was stressing the need for a more effective military policy in Europe. Lumping together the recent coup in Czechoslovakia, Soviet pressure on the Finnish government, civil war in Greece, and the real chance of a Communist electoral victory in Italy, Truman charged that the Soviet Union and "its agents" were committed to destroying the freedom and independence of those countries. While conceding that the economic recovery of Europe had to be assured, Truman further argued that the European states should also be provided with the means of protecting themselves against both internal and external aggression. Specifically, he praised and expressed full U.S. support for the Brussels Pact, which he believed thoroughly consistent with the principles of the United Nations Charter and the cause of world peace.

At the same time, the administration renewed its efforts to secure congressional enactment of universal military training. Its spokesmen persistently emphasized the gravity of the world crisis, the necessity for "immediate" action, and the propriety of a policy that relied on military strength. Peace, Truman argued, could best be secured through superior military strength; he disparaged both traditional diplomacy and the historic American opposition to a strong military. . . .

In a St. Patrick's Day address in 1948, Truman openly identified the Soviet Union as the primary source of potential aggression in the contemporary world. In so doing he established an essentially bipolar framework for international politics. Soviet "agents," Truman argued, were fighting in Greece, working to subvert the freedom of

Italy, and attempting to undermine domestic support for a strong American defense program. Those who opposed that program, he said, were deceiving the public and weakening the country. He then went on to contrast the false, atheistic doctrine of Communist progress with the morally upright nature of American defense policy:

> *The United States has become the principal protector of the free world.*
> *To carry out that responsibility we must maintain our strength—military, economic and moral. . . .*
> *We must beware of those who are devoting themselves to sowing the seeds of disunity among our people. . . .*
> *We must not fall victim to the insidious propaganda that peace can be obtained solely by wanting peace. This theory is advanced in the hope that it will deceive our people and that we will permit our strength to dwindle because of the false belief that all is well in the world. . . .*
> *We must not be confused about the issue which confronts the world today. . . . It is tyranny and freedom. . . .*
> *And even worse, communism denies the very existence of God. Religion is persecuted because it stands for freedom under God. This threat to our liberty and to our faith must be faced by each of us. . . .*

In the end, the oversimplified moralism of this rhetoric was to effectively reduce the administration's own political maneuverability. If confrontation was the only means to fulfill a holy mission, and if, in addition, the nation's major adversary was wholly evil, then to compromise or counsel restraint was not merely immoral but impolitic. Since only a loss of faith, a weakness of purpose, or a lack of vision could impede America's attaining victory, and since the Soviet threat was represented as being essentially subversive and not the result of international strategic realities, Truman's rhetoric buttressed a popular belief in American omnipotence. If it chose, or so the thread of this rhetoric ran, the United States could impose its principles on the world. This being the case, the country's main problem was less the Soviet Union than the will, purpose, and wisdom of the American people and their government. . . .

To first contain Communist expansion and then to overturn Communist domination—these, rhetorically at least, had by 1950 become administration goals. They called for a dual policy of eternal vigilance and superior military strength. Whether championing a large, well-equipped standing army, an improved nuclear technology, an increase in foreign aid—military, technical, or economic—or a greater awareness of the Soviet threat, the administration continually raised both themes. Simultaneously, it sought to represent any negotiations with the Soviet Union as potentially harmful. Negotiations would be desirable, Truman declared, only when the leaders of the Kremlin were convinced that the West would not succumb and when Communist societies were reformed along the lines of Western Christian democracy.

By 1950 this playing off of a crisis atmosphere against a confident optimism about U.S. power had made the American public distinctly anxious. Prodded by administration rhetoric, popular demands for the maximum use of military power against the Russians had increased: America had to *win* over communism. The administration meanwhile sought to undercut every plea for restraint. As much as any other cause, administration rhetoric set the tone of the policy debate over the Korean War.

The North Korean invasion of South Korea created a true political crisis for the Truman administration. It had to enlist popular support for a distant, costly, and seemingly minor conflict and at the same time take care not to provoke the Soviet Union into escalating that conflict into a world war. Since these two objectives were almost diametrically opposed, certain glaring inconsistencies began to appear in administration rhetoric. Thus, while the president on the one hand declared that the "gravity" of the situation required a forthright American military commitment, on the other hand he counseled a limited use of American military resources. While administration rhetoric might emphasize the importance of the Korean conflict by portraying it in moralistic (Holy Crusade) or strategic (domino theory) terms, administration actions reflected a real appreciation of Soviet interests and the limits to American power.

The continuance of the Korean War heightened popular anxieties that Korea was merely the prelude to future, much larger military confrontations with Russia. Seeking to explain the outbreak of the war in terms of its earlier assurances that containment would ensure an effective peace, the administration only intensified these anxieties. This tack failing, the administration next categorically denied that it had failed to deter aggression. Truman now declared that North Korea's attack confirmed the success of his administration's past policies. The Russians' earlier subversive efforts had indeed been frustrated by American economic aid. Truman explained: "The attack upon Korea makes it plain beyond all doubt that communism has passed beyond the use of subversion to conquer independent nations and will now use armed invasion and war."

America responded in kind. Since, as Truman argued, the North Korean attack amounted to a clear-cut act of aggression, one which posed the threat of a third world war, a forceful demonstration of American power was essential to deter any further Soviet armed moves. To demonstrate America's resolve, the administration instituted a series of far-reaching commitments: it assigned American ground troops to South Korea, strengthened American forces in the Philippines, dispatched the Seventh Fleet to Formosa, and provided military assistance to both the Philippine Army and French forces in Indochina. In related moves, the administration sought increased congressional appropriations for the Atomic Energy Commission and military aid to Greece, Turkey, and Iran. It also pressed for congressional approval of a military aid program to establish a well-equipped standing army in Western Europe; this program included West German rearmament and the deployment of American troops in Europe. As evidenced by a December 1, 1950, presidential request for additional defense appropriations from Congress, all these military movements and appropriations requests were made in crisis-laden, moralistic terms.

> The gravity of the world situation requires that these funds be made available with the utmost speed.
> ... These funds are needed to support our part in the United Nations military action in Korea, and to increase the size and readiness of our armed forces should action become necessary in other parts of the world.
> ... The further expansion of our military forces and of our atomic energy enterprise are directed toward strengthening the defenses of the United States and of the entire free world. This expansion is a matter of great urgency, which can be understood and evaluated against the background of present critical world conditions.
> United States troops ... are fighting for freedom and against tyranny —for law and order and against brutal aggression. The attack of the North Korean Communists ..., if unchecked, would have blasted all hope of a just and lasting peace—for if open aggression had been unopposed in Korea, it would have been an invitation to aggression elsewhere. ...

By 1951 Truman's hotted-up rhetoric had caused a loss of credibility in his administration. On the one hand, the administration repeatedly emphasized the gravity of the crisis posed by Soviet subversion and expansionism and expressed confidence in eventual success if the American public only possessed the necessary will and purpose to carry out Truman's policies. All the while it continued to characterize the U.S.-Soviet opposition as a confrontation between American Christian selflessness and Communist atheistic expansionism. On the other hand, quite apart from the forcefulness of its rhetoric, the administration was actually pursuing a policy of restraint in its use of military power, conducting its military operations within firm strategic guidelines. In point of fact, American military potential, particularly nuclear weapons, was by no means fully utilized in Korea: the air war was limited to the Korean peninsula, and Chinese Nationalist troops were confined to Formosa. Nor did the administration use either potential military resources or diplomatic pressure to effect the liberation of the "satellite" peoples. The Chinese Nationalists were prevented from attempting to free the mainland Chinese; Eastern European exiles were neither encouraged nor supplied with weapons; and, despite Soviet violations, the administration opposed congressional efforts to repudiate the Yalta agreements.

These military and political restrictions were inconsistent with the total war against communism which the administration advertised in its rhetoric, and they were in direct contradiction to its projection of what would come about if Soviet subversion were not vigorously confronted. Indeed, if the Soviet threat was world-wide, if world peace and the very liberties of the American people were ultimately threatened by the Korean conflict—and the Truman administration had repeatedly said as much—then nothing less than the full use of American military might in Korea was required. Thus, to countenance military and political restraint, as Truman and his administration clearly did, seemed to be either a misunderstanding of the seriousness of the Communist threat to American security or a dereliction of duty. To argue that restraint was necessary to prevent the escalation of Korea into a world war seemed to reflect a staggering ignorance of the Soviet Union's basic intention—as Truman had time and again declared it to be—of utterly destroying Western Christian democracy.

The inconsistencies between the Truman administration's go-for-broke rhetoric and its cautious military response in Korea paved the way for the success of Joseph McCarthy and his followers. The moralistic and defensive tenor of administration rhetoric, its stress on the American "mission," its emphasis on national security, and its strained definition of Communist subversion—all served to create a climate in which such terms as "sell-out," "betrayal," "liberation," and "victory," could be successfully used by the McCarthyites against the Truman administration. By exploiting the inconsistencies between administration rhetoric and response, McCarthy and other congressional conservatives were able to "explain" that the real Soviet threat to the national security was internal subversion. They thereby capitalized on both fears of a third world war and doubts about the administration's methods and intentions in foreign affairs.

The McCarthyites never did, nor were they required to, formulate an alternative course to Truman's. Instead, because of the inconsistency between administration rhetoric and response, they were able to concentrate on criticizing past administration policy decisions and personnel. Because the administration had set an American peace as its rhetorical goal, the McCarthyites could blame the "failure" to achieve that peace on either the administration's ignorance of the threat of communism, or its lax security procedures which enabled Communists and their sympathizers to infiltrate the government and help bring about pro-Soviet policies. Although this critique was simplisitic, conspiratorial at its base, and rather sleazily moralistic, it nonetheless neatly used administration rhetoric to condemn administration policy. Through its own rhetoric, the Truman administration had closed the vicious circle on itself. All the McCarthyites had to do was chase around it.

"The Other Fellow Started it . . ." (From United Nations World, Vol. 1 [April 1947], p. 12)

# III The Root Causes: The Scholars Debate

*Arthur M. Schlesinger, Jr.*

# LENINIST IDEOLOGY AND
# STALINIST PARANOIA

*Historians have pointed to many root causes of the Cold War. Some argue that the United States and Russia were destined to collide because both tried to fill the European power vacuum left by the defeat of Germany. Others emphasize the "tradition" of great power rivalry and the shaky "structure" of international relations which invited conflict. Some scholars single out American capitalism, with its imperialist impulse, or an American ideology of expansion. Other root causes could include misperceptions by Americans and Russians of the other as an immoral aggressor ("mirror image"), the drawing of incorrect lessons from the past ("historical lessons"), the diplomatic "style" of a brutally blunt Stalin and a short-tempered, frank Truman, and the domestic political and economic imperatives in both countries which forced key decisions. Arthur M. Schlesinger, Jr., in the following essay, discovers the root causes of the Cold War in Stalin's excessive paranoia and the Russian's adherence to an uncompromising Leninist ideology. There was little the United States could have done to change the course of events. He concedes that Russia had major recovery problems and security fears and that American policy was sometimes rigid. But he places responsibility for postwar confrontation squarely in Moscow. Schlesinger also discusses the American "universalist" (as opposed to "sphere of influence") view of world order. Schlesinger has served in a number of academic and government posts and is the prolific author of award-winning studies of the Jacksonian and New Deal eras, as well as* A Thousand Days *(1965, on the John F. Kennedy years),* The Bitter Heritage *(1966, on Vietnam), and* The Imperial Presidency *(1973, on the modern president).*

The Cold War in its original form was a presumably mortal antagonism, arising in the wake of the Second World War, between two rigidly hostile blocs, one led by the Soviet Union, the other by the United States. For nearly two somber and dangerous decades this antagonism dominated the fears of mankind; it may even, on occasion, have come close to blowing up the planet. In recent years, however, the once implacable struggle has lost its familiar clarity of outline. With the passing of old issues and the emergence of new

From Arthur M. Schlesinger, Jr., "Origins of the Cold War," *Foreign Affairs* 46 (October 1967): 22–25, 26–27, 28–30, 31–32, 34–35, 42–47, 48–50, 52. Copyright © 1967 by Council on Foreign Relations, Inc., New York. Excerpted by special permission from *Foreign Affairs*, October 1967, and by permission of the author.

conflicts and contestants, there is a natural tendency, especially on the part of the generation which grew up during the Cold War, to take a fresh look at the causes of the great contention between Russia and America.

Some exercises in reappraisal have merely elaborated the orthodoxies promulgated in Washington or Moscow during the boom years of the Cold War. But others, especially in the United States (there are no signs, alas, of this in the Soviet Union), represent what American historians call "revisionism"—that is, a readiness to challenge official explanations. No one should be surprised by this phenomenon. Every war in American history has been followed in due course by skeptical reassessments of supposedly sacred assumptions. So the War of 1812, fought at the time for the freedom of the seas, was in later years ascribed to the expansionist ambitions of congressional war hawks; so the Mexican War became a slaveholders' conspiracy. So the Civil War has been pronounced a "needless war," and Lincoln has even been accused of maneuvering the rebel attack on Fort Sumter. So too the Spanish-American War and the First and Second World Wars have, each in its turn, undergone revisionist critiques. It is not to be supposed that the Cold War would remain exempt.

In the case of the Cold War, special factors reinforce the predictable historiographical rhythm. The outburst of polycentrism in the Communist empire has made people wonder whether communism was ever so monolithic as official theories of the Cold War supposed. A generation with no vivid memories of Stalinism may see the Russia of the forties in the image of the relatively mild, seedy and irresolute Russia of the sixties. And for this same generation the American course of widening the war in Vietnam—which even nonrevisionists can easily regard as folly—has unquestionably stirred doubts about the wisdom of American foreign policy in the sixties which younger historians may have begun to read back into the forties.

It is useful to remember that, on the whole, past exercises in revisionism have failed to stick. Few historians today believe that the war hawks caused the War of 1812 or the slaveholders the Mexican War, or that the Civil War was needless, or that the House of Morgan brought America into the First World War or that Franklin Roosevelt schemed to produce the attack on Pearl Harbor. But this does not mean that one should deplore the rise of Cold War revisionism. For revisionism is an essential part of the process by which history, through the posing of new problems and the investigation of new possibilities, enlarges its perspectives and enriches its insights.

More than this, in the present context, revisionism expresses a deep, legitimate and tragic apprehension. As the Cold War has begun to lose its purity of definition, as the moral absolutes of the fifties become the moralistic clichés of the sixties, some have begun to ask whether the appalling risks which humanity ran during the Cold War were, after all, necessary and inevitable; whether more restrained and rational policies might not have guided the energies of man from the perils of conflict into the potentialities of collaboration. The fact that such questions are in their nature unanswerable does not mean that it is not right and useful to raise them. Nor does it mean that our sons and daughters are not entitled to an accounting from the generation of Russians and Americans who produced the Cold War.

The orthodox American view, as originally set forth by the American government and as reaffirmed until recently by most American scholars, has been that the Cold War was the brave and essential response of free men to Communist aggression. Some have gone back well before the Second World War to lay open the sources of Russian expansionism. Geopoliticians traced the Cold War to imperial Russian strategic ambitions which in the nineteenth century led to the Crimean War, to Russian penetration of the Balkans and the Middle East and to Russian pressure on Britain's "lifeline" to India. Ideologists traced it to the Communist Manifesto of 1848 ("the violent overthrow of the bourgeoisie lays the foundation for the sway of the proletariat"). Thoughtful observers (a phrase meant to exclude those who speak in Dullese about the unlimited evil of godless, atheistic, militant communism) concluded that classical Russian imperialism and Pan-Slavism, compounded after 1917 by Leninist messianism, confronted the West at the end of the Second World War with an inexorable drive for domination.

The revisionist thesis is very different. In its extreme form, it is that, after the death of Franklin Roosevelt and the end of the Second

World War, the United States deliberately abandoned the wartime policy of collaboration and, exhilarated by the possession of the atomic bomb, undertook a course of aggression of its own designed to expel all Russian influence from Eastern Europe and to establish democratic-capitalist states on the very border of the Soviet Union. As the revisionists see it, this radically new American policy—or rather this resumption by Truman of the pre-Roosevelt policy of insensate anticommunism—left Moscow no alternative but to take measures in defense of its own borders. The result was the Cold War. . . .

Peacemaking after the Second World War was not so much a tapestry as it was a hopelessly raveled and knotted mess of yarn. Yet, for purposes of clarity, it is essential to follow certain threads. One theme indispensable to an understanding of the Cold War is the contrast between two clashing views of world order: the "univeralist" view, by which all nations shared a common interest in all the affairs of the world, and the "sphere-of-influence" view, by which each great power would be assured by the other great powers of an acknowledged predominance in its own area of special interest. The universalist view assumed that national security would be guaranteed by an international organization. The sphere-of-interest view assumed that national security would be guaranteed by the balance of power. While in practice these views have by no means been incompatible (indeed, our shaky peace has been based on a combination of the two), in the abstract they involved sharp contradictions.

The tradition of American thought in these matters was universalist—i.e., Wilsonian. Roosevelt had been a member of Wilson's subcabinet; in 1920, as candidate for vice-president, he had campaigned for the League of Nations. It is true that, within Roosevelt's infinitely complex mind, Wilsonianism warred with the perception of vital strategic interests he had imbibed from Mahan. Moreover, his temperamental inclination to settle things with fellow princes around the conference table led him to regard the Big Three—or Four—as trustees for the rest of the world. On occasion, as this narrative will show, he was beguiled into flirtation with the sphere-of-influence heresy. But in principle he believed in joint action and remained a Wilsonian. His hope for Yalta, as he told the Congress on his return, was that it would "spell the end of the system of unilateral action, the exclusive alliances, the spheres of influence, the balances of power, and all the other expedients that have been tried for centuries—and have always failed."

Whenever Roosevelt backslid, he had at his side that Wilsonian fundamentalist, Secretary of State Cordell Hull, to recall him to the pure faith. After his visit to Moscow in 1943, Hull characteristically said that, with the Declaration of Four Nations on General Security (in which America, Russia, Birtain and China pledged "united action . . . for the organization and maintenance of peace and security"), "there will no longer be need for spheres of influence, for alliances, for balance of power, or any other of the special arrangements through which, in the unhappy past, the nations strove to safeguard their security or to promote their interests."

Remembering the corruption of the Wilsonian vision by the secret treaties of the First World War, Hull was determined to prevent any sphere-of-influence nonsense after the Second World War. He therefore fought all proposals to settle border questions while the war was still on and, excluded as he largely was from wartime diplomacy, poured his not inconsiderable moral energy and frustration into the promulgation of virtuous and spacious general principles. . . .

It is true that critics, and even friends, of the United States sometimes noted a discrepancy between the American passion for universalism when it applied to territory far from American shores and the preeminence the United States accorded its own interests nearer home. Churchill, seeking Washington's blessing for a sphere-of-influence initiative in Eastern Europe, could not forbear reminding the Americans, "We follow the lead of the United States in South America"; nor did any universalist of record propose the abolition of the Monroe Doctrine. But a convenient myopia prevented such inconsistencies from qualifying the ardency of the universalist faith.

There seem only to have been three officials in the United States government who dissented. One was the secretary of war, Henry L. Stimson, a classical balance-of-power man, who in 1944 opposed the creation of a vacuum in Central Europe by the pastoralization of Germany and in 1945 urged "the settlement of all territorial acquisitions in the shape of defense posts which each of these four powers may deem to be necessary for their own safety" in advance of any effort to establish a peacetime United Nations. Stimson considered the claim of Russia to a preferred position in Eastern Europe as not unreasonable: As he told President Truman, "he thought the Russians perhaps were being more realistic than we were in regard to their own security." Such a position for Russia seemed to him comparable to the preferred American position in Latin America; he even spoke of "our respective orbits." Stimson was therefore skeptical of what he regarded as the prevailing tendency "to hang on to exaggerated views of the Monroe Doctrine and at the same time butt into every question that comes up in Central Europe." Acceptance of spheres of influence seemed to him the way to avoid "a head-on collision."

A second official opponent of universalism was George Kennan, an eloquent advocate from the American Embassy in Moscow of "a prompt and clear recognition of the division of Europe into spheres of influence and of a policy based on the fact of such division." Kennan argued that nothing we could do would possibly alter the course of events in Eastern Europe; that we were deceiving ourselves by supposing that these countries had any future but Russian domination; that we should therefore relinquish Eastern Europe to the Soviet Union and avoid anything which would make things easier for the Russians by giving them economic assistance or by sharing moral responsibility for their actions.

A third voice within the government against universalism was (at least after the war) Henry A. Wallace. As secretary of commerce, he stated the sphere-of-influence case with trenchancy in the famous Madison Square Garden speech of September 1946 which led to his dismissal by President Truman:

> On our part, we should recognize that we have no more business in the political affairs of Eastern Europe than Russia has in the political affairs of Latin America, Western Europe, and the United States. . . . Whether we like it or not, the Russians will try to socialize their sphere of influence just as we try to democratize our sphere of influence. . . . The Russians have no more business stirring up native Communists to political activity in Western Europe, Latin America, and the United States than we have in interfering with the politics of Eastern Europe and Russia.

Stimson, Kennan and Wallace seem to have been alone in the government, however, in taking these views. They were very much minority voices. Meanwhile universalism, rooted in the American legal and moral tradition, overwhelmingly backed by contemporary opinion, received successive enshrinements in the Atlantic Charter of 1941, in the Declaration of the United Nations in 1942 and in the Moscow Declaration of 1943.

The Kremlin, on the other hand, thought *only* of spheres of interest; above all, the Russians were determined to protect their frontiers, and especially their border to the west, crossed so often and so bloodily in the dark course of their history. These western frontiers lacked natural means of defense—no great oceans, rugged mountains, steaming swamps or impenetrable jungles. The history of Russia had been the history of invasion, the last of which was by now horribly killing up to 20 million of its people. The protocol of Russia therefore meant the enlargement of the area of Russian influence. Kennan himself wrote (in May 1944), "Behind Russia's stubborn expansion lies only the age-old sense of insecurity of a sedentary people reared on an exposed plain in the neighborhood of fierce nomadic peoples," and he called this "urge" a "permanent feature of Russian psychology. . . ."

The unconditional surrender of Italy in July 1943 created the first major test of the Western devotion to universalism. America and Britain, having won the Italian war, handled the capitulation, keeping Moscow informed at a distance. Stalin complained

> The United States and Great Britain made agreements but the Soviet Union received information about the results . . . just as a passive third observer I have to tell you that it is impossible to tolerate the situation any longer. I propose that the [tripartite military-political commission] be established and that Sicily be assigned . . . as its place of residence.

Roosevelt, who had no intention of sharing the control of Italy with the Russians, suavely replied with the suggestion that Stalin send an officer "to General Eisenhower's headquarters in connection with the commission." Unimpressed, Stalin continued to press for a tripartite body; but his Western allies were adamant in keeping the Soviet Union off the Control Commission for Italy, and the Russians in the end had to be satisfied with a seat, along with minor Allied states, on a meaningless Inter-Allied Advisory Council. Their acquiescence in this was doubtless not unconnected with a desire to establish precedents for Eastern Europe.

Teheran in December 1943 marked the high point of three-power collaboration. Still, when Churchill asked about Russian territorial interests, Stalin replied a little ominously, "There is no need to speak at the present time about any Soviet desires, but when the time comes we will speak." In the next weeks, there were increasing indications of a Soviet determination to deal unilaterally with Eastern Europe—so much so that in early February 1944 Hull cabled Harriman in Moscow:

> *Matters are rapidly approaching the point where the Soviet government will have to choose between the development and extension of the foundation of international cooperation as the guiding principle of the postwar world as against the continuance of a unilateral and arbitrary method of dealing with its special problems even though these problems are admittedly of more direct interest to the Soviet Union than to other great powers.*

As against this approach, however, Churchill, more tolerant of sphere-of-influence deviations, soon proposed that, with the impending liberation of the Balkans, Russia should run things in Rumania and Britain in Greece. Hull strongly opposed this suggestion but made the mistake of leaving Washington for a few days; and Roosevelt, momentarily free from his Wilsonian conscience, yielded to Churchill's plea for a three-months' trial. Hull resumed the fight on his return, and Churchill postponed the matter. . . .

Meanwhile Eastern Europe presented the Alliance with still another crisis that same September. Bulgaria, which was not at war with Russia, decided to surrender to the Western Allies while it still could; and the English and Americans at Cairo began to discuss armistice terms with Bulgarian envoys. Moscow, challenged by what it plainly saw as a Western intrusion into its own zone of vital interest, promptly declared war on Bulgaria, took over the surrender negotiations and, invoking the Italian precedent, denied its Western Allies any role in the Bulgarian Control Commission. In a long and thoughtful cable, Ambassador Harriman meditated on the problems of communication with the Soviet Union. "Words," he reflected, "have a different connotation to the Soviets than they have to us. When they speak of insisting on 'friendly governments' in their neighboring countries, they have in mind something quite different from what we would mean." The Russians, he surmised, really believed that Washington accepted "their position that although they would keep us informed they had the right to settle their problems with their western neighbors unilaterally." But the Soviet position was still in flux: "the Soviet government is not one mind." The problem, as Harriman had earlier told Harry Hopkins, was "to strengthen the hands of those around Stalin who want to play the game along our lines." The way to do this, he now told Hull, was to

*be understanding of their sensitivity, meet them much more than half way, encourage them and support them wherever we can, and yet oppose them promptly with the greatest firmness where we see them going wrong. . . . The only way we can eventually come to an understanding with the Soviet Union on the question of noninterference in the internal affairs of other countries is for us to take a definite interest in the solution of the problems of each individual country as they arise.*

As against Harriman's sophisticated universalist strategy, however, Churchill, increasingly fearful of the consequences of unrestrained competition in Eastern Europe, decided in early October to carry his sphere-of-influence proposal directly to Moscow. Roosevelt was at first content to have Churchill speak for him too and even prepared a cable to that effect. But Hopkins, a more rigorous universalist, took it upon himself to stop the cable and warn Roosevelt of its possible implications. Eventually Roosevelt sent a message to Harriman in Moscow emphasizing that he expected to "retain complete freedom of action after this conference is over." It was now that Churchill quickly proposed—and Stalin as quickly accepted—the celebrated division of southeastern Europe: ending (after further haggling between Eden and Molotov) with 90 percent Soviet predominance in Rumania, 80 percent in Bulgaria and Hungary, 50–50 in Jugloslavia, 90 percent British predominance in Greece.

Churchill in discussing this with Harriman used the phrase "spheres of influence." But he insisted that these were only "immediate wartime arrangements" and received a highly general blessing from Roosevelt. Yet, whatever Churchill intended, there is reason to believe that Stalin construed the percentages as an agreement, not a declaration; as practical arithmetic, not algebra. For Stalin, it should be understood, the sphere-of-influence idea did not mean that he would abandon all efforts to spread communism in some other nation's sphere; it did mean that, if he tried this and the other side cracked down, he could not feel he had serious cause for complaint.

*         *         *

Yalta remains something of an historical perplexity—less, from the perspective of 1967, because of a mythical American deference to the sphere-of-influence thesis than because of the documentable Russian deference to the universalist thesis. Why should Stalin in 1945 have accepted the Declaration on Liberated Europe and an agreement on Poland pledging that "the three governments will jointly" act to assure "free elections of governments responsive to the will of the people"? There are several probable answers: that the war was not over and the Russians still wanted the Americans to intensify their military effort in the West; that one clause in the Declaration premised action on "the opinion of the three governments" and thus implied a Soviet veto, though the Polish agreement was more definite; most of all that the universalist algebra of the Declaration was plainly in Stalin's mind to be construed in terms of the practical arithmetic of his sphere-of-influence agreement with Churchill the previous October. Stalin's assurance to Churchill at Yalta that a proposed Russian amendment to the Declaration would not apply to Greece makes it clear that Roosevelt's pieties did not, in Stalin's mind, nullify Churchill's percentages. He could well have been strengthened in this supposition by the fact that *after* Yalta, Churchill himself repeatedly reasserted the terms of the October agreement as if he regarded it, despite Yalta, as controlling.

Harriman still had the feeling before Yalta that the Kremlin had "two approaches to their postwar policies" and that Stalin himself was "of two minds." One approach emphasized the internal reconstruction and development of Russia; the other its external expansion. But in the meantime the fact which dominated all political decisions—that is, the war against Germany—was moving into its final phase. In the weeks after Yalta, the military situation changed with great rapidity. As the Nazi threat declined, so too did the need for cooperation. The Soviet Union, feeling itself menaced by the American idea of self-determination and the borderlands diplomacy to which it was leading, skeptical whether the United Nations would protect its frontiers as reliably as its own domination in Eastern Europe, began to fulfill its security requirements unilaterally.

In March Stalin expressed his evaluation of the United Nations by rejecting Roosevelt's plea that Molotov come to the San Francisco conference, if only for the opening sessions. In the next weeks the Russians emphatically and crudely worked their will in Eastern Europe, above all in the test country of Poland. They were ignoring the Declaration on Liberated Europe, ignoring the Atlantic Charter, self-determination, human freedom and everything else the Americans considered essential for a stable peace. "We must clearly recognize," Harriman wired Washington a few days before Roosevelt's death, "that the Soviet program is the establishment of totalitarianism, ending personal liberty and democracy as we know and respect it."

At the same time, the Russians also began to mobilize Communist resources in the United States itself to block American universalism. In April 1945 Jacques Duclos, who had been the Comintern official responsible for the Western Communist parties, launched in *Cahiers du Communisme* an uncompromising attack on the policy of the American Communist party. Duclos sharply condemned the revisionism of Earl Browder, the American Communist leader, as "expressed in the concept of a long-term class peace in the United States, of the possibility of the suppression of the class struggle in the postwar period and of establishment of harmony between labor and capital." Browder was specifically rebuked for favoring the "self-determination" of Europe "west of the Soviet Union" on a bourgeois-democratic basis. The excommunication of Browderism was plainly the Politburo's considered reaction to the impending defeat of Germany; it was a signal to the Communist parties of the West that they should recover their identity; it was Moscow's alert to Communists everywhere that they should prepare for new policies in the postwar world.

The Duclos piece obviously could not have been planned and written much later than the Yalta Conference—that is, well before a number of events which revisionists now cite in order to demonstrate American responsibility for the Cold War: before Allen Dulles, for example, began to negotiate the surrender of the German armies in Italy (the episode which provoked Stalin to charge Roosevelt with seeking a separate peace and provoked Roosevelt to denounce the "vile misrepresentations" of Stalin's informants); well before Roosevelt died; many months before the testing of the atomic bomb; even more months before Truman ordered that the bomb be dropped on Japan. William Z. Foster, who soon replaced Brower as the leader of the American Communist party and embodied the new Moscow line, later boasted of having said in January 1944, "A postwar Roosevelt administration would continue to be, as it is now, an imperialist government." With ancient suspicions revived by the American insistence on universalism, this was no doubt the conclusion which the Russians were reaching at the same time. The Soviet canonization of Roosevelt (like their present-day canonization of Kennedy) took place after the American President's death.

The atmosphere of mutual suspicion was beginning to rise. In January 1945 Molotov formally proposed that the United States grant Russia a $6 billion credit for postwar reconstruction. With characteristic tact he explained that he was doing this as a favor to save America from a postwar depression. The proposal seems to have been diffidently made and diffidently received. Roosevelt requested that the matter "not be pressed further" on the American side until he had a chance to talk with Stalin; but the Russians did not follow it up either at Yalta in February (save for a single glancing reference) or during the Stalin-Hopkins talks in May or at Potsdam. Finally the proposal was renewed in the very different political atmosphere of August. This time Washington inexplicably mislaid the request during the transfer of the records of the Foreign Economic Administration to the State Department. It did not turn up again until March 1946. Of course this was impossible for the Russians to believe; it is hard enough even for those acquainted with the capacity of the American government for incompetence to believe; and it only strengthened Soviet suspicions of American purposes.

The American credit was one conceivable form of Western contribution to Russian reconstruction. Another was lend-lease, and the possibility of reconstruction aid under the lend-lease protocol had already been discussed in 1944. But in May 1945 Russia, like Britain, suffered from Truman's abrupt termination of lend-lease shipments— "unfortunate and even brutal," Stalin told Hopkins, adding that, if it was "designed as pressure on the Russians in order to soften them up, then it was a fundamental mistake." A third form was German reparations. Here Stalin in demanding $10 billion in reparations for the Soviet Union made his strongest fight at Yalta. Roosevelt, while agreeing essentially with Churchill's opposition, tried to post-pone the matter by accepting the Soviet figure as a "basis for dis-cussion"—a formula which led to future misunderstanding. In short, the Russian hope for major Western assistance in postwar recon-struction foundered on three events which the Kremlin could well have interpreted respectively as deliberate sabotage (the loan request), blackmail (lend-lease cancellation) and pro-Germanism (reparations).

Actually the American attempt to settle the fourth lend-lease protocol was generous and the Russians for their own reasons de-clined to come to an agreement. It is not clear, though, that satisfy-ing Moscow on any of these financial scores would have made much essential difference. It might have persuaded some doves in the Kremlin that the U.S. government was genuinely friendly; it might have persuaded some hawks that the American anxiety for Soviet friendship was such that Moscow could do as it wished without in-viting challenge from the United States. It would, in short, merely have reinforced both sides of the Kremlin debate; it would hardly have reversed deeper tendencies toward the deterioration of political relationships. Economic deals were surely subordinate to the quality of mutual political confidence; and here, in the months after Yalta, the decay was steady.

The Cold War had now begun. It was the product not of a decision but of a dilemma. Each side felt compelled to adopt policies which the other could not but regard as a threat to the principles of the peace. Each then felt compelled to undertake defensive measures. Thus the Russians saw no choice but to consolidate their security in Eastern Europe. The Americans, regarding Eastern Europe as the first step toward Western Europe, responded by asserting their in-terest in the zone the Russians deemed vital to their security. The Russians concluded that the West was resuming its old course of capitalist encirclement; that it was purposefully laying the founda-tion for anti-Soviet regimes in the area defined by the blood of cen-turies as crucial to Russian survival. Each side believed with pas-sion that future international stability depended on the success of its own conception of world order. Each side, in pursuing its own clearly indicated and deeply cherished principles, was only con-firming the fear of the other that it was bent on aggression.

Very soon the process began to acquire a cumulative momentum. The impending collapse of Germany thus provoked new troubles: the Russians, for example, sincerely feared that the West was planning a separate surrender of the German armies in Italy in a way which would release troops for Hitler's eastern front, as they subsequently feared that the Nazis might succeed in surrendering Berlin to the West. This was the context in which the atomic bomb now appeared. Though the revisionist argument that Truman dropped the bomb less to defeat Japan than to intimidate Russia is not convincing, this thought unquestionably appealed to some in Washington as at least an advantageous side-effect of Hiroshima.

So the machinery of suspicion and countersuspicion, action and counteraction, was set in motion. But, given relations among traditional national states, there was still no reason, even with all the postwar jostling, why this should not have remained a manageable situation. What made it unmanageable, what caused the rapid escalation of the Cold War and in another two years completed the division of Europe, was a set of considerations which this account has thus far excluded.

Up to this point, the discussion has considered the schism within the wartime coalition as if it were entirely the result of disagreements among national states. Assuming this framework, there was unquestionably a failure of communication between America and Russia, a misperception of signals and, as time went on, a mounting tendency to ascribe ominous motives to the other side. It seems hard, for example, to deny that American postwar policy created genuine difficulties for the Russians and even assumed a threatening aspect for them. All this the revisionists have rightly and usefully emphasized.

But the great omission of the revisionists—and also the fundamental explanation of the speed with which the Cold War escalated —lies precisely in the fact that the Soviet Union was *not* a traditional national state. This is where the "mirror image," invoked by some psychologists, falls down. For the Soviet Union was a phenomenon very different from America or Britain: it was a totalitarian state, endowed with an all-explanatory, all-consuming ideology, committed to the infallibility of government and party, still in a somewhat messianic mood, equating dissent with treason, and ruled by a dictator who, for all his quite extraordinary abilities, had his paranoid moments.

Marxism-Leninism gave the Russian leaders a view of the world according to which all societies were inexorably destined to proceed along appointed roads by appointed stages until they achieved the classless nirvana. Moreover, given the resistance of the capitalists to this development, the existence of any non-Communist state was *by definition* a threat to the Soviet Union. "As long as capitalism and socialism exist," Lenin wrote, "we cannot live in peace: in the end, one or the other will triumph—a funeral dirge will be sung either over the Soviet Republic or over world capitalism."

Stalin and his associates, whatever Roosevelt or Truman did or failed to do, were bound to regard the United States as the enemy, not because of this deed or that, but because of the primordial fact that America was the leading capitalist power and thus, by Leninist syllogism, unappeasably hostile, driven by the logic of its system to oppose, encircle and destroy Soviet Russia. Nothing the United States could have done in 1944–45 would have abolished this mistrust, required and sanctified as it was by Marxist gospel—nothing short of the conversion of the United States into a Stalinist despotism; and even this would not have sufficed, as the experience of Jugoslavia and China soon showed, unless it were accompanied by total subservience to Moscow. So long as the United States remained a capitalist democracy, no American policy, given Moscow's theology, could hope to win basic Soviet confidence, and every American action was poisoned from the source. So long as the Soviet Union remained a messianic state, ideology compelled a steady expansion of Communist power. . . .

A temporary recession of ideology was already taking place during the Second World War when Stalin, to rally his people against the invader, had to replace the appeal of Marxism by that of nationalism. ("We are under no illusions that they are fighting for us," Stalin once said to Harriman. "They are fighting for Mother Russia.") But this was still taking place within the strictest limitations. The Soviet Union remained as much a police state as ever; the regime was as infallible as ever; foreigners and their ideas were as suspect as ever. "Never, except possibly during my later experience as ambassador in Moscow," Kennan has written, "did the insistence of the Soviet authorities on isolation of the diplomatic corps weigh more heavily on me . . . than in these first weeks following my return to Russia in the final months of the war. . . . [We were] treated as though we were the bearers of some species of the plague"—which, of course, from the Soviet viewpoint, they were: the plague of skepticism.

Paradoxically, of the forces capable of bringing about a modification of ideology, the most practical and effective was the Soviet dictatorship itself. If Stalin was an ideologist, he was also a pragmatist. If he saw everything through the lenses of Marxism-Leninism, he also, as the infallible expositor of the faith, could reinterpret Marxism-Leninism to justify anything he wanted to do at any given moment. No doubt Roosevelt's ignorance of Marxism-Leninism was inexcusable and led to grievous miscalculations. But Roosevelt's efforts to work on and through Stalin were not so hopelessly naive as it used to be fashionable to think. With the extraordinary instinct of a great political leader, Roosevelt intuitively understood that Stalin was the *only* lever available to the West against the Leninist ideology and the Soviet system. If Stalin could be reached, then alone was there a chance of getting the Russians to act contrary to the prescriptions of their faith. The best evidence is that Roosevelt retained a certain capacity to influence Stalin to the end; the nominal Soviet acquiescence in American universalism as late as Yalta was perhaps an indication of that. It is in this way that the death of Roosevelt was crucial—not in the vulgar sense that his policy was then reversed by his successor, which did not happen, but in the sense that no other American could hope to have the restraining impact on Stalin which Roosevelt might for a while have had.

Stalin alone could have made any difference. Yet Stalin, in spite of the impression of sobriety and realism he made on Westerners who saw him during the Second World War, was plainly a man of deep and morbid obsessions and compulsions. When he was still a young man, Lenin had criticized his rude and arbitrary ways. A reasonably authoritative observer (N. S. Khrushchev) later commented, "These negative characteristics of his developed steadily and during the last years acquired an absolutely insufferable character." His paranoia, probably set off by the suicide of his wife in 1932, led to the terrible purges of the mid-thirties and the wanton murder of thousands of his Bolshevik comrades. "Everywhere and in everything," Khrushchev says of this period, "he saw 'enemies,' 'double-dealers' and 'spies.' " The crisis of war evidently steadied him in some way, though Khrushchev speaks of his "nervousness and hysteria . . . even after the war began." The madness, so rigidly controlled for a time, burst out with new and shocking intensity in the postwar years. "After the war," Khrushchev testifies,

> the situation became even more complicated. Stalin became even more capricious, irritable and brutal; in particular, his suspicion grew. His persecution mania reached unbelievable dimensions. . . . He decided everything, without any consideration for anyone or anything.
> Stalin's willfulness showed itself . . . also in the international relations of the Soviet Union. . . . He had completely lost a sense of reality; he demonstrated his suspicion and haughtiness not only in relation to individuals in the USSR, but in relation to whole parties and nations.

A revisionist fallacy has been to treat Stalin as just another Realpolitik statesman, as Second World War revisionists see Hitler as just another Stresemann or Bismarck. But the record makes it clear that in the end nothing could satisfy Stalin's paranoia. His own associates failed. Why does anyone suppose that any conceivable American policy would have succeeded?

An analysis of the origins of the Cold War which leaves out these factors—the intransigence of Leninist ideology, the sinister dynamics of a totalitarian society and the madness of Stalin—is obviously incomplete. It was these factors which made it hard for the West to accept the thesis that Russia was moved only by a desire to protect its security and would be satisfied by the control of Eastern Europe; it was these factors which charged the debate between universalism and spheres of influence with apocalyptic potentiality.

Leninism and totalitarianism created a structure of thought and behavior which made postwar collaboration between Russia and America—in any normal sense of civilized intercourse between national states—inherently impossible. The Soviet dictatorship of 1945 simply could not have survived such a collaboration. Indeed, nearly a quarter-century later, the Soviet regime, though it has meanwhile moved a good distance, could still hardly survive it without risking the release inside Russia of energies profoundly opposed to Communist despotism. As for Stalin, he may have represented the only force in 1945 capable of overcoming Stalinism, but the very traits which enabled him to win absolute power expressed terrifying instabilities of mind and temperament and hardly offered a solid foundation for a peaceful world. . . .

The point of no return came on July 2, 1947, when Molotov, after bringing eighty-nine technical specialists with him to Paris and evincing initial interest in the project for European reconstruction, received the hot flash from the Kremlin, denounced the whole idea and walked out of the conference. For the next fifteen years the Cold War raged unabated, passing out of historical ambiguity into the realm of good versus evil and breeding on both sides simplifications, stereotypes and self-serving absolutes, often couched in interchangeable phrases. Under the pressure even America, for a deplorable decade, forsook its pragmatic and pluralist traditions, posed as God's appointed messenger to ignorant and sinful man and followed the Soviet example in looking to a world remade in its own image.

In retrospect, if it is impossible to see the Cold War as a case of American aggression and Russian response, it is also hard to see it as a pure case of Russian aggression and American response. "In what is truly tragic," wrote Hegel, "there must be valid moral powers on both the sides which come into collision. . . . Both suffer loss and yet both are mutually justified." In this sense, the Cold War had its tragic elements. The question remains whether it was an instance of Greek tragedy—as Auden has called it, "the tragedy of necessity," where the feeling aroused in the spectator is "What a pity it had to be this way"—or of Christian tragedy, "the tragedy of possibility," where the feeling aroused is "What a pity it was this way when it might have been otherwise."

Once something has happened, the historian is tempted to assume that it had to happen; but this may often be a highly unphilosophical assumption. The Cold War could have been avoided only if the Soviet Union had not been possessed by convictions both of the infallibility of the Communist word and of the inevitability of a Communist world. These convictions transformed an impasse between national states into a religious war, a tragedy of possibility into one of necessity. One might wish that America had preserved the poise and proportion of the first years of the Cold War and had not in time succumbed to its own forms of self-righteousness. But the most rational of American policies could hardly have averted the Cold War. Only today, as Russia begins to recede from its messianic mission and to accept, in practice if not yet in principle, the permanence of the world of diversity, only now can the hope flicker that this long, dreary, costly contest may at last be taking on forms less dramatic, less obsessive and less dangerous to the future of mankind.

## *William A. Williams*
# AMERICAN INNOCENCE QUESTIONED

*In his rebuttal to Schlesinger and in his defense of revisionism, William A. Williams of Oregon State University denies that America was helpless in the early Cold War and that Stalin was uniquely paranoid. Williams finds Schlesinger short on evidence and remiss in not discussing as stimulants to Soviet behavior the dropping of the atomic bomb, the American thrust into Eastern Europe, and the global interventionism of the United States. For many years an historian at the University of Wisconsin, Williams was one of the first scholars to question the traditional Department of State explanation for the coming of the Cold War in his* American-Russian Relations, 1761–1947 *(1952). His other books include* The Tragedy of American Diplomacy *(1959 and 1962) and* The Roots of the Modern American Empire *(1969).*

There is a great book to be written some day explaining how Schlesinger and a good many other historians of his generation came by the power to render such flat-out psychiatric judgments without professional training and without direct access to their subjects. My own candidates for that undertaking are Robert Coles, Abraham H. Maslow or Rollo May, men who somehow acquired a sense of the limits of their approach even as they mastered its discipline.

Meanwhile, the first point to be made about Schlesinger's attempt to fix the origins of the Cold War in Stalin's paranoia is that *no major American policy maker between 1943 and 1948 defined and dealt with the Soviet Union in those terms.* Schlesinger offers not the slightest shred of evidence that such was the case. The reason is simple: there is no such evidence.

From William A. Williams, "The Cold War Revisionists," *The Nation* 205 (November 13, 1967): 492–95. Reprinted by permission.

Even if Schlesinger's characterization of Stalin as a paranoid were granted, the argument would still be unable to account either for the nature or the adoption of American policy. There is only one circumstance in which his proposition would become directly relevant: If a different American policy had been carefully formulated and then seriously tried over a significant period of time, only to fail because of Russian intransigence, then Schlesinger's argument that Stalin's paranoia caused the Cold War would bear on the case.

It is particularly important to grasp that point because Schlesinger does not introduce paranoia until after he has demonstrated that Stalin was acting on a rational and conservative basis. Long before he mentions paranoia, Schlesinger notes the ambivalence of Soviet leaders toward an accommodation with the United States, and makes it clear that American leaders were operating on that estimate of the situation—not on the proposition that the Russians were paranoid. While entering the caveat that "no one, of course, can know what was really in the minds of the Russian leaders," he nevertheless concludes that "it is not unreasonable to suppose that Stalin would have been satisfied at the end of the war to secure ... 'a protective glacis along Russia's western border.' ... His initial objective was very probably not world conquest but Russian security." And he makes it clear that Stalin kept his word about giving the British the initiative in Greece.

Schlesinger does not resort to explaining Soviet action in terms of paranoia until he has to deal with American efforts to exert direct influence on affairs in Eastern Europe. Then he casually asserts that it was a factor: "given the paranoia produced alike by Russian history and Leninist ideology, [American action] no doubt seemed not only an act of hypocrisy but a threat to security."

That offhand introduction of paranoia as a primary operational factor in historical explanation staggers the mind. It is simply not convincing to hold that a man (in this instance, Stalin) who believes he has negotiated a clear security perimeter is paranoid because he reacts negatively when one of the parties to the understanding (in this case the United States) unilaterally asserts and acts on a self-proclaimed right to intervene within that perimeter. When examined closely in connection with foreign affairs, the most that can be made of Schlesinger's argument is that Stalin may have had strong paranoid tendencies, and that the American thrust into Eastern Europe (and elsewhere throughout the world) could very well have pushed him gradually into, and perhaps through, the psychic zone separating neurosis from psychosis.

The most significant aspect of Schlesinger's argument that emerges at this point is his admission that America's assertion of its right to intervene anywhere in the world, and its action in doing so in Eastern Europe, had a primary effect on Soviet behavior. For in saying that, however he qualifies it later, Schlesinger has granted the validity of one of the major points made by the critics of the official line on the Cold War. Many criticisms could be made of his description of the nature and dynamism of American global interventionism, which he labels "universalism," but the most important weakness in his analysis is the failure to discuss the explicit and implicit anticommunism that was a strong element in the American outlook from the moment the Bolsheviks seized power in 1917. That omission gravely undercuts the attempt he makes later to substantiate a vital part of his argument.

For, having admitted the reality and the consequences of American interventionism, Schlesinger faces the difficult problem of demonstrating the truth of three propositions if he is to establish Soviet responsibility for the Cold War. First, he must show that a different American policy could not have produced other results. Second, he must sustain the thesis that the Soviet response to American universalism was indeed paranoid. Third, he must prove that the American counterresponse was relevant and appropriate.

Schlesinger's argument that an alternate American policy would not have made any difference has two themes. He says that a serious effort to negotiate around the Soviet bid for a $6 billion loan would "merely have reinforced both sides of the Kremlin debate" because "economic deals were merely subordinate to the quality of mutual political confidence." That judgment completely overlooks the impact which a serious American economic proposal would have made on the "quality of political confidence."

In the end, however, Schlesinger falls back on Soviet paranoia as the reason that a different approach would have made no difference. Here, however, he introduces a new factor in his explanation. In the early part of the argument, he holds that the Soviets "thought *only* of spheres of influence; above all, the Russians were determined to protect their frontiers, and especially their border to the west,

crossed so often and so bloodily in the dark course of their history."
But later Schlesinger suggests that the paranoia was partially
caused, and significantly reinforced, by the Marxist ideology of capitalist antagonism and opposition.

However, Soviet leaders did not detect capitalist hostility merely
because they were viewing the world through a Marxist prism. Such
enmity had existed, and had been acted upon, since November, 1917,
and anticommunism was an integral part of the universalism that
guided American leaders at the end of World War II. As Schlesinger
demonstrates, willy-nilly if not intentionally, American leaders were
prepared to work with Russian leaders if they would accept key features of the American creed. It is possible, given that truth, to con-
struct a syllogism proving that Stalin was paranoid because he did
not accept the terms. But that kind of proof has nothing to do with
serious historical inquiry, analysis and interpretation.

The real issue at this juncture, however, is not how Schlesinger attempts to establish Stalin's paranoia. The central question is whether
or not Soviet actions are accurately described as paranoid. The evidence does not support that interpretation. Consider the nature of
Soviet behavior in three crucial areas.

First, the Russians reacted to American intervention in Eastern
Europe by consolidating their existing position in that region. Many
Soviet actions implementing that decision were overpowering, cruel
and ruthless, but the methods do not bear on the nature of the policy
itself. The Soviet choice served to verify an important point that
Schlesinger acknowledges: Stalin told Harriman in October, 1945,
that the Soviets were "going isolationist" in pursuit of their national
interests. Russian policy at that time in Eastern Europe was neither
paranoid nor messianic Marxism.

Second, the Soviets pulled back in other areas to avoid escalating
a direct national or governmental confrontation with the United
States. They did so in the clash over rival claims for oil rights in Iran;
and that policy was even more strikingly apparent in Stalin's attempt
to postpone Mao's triumph in China. In the first instance, prudence
belies paranoia. In the second, any messianic urges were sup-
pressed in the national interest.

Third, the Soviets acquiesced in the activities of non-Russian
Communist movements. While the term *acquiesced* is not perfect for
describing the complex process that was involved, it is nevertheless

used advisedly as the best single term to describe the *effect* of Soviet action. Stalin and his colleagues no doubt sought results other than those that occurred in many places—China and Yugoslavia come particularly to mind—and clearly tried to realize their preferences. Nevertheless, they did acquiesce in results that fell far short of their desires.

Schlesinger makes a great deal, as do all official interpreters of the Cold War, of the April, 1945, article by Jacques Duclos of the French Communist party. Let us assume that Duclos wrote the article on orders from Moscow, even though the process that produced the action was probably far more complex than indicated by that simple statement. The crucial point about Duclos' article is that it can be read in two ways. It can be interpreted as a messianic cry for non-Soviet Communist parties to strike for power as part of a general push to expand Russian boundaries or the Soviet sphere of influence. But it can as persuasively be read as primarily a call for non-Soviet Communists to reassert their own identity and become militant and disruptive as part of the Russian strategy of consolidation in the face of American universalism.

Official explanations of the Cold War generally imply that American leaders heard the Duclos piece as a bugle call for Communist aid in behalf of Soviet expansion. In truth, no significant number of American leaders feared a Russian military offensive at any time during the evolution of the Cold War. When the Duclos article appeared, and for a long period thereafter, they were far more concerned with devising ways to use the great preponderance of American power to further the universalism and interventionism of the United States in Eastern Europe and elsewhere.

But the most astonishing use of the Duclos article by any defender of the official line on the Cold War is made by Schlesinger when he employs it to avoid any serious discussion of the impact of the dropping of two atomic bombs in August, 1945. In truth, astonishing is a very mild word for Schlesigner's performance on this point. He says merely that the Duclos article came many months before the bombs were dropped, and then proceeds to ignore the *effect* of the bomb on Soviet leaders. All he adds is a flat assertion that the critics are "not convincing" in their argument that "the bomb was dropped less to defeat Japan than to intimidate Russia" (which is a strained interpretation of what they have said). That is not even to the point, for one could agree that the bomb was dropped only to finish the Japanese and still insist that it had a powerful effect on Soviet thought and action in connection with its future relations with the United States.

The argument could be made, of course, that only a Russia gone paranoid would have been upset by the American act. The issue of psychotic behavior might better be raised about the Americans. It could also be maintained that the United States had no responsibility for the effects of the bomb on Soviet leaders because the motive in using it was not anti-Soviet. That is about like saying that a man who constantly interferes in the affairs of his neighbors, and who suddenly starts using a 40-millimeter cannon to kill cats in his back yard, bears no responsibility for the neighbors' skepticism about his good intentions. Schlesinger is fully warranted in making a careful examination of the period before the bomb, but he has no justification for so nearly ignoring the role of the bomb in the origins of the Cold War.

Finally, there is the question of the relevance and appropriateness of the American response to the Soviet policy of consolidation in Eastern Europe, and the related call for non-Russian Communists to reassert their identity and policies. The answer, put simply and directly, is that the increasingly militarized holy war mounted by American leaders was grossly irrelevant to the situation and highly conducive to producing problems that were more dangerous than those the policy was supposed to resolve.

## *Melvin Croan*
# STALIN'S RATIONALITY AND DOMESTIC IMPERATIVES

*In a 1967 London meeting of the Institute of Contemporary History held in association with the University of Reading, Melvin Croan disputed Schle-*

From "Origins of the Post-War Crisis—A Discussion," *Journal of Contemporary History* 3 (April 1968): 233–37. Reprinted by permission of George Weidenfeld & Nicolson Ltd., London.

*singer's emphasis on Stalin's paranoia. Although essentially agreeing with Schlesinger that Russia was responsible for the Cold War, Croan noted that Stalin was quite rational in measuring his nation's postwar weakness, his somewhat precarious position in the Soviet political system, and the importance of a renewed ideological mobilization of the Russian people. Professor Croan teaches the politics and foreign policy of the Soviet Union in the Department of Political Science, University of Wisconsin.*

Let me only suggest that whatever Stalin's aberrations, his abnormal psychology, the Cold War, or something like it, from his point of view made perfectly rational good sense. That is to say the Cold War was . . . "system functional" for the Soviet regime. And I must say that my own view of the Soviet Union in world affairs in those initial postwar years is certainly not the one embodied in the official American view of Soviet policy under Stalin, namely that the Soviet Union was hell-bent on expansion, armed to the teeth, ready to begin the march to the Atlantic. Rather I think I tend to subscribe in this case, not to Karl Deutsch's but to Isaac Deutscher's view of the Soviet Union as really a relatively weak pole in the bipolar system: a system, a country, a regime which showed a fearsome face to the outside world but one which was, in the decisive view of its leaders, seriously weakened as a result of the war and potentially vulnerable in the postwar international political system.

In my reading of them, those kinds of policies and series of actions which so escalated the Cold War from the Soviet side, did not mark any innovation in the general tenor of Stalinist foreign policy. I accept Deutscher's view of Russia as a relatively weak (in its own perception), threatened power (in its leadership's perception—the only perception that counted—namely, Stalin's perception). . . . Furthermore, as I see it, Stalin himself had been pretty much disabused of revolution, or revolutionism, as a result of the disastrous failure in China in 1927. His objectives after that time right up until his death really were primarily, obviously, survival for the Soviet regime, which meant survival for Stalin's own regime. Second, and related, Stalin sought security for the Soviet Stalinist regime. Third, in his quest for security he inclined towards isolationism—not just isolation, but isolationism—as not only a goal but also as a framework, a psychology. The first manifestation of this we find in a kind of Soviet version of splendid—indeed heroic—isolationism during the period of collectivization and industrialization. It was an isolationism that could not be operated only because of aggressive German and Japanese policies. This was an isolationism which, however, could not in its earlier form, say from 1928 to 1934, be recaptured in the post-1945 bipolar world, in which, by virtue of the migration of power to the United States on the one side and the Soviet Union on the other, opting out of international politics was itself no longer a real option.

I think we must begin by looking at the way in which the postwar Soviet Union must have appeared to its ruler, to Stalin himself. He could not have failed to be aware of Russia's weakness and vulnerability. First of all there was the tremendous loss in population, variously estimated between 15 and 20 million casualties. Then there was the precipitous decline of industrial production, so that, despite the relocation of industry to Siberia, to the Urals, at the end of the war industrial production was only 50 percent of what it had been in 1939. Moreover, as Stalin must have seen it, one-third of the Soviet postwar population was deemed to have been exposed to what were then called "harmful ideological influences," that is to say, the population of those Soviet territories that had been under German occupation, the population of areas that had been absorbed into the postwar Soviet state and had never been indoctrinated in Marxist-Leninist ideology, the *Ost-Arbeiter,* slave laborers, who had returned from Germany, and, last but not least, those troops who had seen a standard of living in the liberated and occupied areas of Europe to the west of Soviet Russia which was considerably higher than what they had grown up with and considerably at variance with what they had been given to expect.

Then we must also consider that, to meet the necessities of survival during the war, the entire apparatus of Soviet government had been considerably transformed in a number of ways. All the networks of party control had been modified in the interests of getting specific jobs done. Moreover, the party itself had suffered tremendous losses, in the rank and file and among the cadres. Here is one level at which quantification in history makes some sense. You find that on the eve of the war, in June 1941, there were 4.2 million party members; at the end of the war there were 5.8 million; but some 60 percent of the 5.8 million were new wartime recruits. In fact, in the first months of the war—and this bears testimony to the active role of the party in the war effort—the losses in party lives between June 1941 and December 1941 were well over 1 million. One can also see that though by the end of the war the physical instruments of control were intact, the underlying ideological framework had been badly shaken; in a sense deliberately shaken, in the interests of rallying popular support and of cementing the wartime alliance with the West, precisely because the wartime alliance itself was necessary, or deemed to be necessary, for the survival of the Soviet state. During the war there occurred a profound downplaying of Marxism-Leninism, a dilution of ideology along many lines through the introduction of all sorts of patriotic themes, through the redefinition of bourgeois democracy as almost a special form of Soviet democracy (or vice versa), bourgeois democracy in this case meaning the American and British government and social systems. This kind of thing in turn led intellectuals to hope for a relaxation of the dictatorship after the war and also to think perhaps of the possibility of more fruitful, more purposive, and more continuing cooperation with the West; to envisage, in other words a downplay of ideological conflict, indeed the establishment of that something which to this very day is taboo in the Soviet Union, namely, ideological coexistence between the Soviet regime and Western democratic regimes.

This is the sense in which it seems to me that ideology was enormously important for the origins of the Cold War. Because if one begins with a sense of a badly-shaken Soviet political system, and if one accepts, as I do, Stalin's consciousness of the need for and utility of absolute dictatorial political power, and if one also adds that Stalin, sixty-six years old at the end of the war, was bound to consider the struggle for the succession, it seems to me that one gets a series of domestic imperatives which led to the need for an objective enemy. All this was reinforced by Stalin's desire to reestablish the kind of political controls which he deemed necessary for the massive task of reconstruction. In turn, all these objectives, it seems to me, could have been accomplished only through a regeneration of ideology, through—more specifically—the objectification of an external enemy. If one thinks of the alternatives, if one thinks of the conceivable price, from Stalin's point of view, that the Soviet system would have had to pay, or would have run the risk of having to pay, for a continuation of the cooperation, intermittent though it may have been, which occurred during the war between the Soviet Union and the West, then I think one reaches the conclusion that such an alternative course was quite simply intolerable to Stalin. . . .

. . . But it also seems to me that the very ideological threat to the Soviet system implicit in American universalism—alas, not nearly strong enough to make it at that time a real threat—nonetheless did reinvigorate Stalin's drive for Soviet ideological purity, for it highlighted the need for ideological legitimacy for the Stalinist dictatorship at home and for the reimposition—and I would stress the word "reimposition"—of the Stalinist style of rule *inside* the Soviet Union —all in order to mobilize the Soviet population for the mammoth tasks of reconstruction, a reconstruction of those internal bases of international power which, once successfully completed, made the Soviet Union a truly dynamic global power, but really only in the era of "competitive coexistence" ushered in by Khrushchev some time after Stalin's death.

These observations leave open the question of whether the Cold War at its most intense and rigid was really inevitable or not. The answer to that question depends on one's philosophy of history, I suppose. All I want to suggest is that a continuation of those tentative lines of cooperation between Russia and the West which had developed during the war was, for a variety of quite understandable domestic Soviet considerations, quite unacceptable to Stalin. Given his point of view, which I regard *not* as the assessment of a madman but rather as the perception of a rather shrewd power-attuned leader, conscious of his own objectives and all too aware of those domestic Soviet realities that seemed to call their attainment into question— something like the Cold War as it actually occurred would have been the likely outcome irrespective of Western policies. Perhaps Stalin himself would have preferred noninvolvement in world affairs altogether. But isolationism was no longer a genuine alternative for a Soviet Union which, despite all its manifold postwar weaknesses, still was one of the two major power centers in a bipolar international system. This being the case, further scholarly progress towards excavating the roots of the Cold War, can, it seems to me, come by concentrating more closely than has heretofore been the case upon the domestic foundations of Soviet foreign policy. Once again, in this case as in so many others, a critical reexamination of the sins of commission and ommission of the diplomacy of one side or the other may be necessary, but it can never be sufficient. In the case of the Cold War, it is high time to assert the primacy not of *Aussenpolitik* but rather of *Innenpolitik*.

*Gaddis Smith*

# THE GHOST OF HITLER: LESSONS OF THE PAST

*If Schlesinger sees irrationality in Stalin, Gaddis Smith, in his biography of Secretary of State Dean Acheson (1949–53), finds an irrational element in American leaders. Harry S. Truman considered himself an amateur historian and like many of his advisers he frequently thought in simple, sometimes mistaken, historical parallels. Gaddis notes how the lessons American statesmen drew from the past helped shape their attitude that Stalin's Russia was replacing Hitler's Germany as a new threat to world order. By the premises of the "great cycle theory" of history, only the United States, through an active and resolute foreign policy designed to lead the reconstruction of the world, could prevent a repetition of instability and war so characteristic of the 1930s. Smith concludes that Truman and Acheson were "driven by the ghost of Hitler" in their Cold War diplomacy and buildup of military power. Smith teaches at Yale University and is the author of* American Diplomacy During the Second World War *(1965).*

His [Dean Acheson's] ideas, one must say, were not unique or original. They were, on the contrary, an extraordinarily articulate expression of a strand of thought which guided American foreign policy for a third of a century after outbreak of the Second World War. An appraisal of Acheson must therefore be an appraisal of the nation's behavior in world affairs for an entire generation.

That behavior was rooted in a particular interpretation of twentieth-century international relations, an interpretation which constituted, in effect, a great cycle theory. According to this view, the cycle began with the deterioration of the nineteenth-century Pax Britannica and the appearance of imperial Germany as an aggressive, ruthless foe of the status quo. The First World War was the result of Germany's drive for predominant world power. At the outset the United States had remained complacently neutral, trying to maintain traditional political and military isolation, ignorant of the fact that isolation was no longer possible without the stabilizing influence of the Pax Britannica. Belatedly in 1917 the American nation rose

From Gaddis Smith, *Dean Acheson* (New York, 1972), pp. 414–18, 423–24. Volume 16 of *The American Secretaries of State and Their Diplomacy,* eds. Robert H. Ferrell and Samuel Flagg Bemis. Reprinted by permission of Cooper Square Publishers, Inc.

from isolationism, recognized the threat to security, and saw a responsibility to a beleaguered world. Germany was defeated. President Wilson proposed a glorious new order through the League of Nations. The highpoint in the first turn of the cycle had been reached.

These events coincided with Acheson's youth. As a law student he volunteered for military training in 1916. He joined the Navy when the country entered the war. He applauded President Wilson's vision of world leadership for the United States.

But in 1919 a tragic downturn in the cycle began. The United States Senate and the people rejected Wilson's program and dreamed of finding security in a return to political isolation. Acheson abandoned his faith in the League of Nations more readily than most Wilsonians, but he deplored the consequences of American withdrawal from world politics—impotence in the face of governments seeking change through military aggression. By 1939 the cycle was again in a dangerous phase—war in Europe and irresponsible neutrality in the United States. As a private citizen Acheson joined those individuals seeking to change American public opinion and prod President Roosevelt toward intervention in support of the victims of Germany and Japan. He believed the situation was parallel to 1914, but more dangerous. The outcome depended even more on the behavior of the United States.

Again the cycle turned. The United States, its action accelerated by the Japanese attack at Pearl Harbor, arose from isolation a second time. By 1945 the century's second threat to a stable world order had been defeated. But now the United States alone among democratic nations had the power to maintain that stability. France was shattered; Great Britain bled white. The third and greatest threat was at hand—the Soviet Union. The alternatives, as Acheson and those persons around him understood, were another slide into irresponsibility followed inevitably by a third great war with the dreadful possibility of Soviet victory—or an heroic American effort to stop the terrible cycle by leading and reconstructing the economic and military power of the free world.

According to the great cycle theory, only the United States had the power to grab hold of history and make it conform. Did the American people have the necessary fortitude and will? All of Acheson's efforts in the State Department were directed toward preventing another turn in the cycle. As a private citizen after 1953 he spoke and wrote to the same end. He believed that another slide into isolation was a permanent danger, because totalitarianism was a permanent threat. The United States should never relinquish its leadership or diminish its power.

Acheson represented the dominant military version of the great cycle theory, as opposed to the minority collective security version. He belittled his youthful enthusiasm for the League of Nations and ridiculed the idea of a universal world organization. The Second World War represented a second chance for the United States to exercise military power, not to achieve utopia through collective security. It was ironic that he was assigned as Assistant Secretary of State to lobby in Congress for an institution in whose transcendence he did not believe. After 1945 he denounced any suggestion that the United Nations could provide an alternative to American military power. He looked on neoisolationists and enthusiasts for world organization as equally dangerous to his version of the great cycle theory and thus to American security.

There were numerous consequences and corollaries of the great cycle theory. First, the enemy was ever-present and unchanging. In many respects there was little difference between Hitler's Germany and Stalin's Russia. The enemy was a force of nature responsive to physical power, never to idealistic persuasion or pleas for cooperation in the interest of mankind. Since this was the case, speculation about the enemy's character or intentions was at best a waste of time and at worst an opening wedge of doubt about one's own position. Once Americans began to question the character of the enemy, they became vulnerable to the enemy's wiles and to their own tendency to backslide. Questioning would lead to doubt, doubt to slackened effort, weakened alliances, abandoned positions of strength, and loss of control over the great cycle. . . .

Acheson first took a leading part in the conduct of American foreign affairs when Hitler was at the peak of his terrible power, and this is a fundamental explanation of Acheson's attitudes and those of his colleagues in the State and Defense Departments, his contemporaries in Congress, the press, the universities, his superior in the White House. They were driven by the ghost of Hitler and only secondarily by hatred for Communist ideology or a desire to achieve a world-wide "open door" for American trade, as some later students of American foreign policy were to claim. The lesson which he and the majority of his generation learned was that peace cannot be preserved by good intentions and a small army. The democracies learned that it was impossible to negotiate with Hitler. The word "Munich" became a curse against the "low, dishonest decade" (the phrase is Auden's) of the thirties. Six years of bloody war, four for the United States, were the price of a false faith in appeasement. The generation which came to positions of leadership during the war could never forget the behavior of Hitler. Acheson represented that generation as well as any man of his time. He had seen the consequences of trying to understand the enemy's point of view, of making diplomatic concessions from a position of weakness, failing to create armed forces more powerful than the foe. The image of Hitler seared itself on the eyes of all who fought him. When Hitler was gone, the image lingered.

Stalin's policies were difficult to understand and apparently hostile to the West, and it was impossible for Acheson to conceive of the United States as having too much military power against the Soviet Union, any more than that the democracies could have had too much military power when facing Hitler. But there was one great difference between the two situations which Acheson recognized. Hitler had to be destroyed. War for the destruction of the Soviet Union would, in the atomic age, have no victors. If the United States had to be prepared to fight such a war as a last dreadful resort, the overriding purpose of American policy was deterrence, the prevention of war.

Russian leaders, to judge from the rhetoric of their public statements, also were deeply influenced by the experience of Hitler. They, too, saw their opponents in Hitlerian terms. Thus the Cold War was a process of reciprocal, reinforcing imagery and mutual deterrence. After a quarter century both the old generation of American and Soviet leaders could claim their policies had been correct. There had been no great war.

## Gabriel and Joyce Kolko

# SUSTAINING AND REFORMING
# WORLD CAPITALISM

*In his extensively researched* The Politics of War *(1968) and* The Limits of
Power *(1972, coauthored with Joyce Kolko), Gabriel Kolko argues that it
was not the Soviet Union, but the rise of the revolutionary Left which posed
a threat to America's postwar goal of sustaining and reforming world capitalism so that American business could expand. Flushed with power but fear-
ing a depression, American leaders employed foreign aid as a major tool
to realize that goal. Russia was but one roadblock to American expansion.
Yet the United States easily blamed Moscow for the postwar disorder
created by World War II and the challenge of the Left. Postwar tension,
concluded Kolko, grew not from external pressures on the United States but
from the internal needs of American capitalism which required overseas expansion, a conclusion other revisionists have debated as too monocausal.
Kolko, one of the leading radical critics of American interventionism, is the
author of* The Triumph of Conservatism *(1963) and* The Roots of American
Foreign Policy *(1969). He teaches at York University, Ontario, Canada.*

World War II was a prelude to the profound and irreversible crisis in
world affairs and the structure of societies which is the hallmark of
our times.

The war had come to an end, but no respite allowed the wounds
of the long era of violence to heal completely. Two vast epics of
bloodletting within thirty years' time had inflicted seemingly irreparable damage to traditional societies everywhere. From the moment
World War II ended, civil war, uprisings, and the specter of them replaced the conflict between the Axis and Allies in many nations, and
implacable hostility superseded tense relations between the Soviet
Union and the other members of what had scarcely been more than
a temporary alliance of convenience born wholly out of necessity.
After global conflagration came not peace, but sustained violence in
numerous areas of the world—violence that was to intensify with the
inevitable, broadening process of social transformation and decoloni-
zation that became the dominant experience of the postwar epoch.

For the individual in vast regions of the world, the war's outcome left hunger, pain, and chaos. Politically, conflict and rivalry wracked nations, and civil war spread in Greece and in Asia. Outside of the Western Hemisphere, ruin and the urge toward reconstruction were the defining imperatives in all the areas that war had touched. Affecting the very fabric of world civilization, the postwar strife threatened to undermine the United States' reasons for having fought two great wars and its specific aims in the postwar world.

Surrounded by this vast upheaval, the United States found itself immeasurably enriched and, without rival, the strongest nation on the globe. It emerged from the war self-conscious of its new strength and confident of its ability to direct world reconstruction along lines compatible with its goals. And these objectives, carefully formulated during the war, were deceptively simple: Essentially, the United States' aim was to restructure the world so that American business could trade, operate, and profit without restrictions everywhere. On this there was absolute unanimity among the American leaders, and it was around this core that they elaborated their policies and programs. They could not consider or foresee all the dimensions of what was essential to the attainment of their objective, but certain assumptions were implicit, and these in turn defined the boundaries of future policy options. American business could operate only in a world composed of politically reliable and stable capitalist nations, and with free access to essential raw materials. Such a universal order precluded the Left from power and necessitated conservative, and ultimately subservient, political control throughout the globe. This essential aim also required limitations on independence and development in the Third World that might conflict with the interests of American capitalism.

The United States therefore ended the war with a comprehensive and remarkably precise vision of an ideal world economic order, but with only a hazy definition of the political prerequisites for such a system. With these objectives before it, Washington confronted the major challenges to their fulfillment. Preeminent among these were the prewar system of world capitalism and its accumulation of trade and investment restrictions and autarchic economic nationalism that World War I and the subsequent depression had created. Traditional nationalism, consequently, was an obstacle to America's attainment of its goals, and this shaped the United States' relations to Britain

and its huge economic alliance, the sterling bloc. Washington's dealings with Britain throughout the war had been profoundly troubled
because of London's reticence in collaborating with American plans
for restructuring world trade. To the English such a program looked
very much like expansion in the name of an internationalism that ill
concealed the more tangible advancement of American power along
quite conventional lines. This rivalry among nominal allies was to become a basic theme of the postwar experience as well, because in
attempting to attain the leading role for itself in the international
economy the English had to consider whether the United States
might also recast Britain's once-dominant role in major areas of the
earth.

It was this same effort to foster a reformed world economy that
compelled the United States to turn its attention, with unprecedented
energy and expense, to the future of the European continent and
Germany's special position in it. The failure of Germany and Japan
to collaborate economically with the world throughout the interwar
period was, in Washington's opinion, the source of most of the mis-
fortunes that had befallen mankind. And however weak Europe might
be at the moment, the United States had to consider how its reemer-
gence—with or without Germany—might potentially affect the United
States' contemplated role on the Continent should Europe once again
assume an independent role. Allied with Russia, or even a resurgent
Germany, Western Europe could become the critical, perhaps decisive, factor in international economic and political power. And it was
an unshakable premise of America's policy that world capitalism
[would] become a unified system that would cease being divided into
autonomous rivals.

Its desire and need for global economic reform, integration, and
expansion almost immediately required the United States to confront
the infinitely more complex issue of the political preconditions for
establishing an ideal world order. This meant relating not only to the
forces of nationalism and conservatism that had so aggressively
undermined America's goals until 1945 but more especially to the
ascendant movements of change we may loosely associate with the
Left—forces that posed a fundamental threat to America's future in
the world. The war had brought to fruition all the crises in the civil
war within societies that World War I had unleashed, a conflict that
interwar fascism and reaction had forcibly, but only temporarily, sup-

pressed. The intensity of these national social and class conflicts was to increase with time, spreading to Asia and the Third World even as the United States was now compelled to consider how best to cope with the immediate threat of the radicalized European workers. The manner in which America balanced its desire for the reformation of European capitalism against its need to preserve it immediately as a system in any form, in order to later attempt to integrate it, is a key chapter in postwar history involving all of Europe and Japan. For the sake of its own future in the world, Washington had to resolve whether it wished to aid in the restoration of the traditional ruling classes of Germany and Japan—the very elements who had conducted wars against America in the past. . . .

In much of Asia and Europe a resurgent and formidable Left was a major effect of World War II, just as the Soviet Union was the main outcome of World War I. Each war had generated vast upheavals and a period of flux, and the United States' own goals and interests had colored its responses to them. Washington neither feared nor suspected that the world was irrevocably in transition, decentralized, unpredictable, and beyond the control of any nation—and especially its own mastery. But, in the short run, American leaders had to consider whether the Left had the will and capacity to act and take power—and how to respond in the event it did. At the same time they had to confront the question of the future of the USSR, a prospect that the deepening wartime diplomatic crisis between Russia and the West had left enshrouded in dark pessimism. The Left and Russia usually appeared as synonymous in America's litany, as Washington often assigned the Kremlin powers in the world that must have surprised the quite circumspect rulers of that war-devastated country. For the USSR's very existence was a reminder of the profound weakening of European capitalism and the traditional order after World War I, and potentially a catalyst for undermining capitalism in the future. But was Russia, given America's self-assigned destiny, *the* critical problem for the United States to confront in the postwar era? To place this question in perspective, one has only to ask, given its articulation of its larger goals, what the United States' policy would have been regarding innumerable problems and areas had the Bolshevik Revolution never occurred. As it was, during the war the Russians repeatedly showed their conservatism in their inhibiting advice to the various Communist parties and their refusal to move freely into the power vacuum capitalism's weakness had created everywhere. And what were the possibilities of negotiations and conventional diplomacy in resolving the outstanding issues with the Soviet Union, such as Eastern Europe, the future of Germany, and Russia's future role in the world, especially given America's definitions of the causes of the world's problems as well as its own interests? In light of American needs and perspectives, and the nature of the postwar upheaval and the forces of our age, were expansion and conflict inevitable? Washington never dissociated the USSR from the Left, not only because bolshevism is but one twentieth-century expression of a much larger revolutionary trend but also because it was often politically convenient for America's leaders to fix the blame for capitalism's failures on the cautious men in the Kremlin. . . .

The United States' ultimate objective at the end of World War II was both to sustain and to reform world capitalism. The tension between doing both eventually prevented America from accomplishing either in a shape fully satisfactory to itself. The task confronting Washington was to dissolve the impact not merely of World War II on the structure of the world economy but of the depression of 1929 and World War I as well—to reverse, in brief, most of the consequences of twentieth-century history. "The main prize of the victory of the United Nations," the State Department summed up the United States' vision in November 1945, "is a limited and temporary power to establish the kind of world we want to live in." That was the prodigious task before it.

*       *       *

The deeply etched memory of the decade-long depression of 1929 hung over all American plans for the postwar era. The war had ended that crisis in American society, but the question remained whether peace would restore it. The historical analyst is perpetually challenged and confounded by the danger that the effects of a policy may only rarely reveal its true motives, and specific interests and causal elements may distort its visible roots. But at the end of World War II the leadership of the United States determined on a policy intended to prevent the return of an economic and social crisis in American society—a policy that explicitly demanded that they resolve America's dilemma in the world arena.

The official and unofficial wartime debate on the postwar economic challenge was immense in scope and alone sufficient for a book. Yet the facts—and goals—were clear in the minds of nearly all commentators: the depression had damaged profoundly the United States' position in the world economy, lowering by almost half its share of a far smaller world trade, and the problem in the postwar era was to restore and then extend this share, to maintain the high wartime profits that had followed the parched 1930s, and to utilize a labor force temporarily absorbed in the military services and war plants. By June 1945 the capital assets in American manufacturing had increased 65 percent, largely from federal sources, over the 1939 level. Stated simply, for Washington's planners the question was how to use this vast plant after the end of hostilities. In the farm sector, the return of surplus gluts, largely due to the depression's impact on the world economy, seemd probable if no action were taken to prevent it. Apart from the vague measures and assumptions that Congress wrote into the Full Employment Bill of [1946], steps focused mainly on mitigating the extent and hardships of mass unemployment which the Senate's Committee on Banking anticipated would likely produce 6 or 7 millions out of work by the winter of 1945–1946, tangible proposals occurred mainly in foreign economic policy. "Our international policies and our domestic policies are inseparable," Secretary of State Byrnes informed the Senate on August 21, 1945. In extending its power throughout the globe, the United States hoped to save itself as well from a return of the misery of prewar experience.

From the 1932 low of $1.6 billion in exports, the United States attained $12.8 billion in 1943 and $14.3 billion in 1944, most of the new peak representing a favorable balance of trade. The figure of $14 billion in postwar exports—well over four times the 1939 level—therefore became the target of most wartime planners and their calculated precondition of continued American prosperity. Assistant Secretary of State Dean Acheson, by early 1945, publicly endorsed a $10 billion minimum figure, but Commerce Department experts thought it to be too low. Even if backlogged domestic wartime savings and demand sustained business activity for two or three years after 1946, Commerce experts warned, this alone would not prevent unemployment of as great as 4.5 million men in 1948. The most optimistic estimates calculated that the United States would not import more than $6 billion a year through 1947, and probably much less, and American private business could not, at best, profitably invest more than $3 billion a year for some time—figures that later proved much too high.

At the very least, $5 billion in annual United States loans and grants would for a time be required to attain the $14 billion export target for domestic prosperity, though some estimates ran to $8 billion. For this reason, key Washington officials publicly warned before the end of the war that the United States would have to provide ". . . the necessary financing of our foreign trade during the crucial period of reconversion at home and reconstruction abroad. . . ." From the outset, Washington set the entire question of postwar American foreign economic policy and aid in the context, as Clayton phrased it as late as November 1946, that ". . . let us admit right off that our objective has as its background the needs and interests of the people of the United States." Such a formulation was also based on the premise, as Byrnes had put it one year earlier, that "[p]olitical peace and economic warfare cannot long exist together." The failure to restore world trade would not only affect American prosperity but in addition lead to a continuation of the world trade restrictions which it was a prime American goal to eliminate as part of the reformation of world capitalism. For if the nations of Europe could not finance reconstruction via American aid, they would attempt to find the resources by tight exchange and import controls—in effect, continuing the status quo in the world economy inherited from the debacle of 1929. Loans would also become the key vehicle of structural change in the capitalist world. "We cannot play Santa Claus to the world but we can make loans to governments whose credit is good, provided such governments will make changes in commercial policies which will make it possible for us to increase our trade with them," Byrnes added. Trade, the reformation of foreign capitalism, and American prosperity were all seen as part of one interlocked issue.

From this viewpoint, even before America's leaders could evaluate the specific political and economic conditions of Europe—indeed, even when they were relatively sanguine—they determined on a postwar economic policy compatible with American interests. Not only, therefore, did Washington have to confront both bolshevism and the social-economic consequences of the great upheaval in the war-torn world, but it had also to redefine the nature of world capitalism as it had evolved after 1918. No responsible American leader had any illusions regarding the nation's critical role in the postwar world economy or any grave doubts as to its ability to fulfill its self-appointed role. . . .

The question of foreign economic policy was not the containment of communism, but rather more directly the extension and expansion of American capitalism according to its new economic power and needs. Primarily, America was committed to inhibiting and redirecting other forces and pressures of change abroad in the world among non-, even anti-, Soviet states. Russia and Eastern Europe were an aspect of this problem, but the rest of the world was yet more important even in 1946.

\*       \*       \*

Just as we insist on making an expansive American capitalism the central theme of postwar history, so, too, must we place a distinct emphasis on its relative failures—defeats the outcome and consequences of which have led to an escalation of the American attempts to master its ever more elusive self-assigned destiny. But we must also place the significance of its mounting efforts in the context of whether the multiplying undertakings were ever sufficient for the American economy's needs and for the fulfillment of its ambitious global objectives. For despite the fact that the magnitude of America's postwar program satisfied specific agricultural and industrial interests, in the largest sense it was inadequate to attain its maximum objectives. The British loan of 1946 was followed by the Marshall Plan, which in turn required massive arms aid, Point Four, and the like. By the time the intensifying transformation of the Third World, and evolution in Europe itself, could be gauged, it was evident to all in Washington that the role of capital exporter initially assigned to American business in the postwar world was woefully utopian. The state therefore undertook that key role during the first postwar decade, and wholly assumed the obligation of furnishing the political and military protection it knew an integrated world capitalism demanded. This merger of public and private power and goals, so traditional in American history, despite its vastly greater extent also fell short of the goal's monumental requirements. There were tactical successes and benefits, but the United States never attained the ideal world order it confidently anticipated during World War II.

America's leaders never fully realized the limits of American power in the world, and the use of foreign policy to express and solve the specific needs of American capitalism continued during the first postwar decade and thereafter, circumscribing the nature of American society and the process of social change throughout the globe. This interaction between a nation with universal objectives but finite power and the remainder of mankind is critical in modern history and the essence of the American experience....

*Robert Tucker*

# WOULD A SOCIALIST AMERICA BEHAVE DIFFERENTLY?

*Robert W. Tucker, who deals below with one group of revisionists, takes Kolko to task for his contention that American expansion is generated by the systemic needs of American capitalism. Tucker suggests that factors such as the search for security, a sense of mission, and the expansionist tendencies of any country possessing great power are just as important. In its foreign policy the United States responds not only to internal stimuli but also to external pressures. He chides Kolko and other radicals for ignoring these factors, as well as the structural causes of the Cold War, and he sees an inevitable conflict in the attempt to put international relations back into some form of stability after the war. But Tucker also criticizes Schlesinger and other traditionalists for superficially depicting American foreign policy as "universalist" in the early Cold War. Instead, writes Tucker, it was self-interestedly expansionist and the "course of containment became the course of empire." Finally, he dissents from the radical assumption that in international affairs a Socialist America would have behaved or will behave differently from a capitalist America. A professor of political science at The Johns Hopkins University and Director of the Washington Center of Foreign Policy Research, Tucker is the author of* Nation or Empire? *(1968), The* Radical Left and American Foreign Policy *(1971), from which this selection is taken, and* A New Isolationism *(1972).*

From Robert W. Tucker, *The Radical Left and American Foreign Policy* (Baltimore, 1971), pp. 70–71, 74–75, 89–94, 105–109, 138–43, 148–52. Copyright © 1971 by The Johns Hopkins University Press. Reprinted by permission. (Footnotes deleted.)

... The distinctiveness of the radical Left's critique must be found in the contention that America's foreign policy is essentially a response to the structural needs of American capitalism. If this contention is once abandoned, or seriously modified, differences will still remain between a radical and a more conventional criticism but these differences will no longer appear either profound or irreconcilable. Whatever the waverings and inconsistencies of particular radical critics, whatever the apparently independent role they may give to conviction and to interests that are not essentially rooted in the economic and social structure of American society, in the end it is only this contention that clearly sets them apart. No doubt, the radical position ought not to be pushed to the point of caricature, whether through a mechanical application of its essential contention or through the exclusion of other factors which are admitted to influence the nation's diplomacy. It is not denied that ideology may acquire a momentum of its own and, in the American case, has clearly done so. Even so, the question remains: What is central and what is peripheral to the radical analysis? The answer is not in real doubt. America's expansion—the drive to pacify and to integrate the global environment under American leadership and control— must be understood primarily as the outcome of forces generated by American capitalism. ...

Is it possible ... to understand the radical critics as arguing, despite their insistence to the contrary, that America is exceptional in its aggressiveness and in its insatiable urge to dominate? If this is their meaning, then it is difficult to argue further that the explanation of these exceptional characteristics is to be found in capitalism. At the very least, it must be argued that these characteristics have their source in a distinctively American version of capitalism. But this is only another way of saying that America's persistent expansiveness and aggressiveness are not to be found so much in capitalism as in other factors, which when combined with capitalism produce such unfortunate consequences. (May not one of these factors be an overweening sense of mission, the roots of which can scarcely be traced to capitalism? May not another factor be the very magnitude of American power, particularly since World War II? And, if so, does this not support a view about the nature of power, not capitalistic power but any power?)

Confronted by these obvious considerations, radical critics may fall back upon an argument against which no response appears to be of any avail. By definition, the possibility is ruled out that a capitalist state can pursue any policy other than an expansionist one, just as by definition the possibility is ruled out that a truly Socialist state *would* pursue an expansionist policy. This being so, there is no need to consider whether other factors may plausibly, or even possibly, account for the expansion of American power. By definition, this expansion can have no other explanation. In the words of one radical critic, "imperialism is capitalism which has burst the boundaries of the nation state. . . . [The] two phenomena are inseparable: There can be no end to imperialism without an end to capitalism and to capitalist relations of production."

\*　　　\*　　　\*

The radical interpretation of the Cold War . . . neglects the structural causes of the conflict. On occasion, it is true, radical critics do acknowledge that the Cold War initially resulted from a situation for which neither party can be held responsible. In this more sophisticated version, it is conceded that the real issue is not which side started the Cold War but which side is responsible for the way in which the conflict developed and the lengths to which it was carried. The concession is at best a limited one, however, usually made in passing and then only reluctantly. It could scarcely be otherwise, since an emphasis on the importance of the structural or systemic causes of the Cold War must seriously detract from the central thrust of the argument. Yet no plausible account of Soviet-American hostility can neglect to emphasize the significance of the structural causes of this hostility. What had been prior to the war the center of the international system had suddenly collapsed. By destroying the prewar balance of power—by creating a vacuum in the heart of Europe—the war resulted in a situation that could not but give rise to Soviet-American hostility. In the past, similar circumstances had invariably led to rivalry, often intense, even between states that understood each other because they possessed many similarities of outlook and shared a common diplomatic tradition. Given this history, and given the fact that the Cold War arose between states that did not understand each other, that entertained markedly divergent outlooks and shared no common diplomatic tradition, it seems evidently implausible to assume that conflict—even quite intense conflict—could have been avoided had one of the parties not been determined to pursue an expanionist policy.

If the radical interpretation is implausible in its neglect of the structural causes of the Cold War, it does provide a needed corrective to the conventional portrayal of the American view of the postwar world (and hence the portrayal of American aims in the postwar world). It is the contention of conventional historiography—whether old or new—that the origins of the Cold War must in part be understood in terms of two very different views of how the postwar world was to be organized: the universalist and the spheres-of-influence view. Whereas the Soviet Union was the champion of spheres of influence, the United States was presumably committed to the view that "all nations shared a common interest in all the affairs of the world" and that "national security would be guaranteed by an international organization."

The radical critic is surely right in insisting that there is little in this description of the universalist view that corresponds to American policy during the period in question. Clearly, America's universalism did not mean an opposition to any and all spheres of influence, for that opposition was betrayed by our continued claim to a sphere of influence in the Western Hemisphere and, beyond the hemisphere, to what was tantamount to a similar claim in the western Pacific. Nor can America's universalism be interpreted to mean the commitment to multilateralism as a method for safeguarding American interests. It is vain to point to the United Nations Charter, and to American support of the charter, as evidence of this commitment. The charter did not commit the great powers to multilateralism as a means for guaranteeing their interests. The charter's design of order was made dependent on the condition that the great powers would retain a basic identity of interests. It did not deal with the only contingency that could seriously threaten the vital interests of a great power but merely assumed that in this contingency—conflict between the great powers—each would seek to protect its interests in its own way and that the security system of the charter would become inoperative.

This was clearly the American understanding of the charter. Rather than to interpret our support of the United Nations as representing a serious commitment to multilateralism, this support should be seen as reflecting the belief, or hope, that the organization could be employed as a modest means for more effectively consolidating America's leadership in the postwar world. (The same may be said of the international economic institutions, predominantly of American inspiration, that were to emerge from the war.) In joining the United Nations America retained, and insisted on retaining, substantially the same freedom of action it had enjoyed in the past. A tradition of unilateralism remained very nearly intact even after the decision was made to undertake formal territorial commitments outside the hemisphere. Given America's vast power and the weakness of her allies, not only were America's commitments for all practical purposes unilateral in character but so were her relations generally. . . .

To the radical critic, the answer is clear. America's universalism was little more than a euphemism for an outlook and policy which sought to establish American supremacy in the postwar world. A policy intent upon making the world itself into an American sphere of influence is of necessity universalist in aim, just as it is of necessity opposed to spheres of influence from which its power and influence are excluded. If the radical response is overdrawn, if it fails to acknowledge the security motive that entered into American policy, it nevertheless contains a core of truth. Yet it is only by juxtaposition with an orthodox historiography that this response appears startling. What state that achieved the power and eminence America achieved by the end of World War II has not wanted and sought to have the world evolve in an equilibrium favorable to it? In America's case, a favorable equilibrium was evidently one that comprised the strengthening of capitalism. It is equally apparent that the strengthening of capitalism as a world system was seen as synonymous with the strengthening of American capitalism, the latter requiring the removal of the prewar obstacles to American exports and investments while ensuring American access to needed raw materials. There is no reason to deny the radical claim that the world America sought to achieve in the postwar period, and from which America could only derive maximum advantage in view of her dominant economic and political position, was the familiar one of the Open Door.

At least there is no reason to deny this claim, provided the Open Door is given a sufficiently broad interpretation. To this extent, the interpretation of America's wartime diplomacy by Williams or, for

that matter, by Kolko is unexceptionable. Thus it is scarcely a revela-
tion to be told, as Kolko tells us, that "America's economic war aim
was to save capitalism at home and abroad." Surely, no one argues
that our economic war aim was to promote socialism. It is another
matter to argue, as Kolko does argue, that America's "core objectives were economic" and that "politics was only the instrument
for preserving and expanding America's unprecedented power and
position in the European and world economy." The argument cannot rest simply upon an economic determinism which takes for
granted what needs to be proved.

*     *     *

The radical critics are quite right in concluding that the reasons
that ultimately impelled us to intervene in World War II also impelled
us to a course of action that made the Cold War inevitable. On both
occasions, the prospect was held out of a world outside this hemisphere hostile to American institutions and interests, a world in
which America's economic and political frontiers might become increasingly coextensive with its territorial frontiers, and thus a world
in which prosperity and democracy in America itself might be im-
periled. The issue of physical security apart, on both occasions it
was to prevent this prospect from becoming a reality that either war
or the risk of war was undertaken. As in the case of intervention
in World War II, the threat that prompted America's Cold War policy
evidently followed from the manner in which American leaders defined the nation's security in its greater than physical dimension. . . .
   Security was a principal motive of American policy in the period
in which the Cold War was joined. Under the circumstances, security
apprehensions were not unreasonable, though they were exaggerated. At the same time, American policy was also expansionist, and
it was so whether it is viewed in its objective or in its subjective
meaning. That its objective meaning was expansionist is admitted
by a conventional historiography. What is not generally admitted is
that it was expansionist in motive or intent. Thus the conventional
judgment, already noted, that America's post-World War II empire
came into being by accident, that nobody planned or wanted it.
There is a measure of truth in this judgment. The speed with which
America's postwar expansion occurred, the means by which it was

carried out, and the complacency with which it was viewed, may in part be explained as the unforeseen and unintended results of the search for security. Once the Cold War was fully joined, this expansion followed the seemingly inescapable dynamic of hegemonial conflict in which the intensity of the conflict is matched by its ubiquity.

Even so, the theme of the "accidental empire" has been carried to excess by a conventional historiography. Unless the view is taken that as a nation America is something new under the sun, our postwar expansion must ultimately be traced to our inordinate power and to our determination to use this power to ensure our particular version of a congenial international order. During World War II abundant evidence of this determination antedates serious conflict with our major ally. To be sure, once that conflict arose the security interest could no longer be separated from the more general interest in employing our power to sustain a world favorable to American institutions and interests. But such separation would have proved difficult in any event, given the generous manner in which the nation's security in its greater than physical sense was defined. For this definition was practically indistinguishable from a world stabilized in a pro-American equilibrium.

The radical critic, aware of the expansionist purposes to which our security claims have been put, thereby concludes that what was presented as a security interest was, in reality, little more than a rationalization for expansion. Nearer the truth, it would seem, is that our postwar policy expressed both a conventional security interest and an interest that went well beyond a conventional notion of security. The Truman Doctrine forms the most striking expression of this underlying ambiguity. By interpreting security as a function not only of a balance of power between states but of the internal order maintained by states, and not only by some states but by all states, the Truman Doctrine equated America's security with interests that evidently went well beyond conventional security requirements. This equation cannot be dismissed as mere rhetoric, designed at the time only to mobilize public opinion in support of limited policy actions, though rhetoric taken seriously by succeeding administrations. Instead, it accurately expressed the magnitude of America's conception of its role and interests in the world from the very inception of the Cold War. If this is kept in mind, American policy in the fifties and, even more, in the sixties appears not as a perversion of the conception of role and interests that dominated the early period of the Cold War, as a conventional historiography maintains, but as its logical progression.

Thus, the radical account of the origins of the Cold War reveals a partial, though nonetheless important, insight that a conventional historiography tends to obscure. Although the radical critic will not see the security interest in postwar American policy, he sees the expansionist interest only too clearly. That the deliberate quality of this interest is exaggerated, that the consistency with which it was presumably translated into early postwar policy is overdrawn, does not invalidate the radical's insistence that America's universalism has been throughout indistinguishable from America's expansionism.

In the period that has followed the initial years of the Cold War, it is the expansionist interest that has become increasingly dominant. It was not always so. A conventional security interest was, if not paramount, then of equal significance in the early policy of containment. As initially applied to Europe, containment was more or less synonymous with a balance-of-power policy. Even in an earlier period, though, a narrower and more traditional concept of security coexisted uneasily with a much broader concept and one that implied expansion. In part, then, the contrast conventional critics have so often drawn between the relatively precise and limited purposes of early postwar policy and the globalism of American policy in the 1960s is instead a contrast between the circumstances attending the application of policy then and now. For the circumstances of an earlier period limited the application of containment principally to Europe and made that application, whatever its larger purpose, roughly identical with a balance-of-power policy.

This rough identity of containment with a conventional security interest was questionable by the middle 1950s. A decade later, it ceased to have any real plausibility. Vietnam and the ensuing debate illuminated what should long have been apparent, that a profound change had occurred in the structure of American security and that, in consequence, many, if not most, of America's present interests and commitments were largely the result of a concept of security that could no longer satisfactorily account for these same interests and commitments. A continued emphasis on security, remarkable if only because of its excessiveness, could not obscure the fact that security in its more conventional and limited sense had ceased to be of paramount concern. An emphasis on security that often seemed almost inversely proportional to the security interests at stake may be explained by the continued need to justify policy—particularly the employment of force—in terms of interests which no longer defined this policy.

The triumph of an expansionist and imperial interest over an interest that expressed a narrower and more traditional concept of security reflected a change in circumstances rather than, or as much as, a change in essential outlook. It reflected the relative success of the early policy of containment. It also reflected the expansion— concomitant with that success—of American interests and the diversity of possible threats to those interests. By a dialectic as old as the history of statecraft, expansion proved to be the other side of the coin of containment. To contain the expansion of others, or what was perceived as such, it became necessary to expand ourselves. In this manner, the course of containment became the course of empire. In the same manner, the narrower interest containment expressed was submerged in the larger interest of maintaining a stable world order that would ensure the triumph of liberal-capitalist values.

*          *          *

Would a Socialist America pursue a foreign policy fundamentally different from the foreign policy pursued by a Capitalist America? Would it no longer seek to influence the course of development of other peoples? Would it abandon its hegemonial position along with the advantages this position has conferred? Would it provide a generous measure of assistance to developing nations while neither seeking nor expecting any tangible advantages in return?

Whether explicitly or implicitly, a radical critique answers these questions affirmatively. Whatever the differences otherwise separating them, the belief that a Socialist America would pursue a fundamentally different foreign policy is common to all radical critics. The pervasiveness of this belief is in itself significant. That it is held with equal fervor by those who nevertheless stress the independent force of conviction in the determination of policy must remain inexplicable, unless conviction is seen as not only having grown out of but as continuing to reflect the socioeconomic structure of society.

What may we say of the radical belief? Clearly, a Socialist America would in some respect behave differently from a Capitalist America. It would no longer seek to insure the triumph of liberal-capitalist values. But a radical critique cannot be content with telling us what no one would care to dispute. What many would dispute is the contention that such an America would no longer attempt to control its environment, that it would no longer attempt to fashion some sort of greater order, and that it would no longer entertain imperial relationships with other and weaker states. That these relationships would be undertaken for ostensibly different reasons cannot preclude the prospect that they would still be characterized by inequality and by some form of coercion.

It is not enough, then, to content oneself with saying that a Socialist America would no longer pursue Capitalist ways. For unless the "ways" of capitalism are equated with the ways collectives have displayed from time immemorial, we might be expected to retain interests that have little to do with capitalism but a great deal to do with the pretensions great powers have almost invariably manifested. If history is to prove at all relevant in this regard, there is no apparent reason to assume that the new America would refrain from identifying the collective self with something larger than the self. If this is so, the nation's security and well-being would still be identified with a world that remained receptive to American institutions and interests. No doubt, a Socialist America would define those institutions and interests in a manner different from the definition of a Capitalist America. But this difference cannot be taken to mean that we would refrain from attempting to influence the course of development of other peoples. The possibility—or, rather, the probability—must be entertained that there would still be revolutions, even radical revolutions, the nature and international consequences of which we might oppose. Nor is there any assurance that our opposition would appear less oppressive to others simply because it was no longer motivated by the desire to safeguard private investments or needed sources of raw materials.

That American policy would no longer be concerned with maintaining an environment receptive to the investment of capital follows by definition. Would the same lack of concern be manifested toward safeguarding present sources of raw materials, particularly if they are as critical to the economy as the radicals contend? Radical critics make a great deal of the political and psychological necessity of a Capitalist America to preserve access to needed sources of raw materials. Why is it assumed that this is a "necessity" unique to capitalism? Is it unreasonable to assume that a Socialist America might also wish to preserve similar access? It may of course be argued that a Socialist America would not consume the quantities of raw materials a capitalist America consumes and that for those raw materials it still needed to import it would pay a "just" price. But this argument is one that proceeds by definition, that is, by defining how a truly Socialist society would act, rather than by experience. . . .

The world of a Socialist America would still be a world marked by great inequalities. It would still be a world of the strong and the weak, the rich and the poor. If injustice springs from such inequalities, what are the grounds for believing the new society would act justly toward the weak? It is, after all, not only Capitalist states that have sought to take advantage of their strength when dealing with poor and weak states. The record of the Soviet Union's relations with the underdeveloped states scarcely bears out a reluctance to draw such advantages as it can from its position of strength. It may of course be argued that this only proves that the Soviet Union is not a truly Socialist state. It may also be argued that the Soviet Union's behavior indicates that the real source of injustice and exploitation today stem from the fact that the world is divided into rich and poor states. The latter argument is a striking departure from Marxism or its Leninist adaptation, but it is still not enough of a departure. It is not only the division of humanity into the rich and the poor that gives rise to the various forms of unequal relationships the radical equates with imperialism. It is also the division of humanity into discrete collectives. If advanced states, whether capitalist or Socialist, may behave similarly in many respects toward backward states, it is not simply because they are advanced but because collectives have very little sense of obligation to others. That is why we have no persuasive grounds for assuming that a society which acts justly at home will also act justly abroad. . . .

Whatever influence the radical critique may enjoy, its intrinsic merits must be judged quite separately. Despite the treatment radical criticism has generally received at the hands of conventional critics (who have dismissed it even while responding to its more persuasive features), as an interpretation of American diplomacy this criticism does have merit. If nothing else, the radical critique has forced us to acknowledge the extent to which an obsessive self-interest has been central in American foreign policy. In doing so, it has provided an element of realism that, ironically enough, has often been missing from a conventionally critical historiography which has prided itself precisely on its realism. In its insistence that American diplomacy has been driven throughout by self-interest, the lesson radical criticism conveys is that America has behaved very much as other great nations have behaved, and that if there is a quality unique to American diplomacy it consists in the greater than usual disparity between ideals professed and behavior. This lesson may not have been the intention of radical critics—certainly this was not their primary intention—but its corrective value is not diminished for that reason.

It is also the merit of radical criticism to have shown that American diplomacy scarcely betrays the intellectual error attributed to it by a conventionally critical historiography. To the latter, America's globalism—and interventionism—spring from illusory judgments of the world and particularly from the conviction that America's wants and values are shared by men everywhere. That we persist in this conviction proves to the conventional critic that America is still isolationist in the deeper sense of remaining an "isolated" nation. It is true that the quality of isolation, the sense of political and moral separateness, may manifest itself both in a policy of isolation as well as in a policy of intervention. In either case, however, the root of policy is presumably the same and consists in the inability to recognize and to accept the world for what it is. The radical critic clearly does not deny our inability to accept the world for what it is. To the contrary, this is a central element of his criticism. What he does deny is that this inability, or unwillingness, is explained by intellectual error. Where the conventional critic finds intellectual error or false perceptions, the radical critic finds the will to establish America's hegemony in the world. Here again, the lesson radical criticism conveys is that America has behaved very much as other great nations have behaved and that her messianism has been a means to the end of hegemony. In emphasizing the deliberate and consistent quality of this will, the radical critic no doubt exaggerates. Even in exaggeration, however, the radical emphasis seems nearer the truth than liberal-realist historiography.

Nor does it matter much whether America's expansionism is seen to reflect a will to hegemony or the desire to shape an environment congenial to American institutions and interests. Even if the latter interpretation is taken, the point remains that America has entertained in this century a very expansive concept of security. Although obscuring its deeper roots, radical criticism has nevertheless illuminated this concept of security in a manner conventional historiography has not done. The radical critique has persuasively demonstrated that the manner in which we have defined our security in its greater than physical dimension has been practically indistinguishable from a world stabilized in a pro-American equilibrium. To this extent, there is much to be said for the radical emphasis on the Open Door as the key to American strategy in this century. For the Open Door not only defined the manner in which American leaders viewed the nation's security in its greater than physical dimensions, it also reflected the aspiration to world leadership that was inseparable from this view. The radical critic may interpret the Open Door too narrowly and identify as policy what has often been little more than aspiration. Even in doing so, he provides a needed corrective to conventional criticism.

Despite these considerations, we cannot conclude that such influence as radical criticism has enjoyed may be attributed primarily to its explanatory power. For the merit of the radical critique must still be weighed against defects examined in earlier pages. These defects, and the illusions they must inevitably foster, cannot be redeemed by the provisional realism which makes the radical so effective a critic, not only of American diplomacy but also of the dominant interpretation of this diplomacy. Whereas the radical critic clearly sees—indeed, too clearly sees—the calculation and self-interest that have marked American foreign policy, he persistently ignores the deeper sources of collective self-aggrandizement. Even if it were true that America's security in this century has been totally unconditioned by events occurring beyond our frontiers, it would not follow that our expansion must be attributed to forces generated by a particular socioeconomic structure. There may be few reliable lessons that the study of state relations reveals. But one is surely that the identification of the collective self with something greater than the self is so endemic a trait in the case of great states that it may be considered to form part of their natural history. The radical attempt to find the roots of America's expansion primarily in her institutional forms dismisses this lesson. It necessarily denies that it is power itself, more than a particular form of power, which prompts expansion.

Thus radical criticism will not confront the eternal and insoluble problems inordinate power creates, just as it will not acknowledge that men possessed of this power are always ready to use it if only in order to rule over others. In the radical *weltanschauung* there is little, if any, appreciation that dominion is its own reward and that men may sacrifice material interest in order to rule (or, for that matter, to be emulated). There is also little, if any, appreciation that expansion may be rooted in an insecurity that is not simply self-generated. It is no doubt true that America's expansion is in large measure the result of an expansive concept of security and that this concept is, in part, related to the nature of America's institutions. It is not true that America's security in this century has been un-conditioned by events occurring beyond our frontiers and that, in consequence, to the extent our security has been compromised it has been the result of our own persistent expansionism and aggres-siveness. The issue of physical security apart, the radical case pro-ceeds from the assumption that whatever threat there has been to American security in its greater than physical dimensions, such threat has followed either from the way we have mistakenly defined our security (that is, as a function of what were supposedly our in-stitutional needs) or from the objective needs of America's institu-tions. In neither form, however, does this assumption rest upon a persuasive showing that given different institutions a hostile world would have posed no threat to us. The radical critique takes for granted what must instead be plausibly demonstrated. . . .

# Suggestions for Additional Reading

Any study of the origins of the Cold War must ground itself in the pre-1945 period. For various points of view see Thomas Bailey, *America Faces Russia* (Ithaca, 1950); Desmond Donnelly, *Struggle for the World* (New York, 1965); George Kennan, *Russia and the West Under Lenin and Stalin* (Boston, 1969); B. Ponomaryvov, et al., eds., *History of Soviet Foreign Policy, 1917–1945* (Moscow, 1969); Adam Ulam, *Expansion and Coexistence: The History of Soviet Foreign Policy, 1917–1973* (New York, 1974); and William A. Williams, *American-Russian Relations, 1781–1947* (New York, 1952). For the American intervention in the Bolshevik Revolution, see N. Gordon Levin, *Woodrow Wilson and World Politics* (New York, 1968) and the representative studies in Betty Miller Unterberger, ed., *American Intervention in the Russian Civil War* (Lexington, Mass., 1969). For relations leading to recognition in 1933, and the troubled aftermath, see Edward Bennett, *Recognition of Russia* (Waltham, Mass., 1970); Peter Filene, *Americans and the Soviet Experiment, 1917–1933* (Cambridge, Mass., 1967); Charles Timberlake, "Russian-American Contacts, 1917–1937: A Review Essay," *Pacific Northwest Quarterly* 61 (October 1970):217–21; and Joan Hoff Wilson, *Ideology and Economics* (Columbia, Mo., 1974).

Different perspectives on the diplomacy of World War II can be found in Herbert Feis, *Churchill, Roosevelt, and Stalin* (Princeton, 1957) and *Between War and Peace: The Potsdam Conference* (Princeton, 1960); Gabriel Kolko, *The Politics of War* (New York, 1968); and William H. McNeill, *America, Britain, and Russia* (London, 1953). Other general surveys include Gaddis Smith, *American Diplomacy During the Second World War, 1941–1945* (New York, 1965) and John Snell, *Illusion and Necessity* (Boston, 1963). The Lend-Lease question is studied sympathetically in George Herring, *Aid to Russia, 1941–1946* (New York, 1973) and critically in Robert Jones, *The Roads to Russia* (Norman, Okla., 1969). The president is the central figure in James MacGregor Burns, *Roosevelt: Soldier of Freedom* (New York, 1970) and Robert Divine, *Roosevelt and World War II* (Baltimore, 1969). The link between military decisions and diplomacy is treated in an "official" history by Robert Coakley and Richard Leighton, *Global Logistics and Strategy, 1943–1945* (Washington, 1968; part of *U.S. Army in World War II*) and in Raymond O'Connor, *Diplomacy for Victory: FDR and Unconditional Surrender* (New York, 1971). Secretary of State Cordell Hull relives his participation in his *Memoirs* (New York, 1948; 2 vols.), as does John Deane, *The Strange Alliance* (New York, 1947). Special problems are discussed in George Kirk, *The Middle East in the War* (London, 1952) and Edward Rozek, *Allied Wartime Diplomacy: A Pattern in Poland* (New York, 1958). A useful collection and bibliography is Robert Divine, ed., *Causes and Consequences of World War II* (Chicago, 1969).

General accounts of the origins of the Cold War from the traditional point of view include Seyom Brown, *The Faces of Power* (New York, 1968); Herbert Feis, *From Trust to Terror* (New York, 1970); André Fontaine, *History of the Cold War* (New York, 1968–1969; 2 vols.); Paul Hammond, *The Cold War Years* (New York, 1969); Philip Mosely, *The Kremlin and World Politics* (New York, 1960); Eugene Rostow, *Peace in the Balance* (New York, 1972); Walt Rostow, *The Diffusion of Power* (New York, 1972); Arthur Schlesinger, Jr., "Origins of the Cold War," *Foreign Affairs* 96 (October 1967): 22–52; John Spanier, *American Foreign Policy Since World War II* (New York, 1971); and John Wheeler-Bennett and Anthony Nichols, *The Semblance of Peace* (London, 1972). Especially useful for information and chronology are John Campbell, *The United States in World Affairs, 1945–1947* (New York, 1947), and succeeding volumes.

General revisionist studies include Stephen Ambrose, *Rise to Globalism* (Baltimore, 1971); Richard Barnet, *Roots of War* (Baltimore, 1972); Barton Bernstein, ed., *Politics and Policies of the Truman Administration* (Chicago, 1970); D. F. Fleming, *The Cold War and Its Origins* (Garden City, 1961; 2 vols.); J. William Fulbright, "Reflections: In Thrall to Fear," *New Yorker* 47 (January 8, 1972):41–62; Lloyd Gardner, *Architects of Illusion* (Chicago, 1970); David Horowitz, *Free World Colossus* (New York, 1971); N. D. Houghton, ed., *Struggle Against History* (New York, 1968); Gabriel and Joyce Kolko, *The Limits of Power* (New York, 1972); Gabriel Kolko, *The Roots of American Foreign Policy* (Boston, 1969); Walter LaFeber, *America, Russia, and the Cold War* (New York, 1972); Lynn Miller and Ronald Pruessen, eds., *Reflections on the Cold War* (Philadelphia, 1974); Thomas Paterson, ed., *Cold War Critics* (Chicago, 1971); Frederick Schuman, *The Cold War* (Baton Rouge, 1967); Rexford Tugwell, *A Chronicle of Jeopardy* (Chicago, 1955); and William A. Williams, *Tragedy of American Diplomacy* (New York, 1962).

Other general works, not easily categorized, include John Gaddis, *The United States and the Origins of the Cold War* (New York, 1972); Louis Halle, *The Cold War as History* (New York, 1967); John Lukacs, *A New History of the Cold War* (Garden City, 1966); Ernest May, *"Lessons" of the Past* (New York, 1973); William Neumann, *After Victory* (New York, 1967); Lisle Rose, *After Yalta* (New York, 1973) and *The Coming of the American Age* (Kent, Ohio, 1974; 2 vols.); Marshall Shulman, *Stalin's Foreign Policy Reappraised* (Cambridge, Mass., 1963); Adam Ulam, *The Rivals* (New York, 1971); and Thomas Wolfe, *Soviet Power and Europe, 1945–1970* (Baltimore, 1970).

The debate between the schools of thought on the origins of the Cold War has sparked some provocative interpretative literature. For representative essays by Bernstein, Ferrell, Gardner, and David McLellan, see Richard Kirkendall, *The Truman Period as a Research Field* (Columbia, Mo., 1974). Other works which reveal the intensity of the debate are Norman Graebner, "Cold War Origins and the Contemporary Debate: A Review of Recent Literature," *Journal of Conflict Resolution* 13 (March 1969):123–32; David Horowitz, "Historians and the Cold War," *Ramparts* 12 (August-September 1973):36ff; Walter Laqueur, "Rewriting History," *Commentary* 55 (March 1973):53–63; Christopher Lasch, "The Cold War: Revisited and Re-Visioned," *New York Times Magazine* (January 14, 1968):26ff; Robert Maddox, *The New Left and the Origins of the Cold War* (Princeton, 1973); Charles Maier, "Revisionism and the Interpretation of Cold War Origins," *Perspectives in American History* 4 (1970):313–47; J. L. Richardson, "Cold War Revisionism: A Critique," *World Politics* 24 (July 1972):579–612; Joseph Siracusa, *New Left Histories and Historians* (Port Washington, N.Y., 1973); Joseph Starobin, "Origins of the Cold War: The Communist Dimension," *Foreign Affairs* 47 (July 1969):681–96; Ronald Steel, "The Good Old Days," *New York Review of Books* (June 14, 1973):33–36; Robert Stover, "Responsibility for the Cold War," *History and Theory* 2 (1972):145–78; Robert W. Tucker, *The Radical Left and American Foreign Policy* (Baltimore, 1971); William Welch, *American Images of Soviet Foreign Policy: An Inquiry into Recent Appraisals from the Academic Community* (New Haven, 1970); Norman Wilensky, "Was the Cold War Necessary?" *American Studies* 13 (Spring 1972):177–87; and William A. Williams, "The Cold War Revisionists," *The Nation* 205 (November 13, 1967): 492–95.

The following sections indicate studies which have their primary focus on a particular question. Many of the works cited above also include discussions of specific issues. Gar Alperovitz, in *Atomic Diplomacy* (New York, 1965) and *Cold War Essays* (Garden City, 1970), argues that the decision to drop the bomb had significant diplomatic motivation. Herbert Feis, *The Atomic Bomb and the End of World War II* (Princeton, 1966) disagrees and argues that the bomb was used to end the war quickly to save lives. P. M. S. Blackett gives an earlier suggestive account paralleling Alperovitz in *Fear, War, and the Bomb* (New York, 1948). For the continuity between the Roosevelt and Truman administrations, see Martin Sherwin, "The Atomic Bomb and the Origins of the Cold War: U.S. Atomic-Energy Policy and Diplomacy, 1941–1945," *American Historical Review* 78 (October 1973):945–68 and Barton Bernstein, "The Quest for Security . . . 1942–1946," *Journal of American History* 60 (March 1974):1003–44. For a study which discovers bureaucratic considerations uppermost, see Kenneth Glazier, "The Decision to Use Atomic Weapons Against Hiroshima and Nagasaki," *Public Policy* 18 (Summer 1970):463–516. James Byrnes' thinking is evident in his "We Were Anxious to Get the War Over," *U.S. News and World Report* 49 (August 15, 1960):65–68, and in Thomas Paterson, "Potsdam, the Atomic Bomb and the Cold War," *Pacific Historical Review* 41 (May 1970):225–30. Henry Stimson explains his hesitancy in using the bomb for diplomatic purposes in Stimson and McGeorge Bundy, *On Active Service in Peace and War* (New York, 1948). The place of the scientists in the debate is treated in Alice Smith, *A Peril and a Hope* (Chicago, 1965) and Leo Szilard, "Reminiscences," *Perspectives in American History* 2 (1968):94–151. Subsequent negotiations on atomic disarmament can be followed in Berhard Bechhoefer, *Postwar Negotiations for Arms Control* (Washington, 1961), Joseph Lieberman, *The Scorpion and the Tarantula: The Struggle to Control Atomic Weapons, 1945–1949* (Boston, 1970), David Lilienthal, Vol. III of *Journals: Atomic Energy Years, 1945–1950* (New York, 1964), and John Spanier and Joseph Nogee, *The Politics of Disarmament* (New York, 1962). For the official history of the Atomic Energy Commission, see Richard Hewlett and Oscar Anderson, *The New World* (University Park, Pa., 1962) and Hewlett and Francis Duncan, *Atomic Shield* (University Park, Pa., 1970). See Clarence Lasby, *Operation Paperclip: German Scientists and the*

*Cold War* (New York, 1971), for the competition between Russia and America in the capture of German experts.

The establishment of the United Nations Organization is treated critically by Thomas Campbell, *Masquerade Peace: America's U.N. Policy, 1944–1945* (Tallahassee, Fla., 1973) and traditionally in Ruth Russell, *A History of the United Nations* (Washington, 1958). For background, see Robert Divine, *Second Chance: The Triumph of Internationalism in America During World War II* (New York, 1967). Early participants and their records are accessible in Trygve Lie (secretary general), *In the Cause of Peace* (New York, 1954); Andrew Cordier and Wilder Foote, eds., *Public Papers of the Secretaries-General of the United Nations, Vol. I, Trygve Lie, 1946–1953* (New York, 1969); and Walter Johnson, ed., *Papers of Adlai Stevenson,* Vol. 2 (Boston, 1973). One aspect can be studied in Robert Asher, et al., *The United Nations and Economic and Social Co-operation* (Washington, 1957). For studies of the veto and voting power, all demonstrating a strong U.S. position, see Frederick Gareau, *The Cold War, 1947–1967: A Quantitative Study* (Denver, 1968–69); Edward Rowe, "The United States, the United Nations, and the Cold War," *International Organization* 25 (Winter 1971):59–78; and John Stoessinger, *The United Nations and the Superpowers* (New York, 1970).

For a detailed survey of postwar economic diplomacy, see Thomas Paterson, *Soviet-American Confrontation* (Baltimore, 1973). Background studies include Lloyd Gardner, *Economic Aspects of New Deal Diplomacy* (Madison, 1964); Ernest Penrose, *Economic Planning for the Peace* (Princeton, 1953); and George Herring, *Aid to Russia.* Theodore Wilson and Richard McKenzie are completing a study of foreign aid for the early Cold War years. For aid and trade policy, see David Baldwin, *Economic Development and American Foreign Policy, 1943–62* (Chicago, 1966); William Brown, *The United States and the Restoration of World Trade* (Washington, 1950); William Brown and Redvers Opie, *American Foreign Assistance* (Washington, 1953); Richard Gardner, *Sterling-Dollar Diplomacy* (New York, 1969); George Lenczowski, *Oil and State in the Middle East* (Ithaca, 1960); and Raymond Mikesell, *U.S. Private and Government Investment Abroad* (Corvallis, 1962). Helpful for data are the Department of the Treasury, *Census of American-Owned Assets in Foreign Coun-*

*tries* (Washington, 1947); Department of Commerce, *Foreign Aid, 1940–51* (Washington, 1952); and U.S. Export-Import Bank, *Semiannual Report(s) to Congress.* For other aspects, see Jack Behrman, "Political Factors in U.S. International Financial Cooperation, 1945–1950," *American Political Science Review* 47 (June 1953):431–60; James Clayton, ed., *The Economic Impact of the Cold War* (New York, 1970) and "The Fiscal Cost of the Cold War to the United States: The First 25 Years," *Western Political Quarterly* 25 (September 1972):375–95; Herbert Feis, "The Conflict over Trade Ideologies," *Foreign Affairs* 25 (October 1946):217–28; and David Horowitz, ed., *Corporations and the Cold War* (New York, 1969). For an official history of UNRRA relief, consult George Woodbridge, et al., *UNRRA* (New York, 1950; 3 vols.). The Marshall Plan receives standard treatment in Harry Price, *The Marshall Plan and Its Meaning* (Ithaca, 1955) and a revisionist interpretation in Warren Hickman, *Genesis of the European Recovery Program* (Geneva, 1949). A study of the Marshall Plan as a "bureaucratic process" is Hadley Arkes, *Bureaucracy, the Marshall Plan, and the National Interest* (Princeton, 1973). David Wightman, *Economic Co-operation in Europe* (New York, 1956), studies the ECE. The Point Four program is interpreted in Thomas Paterson, "Foreign Aid Under Wraps: The Point Four Program," *Wisconsin Magazine of History* 56 (Winter 1972–73):119–26.

The Yalta Conference and issues over and in Eastern Europe have stimulated a great deal of literature. For the Yalta Conference, see Diane Shaver Clemens, *Yalta* (New York, 1970); Martin Herz, *Beginnings of the Cold War* (Bloomington, Ind., 1966), which emphasizes Poland; John Snell, ed., *The Meaning of Yalta* (Baton Rouge, 1956); and representative essays in Richard Fenno, ed., *The Yalta Conference* (Lexington, Mass., 1972). A participant discusses it in Edward Stettinius, *Roosevelt and the Russians* (Garden City, 1949). For the conference as an issue in American politics after 1945, see Athan Theoharis, *The Yalta Myths* (Columbia, Mo., 1970). For American and Russian relations with countries in Eastern Europe after the war, see Phyllis Auty, *Tito* (New York, 1970); R. R. Betts, ed., *Central and South East Europe, 1945–1948* (London, 1950); Lynn Etheridge Davis, *The Cold War Begins: Soviet-American Conflict over Eastern Europe* (Princeton, 1974); William Diamond, *Czechoslovakia Between East and West* (London, 1947); Andrew Gyorgy, *Governments of Danubian Europe* (New York, 1949); H. Stuart Hughes, "The Second Year of the Cold War," *Commentary* 48 (August 1969):27–32; Stephen Kertesz, ed., *The Fate of East Central Europe* (Notre Dame, 1956); Joseph Korbel, *The Communist Subversion of Czechoslovakia, 1938–1948* (Princeton, 1959); Bennett Kovrig, *The Myth of Liberation* (Baltimore, 1972); Hugh Seton-Watson, *The East European Revolution* (New York, 1956); James Warburg, *Last Call for Common Sense* (New York, 1949); and Paul Zinner, *Communist Strategy and Tactics in Czechoslovakia, 1918–1948* (New York, 1963). For memoirs and papers largely on Eastern European affairs, see Ambassador to Poland Arthur Bliss Lane's *I Saw Poland Betrayed* (Indianapolis, 1948); Polish leader Stanislaw Mikolajczyk's *The Rape of Poland* (New York, 1948); Czech Foreign Trade Minister Hubert Ripka's *Czechoslovakia Enslaved* (London, 1950); Vladimir Dedijer, *The Battle Stalin Lost: Memoirs of Yugoslavia, 1948–1953* (New York, 1971); and Josip Tito, *Selected Speeches and Articles, 1941–1961* (Zagreb, 1963).

Histories of the great power squabble over postwar Germany include John Backer, *Priming the German Economy: American Occupation Policies, 1945–1948* (Durham, 1971); Michael Balfour and John Mair, *Four Power Control in Germany and Austria, 1945–1946* (London, 1956); Eugene Davidson, *The Death and Life of Germany* (New York, 1959); John Gimbel, *The American Occupation of Germany* (Stanford, 1968), Manuel Gottlieb, *The German Peace Settlement and the Berlin Crisis* (New York, 1960); Bruce Kuklick, *American Policy and the Division of Germany* (Ithaca, 1972); and Harold Zink, *The United States in Germany, 1944–1955* (Princeton, 1957). For a much debated issue, see Stephen Ambrose, *Eisenhower and Berlin, 1945: The Decision to Halt at the Elbe* (New York, 1967). French policy is handled in A. W. Porte, *De Gaulle's Foreign Policy, 1944–1946* (Cambridge, Mass., 1968) and Soviet policy in J. P. Nettl, *The Eastern Zone and Soviet Policy in Germany, 1945–50* (London, 1951) and Robert Slusser, ed., *Soviet Economic Policy in Postwar Germany* (New York, 1953). The Berlin question is discussed in W. Phillips Davidson, *The Berlin Blockade* (Princeton, 1958); William Franklin, "Zonal Boundaries and Access to Berlin," *World Politics* 16 (October 1963):1–31; and Jean Smith, *The Defense of Berlin* (Baltimore, 1963). For German military reconstruction see Laurence Martin, "The American Decision to Rearm Germany," in Harold Stein, ed., *American Civil-Military Decisions* (Birmingham, Ala., 1963). For the vigorous discussion concerning the Morgenthau Plan, see John Gimbel and

Bruce Kuklick (referred to above), as well as Walter Dorn, "The De-bate Over American Occupation in Germany in 1944–1945," *Political Science Quarterly* 72 (December 1957):481–501 and Paul Hammond, "Directives for the Occupation of Germany: The Washington Con-troversy," in Harold Stein, ed., *American Civil-Military Decisions* (Birmingham, Ala., 1963). Henry Morgenthau, Jr., explains his "plan" in *Germany Is Our Problem* (New York, 1945) and in John Blum, *From the Morgenthau Diaries: Years of War, 1941–1945* (Boston, 1967; Vol. 3 of 3 vols.). For provocative commentaries from contem-porary participants, see Lewis Brown, *A Report on Germany* (New York, 1947); James Martin, *All Honorable Men* (Boston, 1950); Gustav Stolper, *German Realities* (New York, 1948); and James Warburg, *Germany—Bridge or Battleground?* (New York, 1947) and *Germany: Key to Peace* (Cambridge, Mass., 1953). Lucius Clay, the military gov-ernor, discusses his policies in *Decision in Germany* (Garden City, 1950). See also Jean Smith, ed., *The Papers of General Lucius Clay: Germany, 1945–1949* (Bloomington, Ind., 1974) and U.S. Department of State, *Germany, 1947–1949: The Story in Documents* (Washington, 1950). A leading German reflects on his role in Konrad Adenauer, *Memoirs* (Chicago, 1966). For a neighboring occupied country, con-sult William Bader, *Austria Between East and West, 1945–1955* (Stan-ford, 1966).

For events in Greece leading to the American response in the Truman Doctrine, see John Iatrides, *Revolt in Athens* (Princeton, 1972); Edgar O'Ballance, *The Greek Civil War* (New York, 1966); and Stephen Xydis, *Greece and the Great Powers, 1944–1947* (Thessalo-nike, 1963). For the formulation of the Truman Doctrine and contain-ment philosophy and the subsequent debate, see Richard Barnet, *Intervention and Revolution* (New York, 1968 and 1972); Richard Freeland, *The Truman Doctrine and the Origins of McCarthyism* (New York, 1972); Joseph Jones, *The Fifteen Weeks* (New York, 1955), a Truman speechwriter; Walter Lippmann, *The Cold War* (New York, 1947); Thomas Paterson, ed., *Containment and the Cold War* (Reading, Mass., 1973), which includes representative opinions and an extensive bibliography; and Thomas Paterson, "The Search for Meaning: George F. Kennan and American Foreign Policy," in Frank Merli and Theodore Wilson, eds., *Makers of American Diplomacy* (New York, 1974).

For the subsequent U.S. impact on Greece, consult Theodore

Couloumbis, *Greek Political Reaction to American and NATO Influences* (New Haven, 1966); Stephen Rousseas, *The Death of a Democracy: Greece and the American Conscience* (New York, 1967); and L. S. Stavrianos, *Greece: American Dilemma and Opportunity* (Chicago, 1952). The problems of British policy are discussed in M. A. Fitzsimmons, *The Foreign Policy of the British Labour Government: 1945–1951* (Notre Dame, 1953); Michael Gordon, *Conflict and Consensus in Labour's Foreign Policy, 1914–1965* (Stanford, 1969); and F. S. Northedge, *British Foreign Policy: The Process of Readjustment, 1945–1961* (New York, 1962).

For the Far East in the early Cold War, see Warren I. Cohen, *America's Response to China* (New York, 1971); Russell Buhite, *Patrick J. Hurley and American Foreign Policy* (Ithaca, 1973); John Paton Davies, Jr., *Dragon by the Tail* (New York, 1972); Herbert Feis, *The China Tangle* (Princeton, 1953) and *Contest Over Japan* (New York, 1967); Edward Friedman and Mark Selden, eds., *America's Asia: Dissenting Essays in Asian-American Relations* (New York, 1971); Akira Iriye, *The Cold War in Asia* (Englewood Cliffs, N.J., 1974); Ross Koen, *The China Lobby in American Politics* (New York, 1974); William Neumann, *America Encounters Japan* (Baltimore, 1963); John Service, *The Amerasia Papers* (Berkeley, 1972); A. T. Steele, *The American People and China* (New York, 1966); Tang Tsou, *America's Failure in China, 1941–1950* (Chicago, 1963); and Barbara Tuchman, *Stilwell and the American Experience in China, 1911–45* (New York, 1971) and "If Mao Had Come to Washington: An Essay in Alternatives," *Foreign Affairs* 51 (October 1972):44–64. For Vietnam, see Joseph Buttinger, *Vietnam: A Political History* (New York, 1968); Theodore Draper, *Abuse of Power* (New York, 1967); Gary Hess, "Franklin Roosevelt and Indochina," *Journal of American History* 59 (September 1972): 353–68; George Kahin and John Lewis, *The United States and Vietnam* (New York, 1969); *The Pentagon Papers* (various editions); Arthur Schlesinger, Jr., *The Bitter Heritage: Vietnam and American Democracy, 1941–1968* (New York, 1968); and U.S. Senate, Committee on Foreign Relations, *The United States and Vietnam: 1944–1947* (Washington, 1972). For the Korean War, consult Joyce and Gabriel Kolko, *Limits of Power* (New York, 1972); Charles Lofgren, "Mr. Truman's War: A Debate and Its Aftermath," *Review of Politics* 31 (April 1969):223–41; David McLellan, "Dean Acheson and the Korean War," *Political Science Quarterly* 83 (March 1968):16–39;

Ernest May, "The Nature of Foreign Policy: The Calculated versus the Axiomatic," *Daedalus* 91 (Fall 1962):653–67; Glenn Paige, *The Korean Decision* (New York, 1968); I. F. Stone, *The Hidden History of the Korean War* (New York, 1952 and 1969); and Allen Whiting, *China Crosses the Yalu* (New York, 1960).

For NATO and the military build-up, see the collection by Lawrence Kaplan, ed., *NATO and the Policy of Containment* (Boston, 1968) and Robert Osgood, *NATO: The Entangling Alliance* (Chicago, 1962). For NSC-68, see Paul Hammond's article in Warner Schilling, Paul Hammond, and Glenn Snyder, eds., *Strategy, Politics, and Defense Budgets* (New York, 1962). For competition in the Middle East and Iran, consult Jacob Hurewitz, *Middle East Dilemmas* (New York, 1953); George Kirk, *The Middle East, 1945–1950* (London, 1954); and George Lenczowski, *Russia and the West in Iran, 1918–1948* (Ithaca, 1949). Also see John Snetsinger, *Truman, The Jewish Vote, and the Creation of Israel* (Stanford, Cal., 1974). Relations with Latin America are discussed in Donald Dozer, *Are We Good Neighbors?* (Gainsville, 1959); David Green, "The Cold War Comes to Latin America," in Barton Bernstein, *Politics and Policies of the Truman Administration* (Chicago, 1970); and J. Lloyd Mecham, *A Survey of United States-Latin American Relations* (New York, 1965). Works on topics relating especially to how the U.S. viewed the Russians include Les Adler and Thomas Paterson, "Red Fascism: The Merger of Nazi Germany and Soviet Russia in the American Image of Totalitarianism, 1930's–1950's," *American Historical Review* 75 (April 1970):1046–1064; Russell Buhite, "Soviet-American Relations and the Repatriation of Prisoners of War, 1945," *The Historian* 25 (May 1973):384–97; Raymond Dennett and Joseph Johnson, eds., *Negotiating with the Russians* (Boston, 1951); Stephen Kertesz, "Reflections on Soviet and American Negotiating Behavior," *Review of Politics* 19 (January 1957):3–36; and Philip Mosely, "Across the Green Table from Stalin," *Current History* 15 (September 1948):129–33.

For domestic politics and public opinion in the early Cold War, see Barton Bernstein, "America in War and Peace: The Test of Liberalism," in Barton Bernstein, ed., *Towards a New Past* (New York, 1968); Robert Divine, *Foreign Policy and U.S. Presidential Elections, 1940–1960* (New York, 1974; 2 vols.); Alonzo Hamby, *Beyond the New Deal: Harry S. Truman and American Liberalism* (New York, 1973); Richard Kirkendall, "Election of 1948," in Arthur Schlesinger, Jr., ed.,

*History of American Presidential Elections,* Vol. 4 (New York, 1971); Richard Neustadt, *Presidential Power* (New York, 1960); Cabel Phillips, *The Truman Presidency* (New York, 1966); Athan Theoharis, "The Truman Presidency: Trial and Error," *Wisconsin Magazine of History* 55 (Autumn 1971):49–58; H. Bradford Westerfield, *Foreign Policy and Party Politics* (New Haven, 1955); and Lawrence Wittner, *Rebels Against War: The American Peace Movement, 1941–1960* (New York, 1969). A handy collection is Barton Bernstein and Allen Matusow, eds., *The Truman Administration: A Documentary History* (New York, 1966). Public opinion polls are assembled in Hadley Cantril and Mildred Strunk, eds., *Public Opinion, 1935–1946* (Princeton, 1951) and George Gallup, ed., *The Gallup Poll* (New York, 1972). For the Communist issue at home and McCarthyism, see Robert Griffith and Athan Theoharis, eds., *The Specter: Original Essays on the Cold War and the Origins of McCarthyism* (New York, 1974); Alan Harper, *The Politics of Loyalty: The White House and the Communist Issue, 1946–1952* (Westport, Conn., 1970); Earl Latham, *The Communist Controversy in Washington* (Cambridge, Mass., 1966); Allen Matusow, ed., *Joseph R. McCarthy* (Englewood Cliffs, N.J., 1970); Richard Rovere, *Senator Joe McCarthy* (New York, 1959); and Athan Theoharis, *Seeds of Repression: Harry S. Truman and the Origins of McCarthyism* (Chicago, 1971).

Many of the leading characters of the early Cold War years can be studied through their own accounts, collected papers, or biographies. The works of Adenauer, Brown, Byrnes, Clay, Dedijer, Lane, Lie, Lilienthal, Martin, Mikolajczyk, Morgenthau, Ripka, the Rostows, Stettinius, Stimson, Stolper, Tito, and Warburg have already been mentioned above for specific topics. President Truman has written his *Memoirs* (Garden City, 1955–56; 2 vols.). *The Public Papers of the Presidents, Truman* (Washington, 1961–65; 8 vols.) contain his formal statements as well as transcripts of press conferences. Biographies include Bert Cochran, *Harry Truman and the Crisis Presidency* (New York, 1973); Jonathan Daniels, *The Man of Independence* (Philadelphia, 1950); Merle Miller, *Plain Speaking: An Oral Biography of Harry S. Truman* (New York, 1974), based on interviews; and Margaret Truman, *Harry S. Truman* (New York, 1973), a simple, flattering story by his daughter. The secretaries of state have produced or stimulated studies, too. James Byrnes has written *Speaking Frankly* (New York, 1947) and *All in One Lifetime* (New

York, 1958). See also George Curry, *James F. Byrnes* (New York, 1965). For George Marshall, see Robert Ferrell, *George C. Marshall* (New York, 1966). Forrest Pogue is completing a multivolume biography of Marshall. For Dean Acheson, see his *Present at the Creation* (New York, 1969); Gaddis Smith, *Dean Acheson* (New York, 1972); and Ronald Steel, "Commissar of the Cold War," *New York Review of Books* (February 12, 1970):17–21. All the secretaries of state are treated in Norman Graebner, ed., *An Uncertain Tradition* (New York, 1961). In Frank Merli and Theodore Wilson, eds., *Makers of American Diplomacy* (New York, 1974), there are essays on Acheson (by Ferrell and McLellan), John Foster Dulles (by Herbert Parmet), George F. Kennan (by Paterson), and Truman (by John Gaddis). For a major architect of economic diplomacy, see Frederick Dobney, ed., *Selected Papers of Will Clayton* (Baltimore, 1971). Accounts by diplomats deeply engaged in making Cold War decisions include Charles Bohlen, *Witness to History, 1929–1969* (New York, 1973) and *The Transformation of American Foreign Policy* (New York, 1969); W. Averell Harriman, *America and Russia in a Changing World* (New York, 1971); George Kennan, *Memoirs, 1925–1950* (Boston, 1967); Foy Kohler, *Understanding the Russians* (New York, 1970); Douglas MacArthur, *Reminiscences* (New York, 1964); Robert Murphy, *Diplomat Among Warriors* (Garden City, 1964); and Walter Bedell Smith, *My Three Years in Moscow* (Philadelphia, 1950). John Blum has edited important comments by Henry Wallace in *The Wallace Diaries* (Boston, 1973). See also Henry Wallace, *Toward World Peace* (Boston, 1948); Norman Markowitz, *The Rise and Fall of the People's Century: Henry A. Wallace and American Liberalism, 1941–1948* (New York, 1973); and Karl Schmidt, *Henry A. Wallace* (Syracuse, 1960). For a presidential adviser see William Leahy, *I Was There* (New York, 1950). James Forrestal, secretary of navy and of defense, is frank in Walter Millis, ed., *The Forrestal Diaries* (New York, 1951). The foreign policy positions of a bipartisan leader in the Senate are revealed in Arthur Vanderberg, Jr., *The Papers of Senator Vandenberg* (Boston, 1952).

For British diplomatic leaders see Clement Atlee, *As It Happened* (New York, 1954); Alan Bullock, *The Life and Times of Ernest Bevin* (London, 1960–67; 2 vols.); Winston Churchill, *Triumph and Tragedy* (Boston, 1953); Hugh Dalton, *High Tide and After* (London, 1962); Anthony Eden, *Full Circle* (London, 1960); Roy Harrod, *The Life of John Maynard Keynes* (New York, 1951); and Harold Macmillan, *Tides of Fortune, 1945–1955* (New York, 1967). For France, consult Georges Bidault, *Resistance* (New York, 1967) and Charles de Gaulle, *The War Memoirs* (New York, 1960). For Soviet leaders, see Seweryn Bialer, comp., *Stalin and His Generals* (New York, 1969); Isaac Deutscher, *Stalin: A Political Biography* (New York, 1967); Milovan Djilas, *Conversations with Stalin* (New York, 1962), *J. V. Stalin on Post-War International Relations* (London, 1947); Adam Ulam, *Stalin* (New York, 1973); V. M. Molotov, *Problems of Foreign Policy* (Moscow, 1949); Harrison Salisbury, ed., *Marshal Zhukov's Greatest Battles by Georgi K. Zhukov* (New York, 1969); and Andrei Zhdanov, *The International Situation* (Moscow, 1947).

Cold War documents—diplomatic correspondence, agreements, press releases, State Department reports—are available in the Department of State's *Foreign Relations of the United States* (multiple volumes for each year and special volumes on conferences); the *Department of State Bulletin;* and Council on Foreign Relations, *Documents on American Foreign Relations* (New York, annual volumes). Reports by agencies such as the Export-Import Bank and Department of Commerce, as well as hearings on important topics such as the Truman Doctrine, can be located in the U.S. Government Printing Office, *Monthly Catalog of United States Government Publications* (annual volumes). In recent years the Senate Foreign Relations Committee has published important but heretofore secret hearings from its executive sessions held in the early Cold War period. Senate and House floor debates can be followed in the *Congressional Record* (multiple volumes by Congress). Russian sources in either Russian or English are quite limited. The Soviet government has released some documentation in *The Teheran, Yalta, and Potsdam Conferences* (Moscow, 1969) and *Correspondence Between the Chairman of the Council of Ministers of the U.S.S.R. and the Presidents of the U.S.A. and the Prime Minister of Great Britain During the Great Patriotic War of 1941–1945* (Moscow, 1957). Various editions of the speeches of Stalin, Molotov, and Andrei Vishinsky have also been published in English. The periodical *New Times* and *Soviet Press Translations* (Seattle, University of Washington, 1946–48) reprint articles. A very useful collection of documents from many countries is published by the Royal Institute of International Affairs, *Documents on International Affairs* (London, annual volumes). The United Nations Organization has published a large number of reports and minutes of its sessions. See also the *United Nations Bulletin.*

$$\begin{array}{r} 2\phantom{0} \\ 85 \\ 69 \\ 69 \\ 65 \end{array}$$

288

4

72

72

7

78

$$5\overline{)38^34}$$